Adorno, Heidegger,
and the Politics of Truth

SUNY series in Contemporary Continental Philosophy
———————
Dennis J. Schmidt, editor

Adorno, Heidegger, and the Politics of Truth

LAMBERT ZUIDERVAART

Photo credit: *Longing for the Wholly Other* (2021), by Joyce A. Recker. Mixed media, 23" × 14" × 8". Photograph by Dana Freeman.

Published by State University of New York Press, Albany

© 2024 State University of New York

All rights reserved

Printed in the United States of America

No part of this book may be used or reproduced in any manner whatsoever without written permission. No part of this book may be stored in a retrieval system or transmitted in any form or by any means including electronic, electrostatic, magnetic tape, mechanical, photocopying, recording, or otherwise without the prior permission in writing of the publisher.

For information, contact State University of New York Press, Albany, NY
www.sunypress.edu

Library of Congress Cataloging-in-Publication Data

Name: Zuidervaart, Lambert, author.
Title: Adorno, Heidegger, and the politics of truth / Lambert Zuidervaart.
Description: Albany, NY : State University of New York Press, [2024] |
  Series: SUNY series in contemporary continental philosophy | Includes bibliographical references and index.
Identifiers: LCCN 2023023331 | ISBN 9781438496412 (hardcover : alk. paper) |
  ISBN 9781438496429 (ebook) | ISBN 9781438296405 (pbk. : alk. paper)
Subjects: LCSH: Adorno, Theodor W., 1903–1969—Knowledge and learning. |
  Heidegger, Martin, 1889–1976. Sein und Zeit. | Truth.
Classification: LCC B3199.A34 Z83 2024 | DDC 121—dc23/eng/20231113
LC record available at https://lccn.loc.gov/2023023331

10 9 8 7 6 5 4 3 2 1

For Martin Jay
In memory of Deborah Ellen Cook (1954–2020)

Contents

Preface		ix
Abbreviations and Citations		xiii
Chapter 1	Adorno's Conception of Truth	1
Chapter 2	The Humanly Promised Other of History	19
Chapter 3	Surplus beyond the Subject	37
Chapter 4	What Is, Is More Than It Is	55
Chapter 5	Politics of Truth: Adorno, Foucault, and Feminist Critical Theory	77
Chapter 6	"Weh spricht vergeh": Truth in Adorno's *Aesthetic Theory*	101
Chapter 7	Promises of Truth	129
Appendix	Reflections from Damaged Life: Theodor W. Adorno (1903–69)	141
Notes		151
Bibliography		179
Index		193

Preface

The impetus for writing this book comes from my work on *Truth in Husserl, Heidegger, and the Frankfurt School* (MIT Press, 2017), the first of two volumes that present a new conception of truth in dialogue with both continental and analytic philosophy. (The second volume is titled *Social Domains of Truth*.) The first volume has less to say about Adorno than about Husserl, Heidegger, Horkheimer, and Habermas. Moreover, the little it does say about Adorno has struck some readers as either insufficient or problematic. This became apparent during a book session at the annual meeting of the Society for Phenomenology and Existential Philosophy (SPEP) in 2018. Both of the commentaries on the book, as well as my own response, focused on how to read Adorno. So I decided I should say more about his conception of truth. Hence the impetus for the current volume.

The book also emerges from decades of studying Adorno's work, beginning with a doctoral dissertation written during the late 1970s and early 1980s, continuing with a monograph (*Adorno's Aesthetic Theory*) and a coedited collection (*The Semblance of Subjectivity*) published by MIT Press in the 1990s, and leading a decade later to the publication of *Social Philosophy after Adorno* (Cambridge University Press, 2007). Adorno's conception of truth has been at the center of these studies, even though I did not always make it thematic. Only after I had begun to spell out my own conception of truth, however, with both its debts to Adorno and distance from him, was I ready to provide a systematic reconstruction and critical retrieval of his conception. This book is the result.

Invitations to present papers on Adorno provided propitious occasions to write first drafts of several chapters. As detailed in an endnote to each chapter-opening page, these occasions included a conference on Adorno's *Negative Dialectics* at Harvard University (chapter 2) as well as annual meetings of the Association for Adorno Studies (chapter 3), SPEP (chapter 4), and the Critical Theory Roundtable (chapter 6). I am grateful to the meeting organizers for their invitations and to the session participants for lively and instructive discussions.

Versions of several chapters appear in other publications. Chapter 2 incorporates and revises "History and Transcendence in Adorno's Idea of Truth," in *The Routledge Companion to the Frankfurt School*, edited by Peter Gordon, Espen Hammer, and Axel Honneth (New York: Routledge, 2018), 121–34. Chapter 3 expands and revises "Surplus beyond the Subject: Truth in Adorno's Critique of Husserl and Heidegger," *Symposium: Canadian Journal of Continental Philosophy* 22, no. 1 (Spring 2018): 123–40. A version of chapter 4 appears under the title "Adorno's Critique of Heidegger: The Temporality of Truth" in *The Oxford Handbook of Adorno*, edited by Henry Pickford and Martin Shuster (Oxford University Press), and one of chapter 5 in *Feminism and the Early Frankfurt School*, edited by Christine Payne and Jeremiah Morelock and published by Brill. The first part of chapter 6 has been published under the title "'Weh spricht vergeh': Die unzeitgemässe Aktualität von Adornos *Ästhetischer Theorie*," in *Eros und Erkenntnis: 50 Jahre "Ästhetische Theorie*," edited by Martin Endres, Axel Pichler, and Claus Zittel (Berlin: Walter DeGruyter, 2019), 193–202. And the appendix stems from "Theodor W. Adorno: Exposing Capitalism's Blind Domination," published in the *Times Literary Supplement* online series *Footnotes to Plato*, at https://www.the-tls.co.uk/articles/public/theodor-adorno-footnotes-to-plato/. Readers unfamiliar with Adorno's writings may want to begin with the appendix, which provides an accessible survey of his life and work. I wish to thank the editors and publishers of the various publications mentioned for their permission to include these materials here. I also thank Joe Kirby for preparing the index to this volume.

Chapter 5 on Adorno, Foucault, and feminism has a unique history. I began work on it in October 2019, in response to an invitation from Professor Hans Hansen, head of the Department of Philosophy at the University of Windsor, to participate in a symposium there honoring Professor Deborah Cook upon her retirement. Because Deborah was best known as a Foucault and Adorno scholar and had recently published a book on their critiques of Western society, I decided to write a paper on Adorno and Foucault. But I never presented it. First the symposium was postponed. Then, when the global coronavirus pandemic broke out, it was canceled. By then I had a sprawling sixty-page manuscript on Foucault, but nothing on Adorno. Nevertheless, I sent the manuscript to Deborah for her comments. That led to an email correspondence over several months about her book manuscript in progress on Adorno and identity and my own proposed book on Adorno's conception of truth. It was a shock to learn a few months later that Deborah had died in October 2020 at the age of sixty-five.

We first met in 2001 when Deborah invited me to speak at the University of Windsor on what I labeled Heidegger's "anti-aesthetics." After I moved to Toronto the next year to take up graduate faculty positions at the Institute for Christian Studies and the University of Toronto, she and my wife Joyce and I visited frequently. Deborah and I also presented papers at our respective schools. Her interest in my work helped bring me back into Adorno studies after research for the books *Artistic Truth* and *Art in Public* had taken me in other directions. I have long admired her patient, persistent, and politically astute contributions to Critical Theory. Although I never had a chance to say that by presenting a paper in her honor, I can say it now, by dedicating this book to her memory.

I completed my dissertation on Adorno's aesthetics during four years of research and writing in Berlin and Amsterdam. When I took up my first faculty position in Edmonton in 1981, I did not know any of the leading English-language scholars on Adorno and Critical Theory, and North American philosophers of art paid scant attention to Adorno's work. Nevertheless, I submitted a paper on Adorno's idea of truth content for the annual meeting of the American Society for Aesthetics in Banff, Alberta. To my surprise and delight, not only did the program committee accept the paper but they also invited as commentators Professors Susan Buck-Morss and Martin Jay, two leading American scholars in this area. Susan's *The Origin of Negative Dialectics* and Martin's *The Dialectical Imagination* had provided crucial lifelines as I navigated the labyrinths of Adorno's writings. Meeting them in October 1982 and receiving their gracious comments on my work helped inspire me to turn the dissertation into a book. By the end of a memorable gondola ride with them above the mountainside in Banff, I felt these two esteemed scholars were also my friends.

Even though our personal paths seldom cross, Martin Jay and I have stayed in touch over the years. Our most recent conversations were at the 2016 Harvard University conference on Adorno's *Negative Dialectics*. He has always been ready to encourage my projects, even as he continues to do pathbreaking work in intellectual history. The field of Adorno studies and, more broadly, research on the history and contemporary relevance of Critical Theory would be inconceivable without his contributions. With gratitude and admiration, I also dedicate this book to Martin Jay, trailblazing scholar and collegial friend.

Abbreviations and Citations

Citations of works listed in both German and English use abbreviations derived from the German title and, except in the case Heidegger's *Being and Time*, give pagination first in the German original and then in the English translation, thus: ND 156/153. Throughout the book I cite existing English translations where possible and silently emend them when necessary. Other translations are my own. Dates immediately after titles indicate when the German or French originals were first presented or published. The bibliography contains additional works by Adorno and other authors.

Books by Adorno

ÄT   *Ästhetische Theorie*, GS 7, ed. Gretel Adorno and Rolf Tiedemann, 2nd ed. (Frankfurt am Main: Suhrkamp, 1972) / *Aesthetic Theory* (1970), trans. Robert Hullot-Kentor (Minneapolis: University of Minnesota Press, 1997).

DA   Max Horkheimer and Theodor W. Adorno, *Dialektik der Aufklärung*, in Max Horkheimer, *Gesammelte Schriften*. Vol. 5, *Dialektik der Aufklärung" und Schriften 1940–1950*, ed. Gunzelin Schmid Noerr (Frankfurt am Main: Fischer Taschenbuch, 1987), 11-290 / *Dialectic of Enlightenment: Philosophical Fragments* (1947), trans. Edmund Jephcott (Stanford, CA: Stanford University Press, 2002).

GS   *Gesammelte Schriften*, 20 vols., ed. Rolf Tiedemann et al. (Frankfurt am Main: Suhrkamp, 1970–86).

H   *Drei Studien zu Hegel*, in GS 5 (Frankfurt am Main: Suhrkamp, 1970), 247–381 / *Hegel: Three Studies* (1963), trans. Shierry Weber Nicholsen (Cambridge, MA: MIT Press, 1993).

K   *Kants "Kritik der reinen Vernunft" (1959)*, NS IV.4, ed. Rolf Tiedemann (Frankfurt am Main: Suhrkamp, 1995) / *Kant's "Critique of Pure Reason" (1959)*, trans. Rodney Livingstone (Stanford, CA: Stanford University Press, 2001).

ME *Zur Metakritik der Erkenntnistheorie: Studien über Husserl und die phänomenologischen Antinomien*, in GS 5 (Frankfurt am Main: Suhrkamp, 1970), 7-245 / *Against Epistemology: A Metacritique; Studies in Husserl and the Phenomenological Antinomies* (1956), trans. Willis Domingo (Cambridge, MA: MIT Press, 1982).

MM *Minima Moralia: Reflexionen aus dem beschädigten Leben*, GS 4, 2nd ed. (Frankfurt am Main: Suhrkamp, 1996) / *Minima Moralia: Reflections from Damaged Life* (1951), trans. E. F. N. Jephcott (London: NLB, 1974).

ND *Negative Dialektik*, in GS 6 (Frankfurt am Main: Suhrkamp, 1973), 7-412 / *Negative Dialectics* (1966, 1967), trans. E. B. Ashton (New York: Seabury Press, 1973). I have also consulted the translation by Dennis Redmond (2001), available online at http://members.efn.org/~dredmond/ndtrans.html.

NS *Nachgelassene Schriften* (Frankfurt am Main: Suhrkamp, 1993–).

OD *Ontologie und Dialektik (1960/61)*, NS IV.7, ed. Rolf Tiedemann (Frankfurt am Main: Suhrkamp, 2002) / *Ontology and Dialectics 1960/61*, trans. Nicholas Walker (Cambridge: Polity, 2019).

Other Authors

SZ Martin Heidegger, *Sein und Zeit* (1927), 15th ed. (Tübingen: Max Niemeyer, 1979). Passages in translation are taken from Martin Heidegger, *Being and Time*, trans. Joan Stambaugh (Albany: State University of New York Press, 1996); the page numbers given are from *Sein und Zeit*, as found in the margins of English translations. I have also consulted *Being and Time*, trans. John Macquarrie and

Edward Robinson (New York: Harper & Row, 1962). I give preference to the Macquarrie/Robinson translation in retaining "Being" (capital "B") for *Sein* and in not hyphenating Dasein. These modifications to the Stambaugh translation are made without comment. Other relevant modifications are marked by square brackets.

TP Michel Foucault, "Truth and Power" (1977), in *Power/Knowledge: Selected Interviews and Other Writings 1972–1977*, ed. Colin Gordon (New York: Pantheon Books, 1980), 109–33.

1

Adorno's Conception of Truth

> The idea of the truth . . . probably can be grasped only in a fragmentary manner.
>
> —Theodor W. Adorno[1]

The idea of truth is central to Theodor Adorno's philosophy, aesthetics, and social critique. *Negative Dialectics* describes it as the most important (*die oberste*) metaphysical idea (ND 394/401); arguably, rescuing the idea of truth is the entire point of Adorno's attempt to show "solidarity with metaphysics in the moment of its collapse" (ND 400/408). So too, his discussion of artistic truth content in *Aesthetic Theory* lies at both the textual and the conceptual heart of this unfinished magnum opus (ÄT 179–205/118–36). Moreover, his wide-ranging contributions to social and cultural criticism revolve around the claim that contemporary society as a whole is false: as his pointed parody of G. W. F. Hegel's *Phenomenology of Spirit* puts it, "The whole is the false" (MM §29, 55/50).

Nowhere, however, does Adorno spell out in detail how he understands the idea of truth. Even in his debate with Lucien Goldmann about the sociology of literature, where their differences revolve around how Adorno understands artistic truth content, he says very little about his general conception of truth. Instead, he suggests one can have only a fragmentary grasp of the idea of truth. This, despite the fact that, when the debate occurred—two years after *Negative Dialektik* appeared and two before the posthumous publication of *Ästhetische Theorie*—Adorno had already arrived at his mature positions about truth in philosophy, art, and society.[2]

Consequently, readers of Adorno face a continual challenge. On the one hand, he emphasizes the idea of truth and repeatedly appeals to it throughout his writings. On the other hand, Adorno never systematically lays out his conception of truth. Nor does he provide thorough criticisms of other conceptions. His conception of truth and its critical implications lie scattered across his many writings. It seems then that, like the idea of truth, Adorno's own conception of truth can be grasped only in a fragmentary way.

Yet this suggests the idea of truth, and Adorno's conception of it, can in fact be grasped. And it leaves open the possibility that from the fragments something like a coherent account can emerge. That is the wager of this book. Concentrating on Adorno's mature writings, I aim to piece together the most prominent patterns that make up his conception of truth and test their viability. I plan to ask how such patterns sustain Adorno's aesthetics and social philosophy, inform his critique of Martin Heidegger's work, and raise issues like those that confront Foucaultian and feminist critiques of power. Throughout the book, I also explore the adequacy of Adorno's conception and, where appropriate, suggest ways to address its flaws. The book attempts a systematic reconstruction for the sake of critical retrieval.

As I explain at greater length elsewhere,[3] critical retrieval is the project of recovering insights on issues of contemporary relevance through a careful and critical reading of another philosopher's work. As pursued in this book and closely related publications,[4] critical retrieval examines the most significant texts within an author's oeuvre for the issues in question, and it places them in dialogue with significant texts by other philosophers that have a contrary position. Sometimes the dialogue is explicit in the texts under consideration. At other times, however, it must be reconstructed in the process of critical retrieval. Adorno's differences with Heidegger concerning the idea of truth, for example, lie near the surface of Adorno's writings. But a dialectical dialogue between Adorno and Michel Foucault on the politics of truth can only be reconstructed from their respective writings, for neither one said anything of substance about the other's position.

Because I focus on recovering insights of contemporary relevance from the most significant texts, this book's attempt at critically retrieving Adorno's insights into truth does not aim for the comprehensiveness one might expect from a different sort of book. It does not seek to address the entire array of secondary literature germane to the topic, even though I do selectively engage with this literature. I also do not try to fill in the complex historical background to Adorno's conception of truth. That would require more detailed discussions of Kant, Hegel, Kierkegaard, Marx, Nietzsche, and Freud, not to mention the various twentieth-century figures with whom Adorno interacted. Instead, I concentrate on Adorno's own writings, especially *Negative Dialectics* and *Aesthetic Theory*, and try, in the manner already described, to recover his insights into truth. And I pay special attention to his long-standing critique of Heidegger's conception of Being (*Sein*) and his apparent proximity to Foucault's politics of truth. In this way, I hope to uncover issues and insights of relevance not only to Adorno scholars but also to anyone concerned about the philosophical idea of truth.

To lay the groundwork for such a critical retrieval, this chapter introduces Adorno's conception of truth as a dynamic constellation. Then it considers three possible objections to my emphasis on systematic reconstruction and critical retrieval. And it concludes with a preview of the chapters that follow.

Dynamic Constellation

In an essay dedicated to Herbert Marcuse on his seventieth birthday, Adorno describes truth as "a constantly evolving constellation [*werdende Konstellation*]."[5] Similar descriptions occur in *Negative Dialectics* and in Adorno's books on Edmund Husserl and Hegel. With this single phrase—*werdende Konstellation*—Adorno captures the Walter Benjamin–inspired revision of Hegel's conception of truth that permeates his philosophy.

Benjamin's "Epistemo-Critical Foreword" to his book on the German *Trauerspiel* describes ideas as "eternal constellations" in which the phenomena are saved: "Ideas are eternal constellations, and inasmuch as the elements are grasped as points in such constellations, the phenomena are simultaneously divided out and saved."[6] Like Benjamin, Adorno says the idea of truth is a constellation. It is an arrangement of elements that illuminates them by virtue of their interrelations. Unlike Benjamin, however, Adorno does not think the idea of truth (or any idea, for that matter) is a *timeless* or *eternal* constellation. Rather, the idea of truth is temporal and historical: it is a dynamic or processual (*werdende*) constellation. So too, unlike Benjamin, Adorno does not separate ideas from concepts.[7] Instead, he regards ideas as intrinsically conceptual. Accordingly, Adorno regards the idea of truth as a dynamic constellation of concepts.

In both of these respects—the emphasis on temporality and the embrace of conceptuality—Adorno shows his indebtedness to Hegel, with whom Benjamin never seriously engaged. Like Hegel, Adorno regards truth as an idea in which dialectical relations between concepts play out and the limits of each concept are overcome. Unlike Hegel, however, Adorno does not think we can currently have a conceptual grasp of truth as a whole. Nor does he think that the limits to existing concepts can be overcome by conceptual thought alone. The reason for this, which subsequent chapters explain, is that Adorno thinks concepts typically *impose* a universal identity on objects and thereby fail to do justice to the objects' unique individuality.

For Adorno, placing concepts in constellations relaxes their imposition and helps attune them to the unique individuality of intrinsically nonconceptual matters. This attunement can happen because objects themselves, in their individual identity, exist in historical constellations. As Alison Stone puts it, "Adorno suggests that each object is itself a constellation of different past relations with other objects, all of which have shaped it. On this account, an object is a constellation of historical processes, and a constellation of concepts is a range of concepts, each of which grasps one of the various historical relations that has left its mark on the object. Taken together, these concepts 'gather around' the unique history of the object where this history makes the object the unique thing that it is."[8] Moreover, each object has a possible future toward which a constellation of concepts can point. In David Kaufmann's words, for Adorno "the truth of an object . . . is not only what it has become, but also what it should be."[9]

Accordingly, the dynamic character of a conceptual constellation is supposed to mime the historical interrelatedness of things, while leaving open what both the object and an appropriate understanding might look like in the future. It thereby counteracts the tendency of concepts to freeze-frame objects under an imposed identity: "Only constellations represent from outside what the concept has cut away inside, the 'more' that the concept wants to be just as much as it cannot be. By gathering around the matter [*Sache*] to be known, the concepts potentially determine its inner core, thoughtfully attaining what thought itself necessarily cut out" (ND 164–65/162). In this way, Adorno partially reclaims Benjamin's notion of the (ideational) constellation as a way to "save the phenomena."

At the same time, however, Adorno follows what he takes to be Hegel's lead: an emphasis on the truth of philosophical thought in relation to its subject matter;[10] the conception of truth as "process and result in one";[11] the understanding of truth as an "emphatic idea" that far exceeds "a mere relationship between judgment [*Urteil*] and object [*Gegenstand*]" or, in the parlance of more recent philosophy, between propositions and facts (H 281/36); the insistence that thought's critical self-reflection is intrinsic to truth as such (H 282/37); the transposition of the concept of truth from "predicative logic," with its notion of truth as an *adaequatio rei atque cogitationis* (Latin: making the thing equal with what is thought), into "the dialectic as a whole" (H 283/38); the emphasis on a mutual mediation between epistemic subject and epistemic object, between "thoughtful synthesis [*denkende Synthesis*]" and the "judged states of affairs [*Urteilssachverhalten*]," that goes beyond both (H 284/39); and the assumption that, at bottom, there is an affinity (but, for Adorno, not an identity) between subject and object, one that thought's critical self-reflection can uncover. As Adorno concludes in a long paragraph that defends Hegel's conception of truth against Heidegger's ontological critique of idealism: "The speculative Hegelian concept [of truth] rescues mimesis through spirit's self-reflection: truth is not *adaequatio* but affinity, and in the decline of idealism reason's mindfulness [*Eingedenken*] of its mimetic nature is revealed by Hegel to be its human right" (H 285/41). Conceptual constellations are Adorno's Benjamin-inspired way to appropriate Hegel's conception of truth.

Yet the idea of truth is unlike other conceptual constellations in two respects. First, strictly speaking there is no "thing" (*Sache*) or "object" (*Gegenstand*) around which the concepts in this truth-constellation must gather. For the idea of truth pertains to relations among all concepts as well as between every concept and object. It cannot be reduced to specific relations between certain concepts and objects. Second, as Adorno's own usages indicate, the idea of truth pertains in the first instance to the mediation of philosophically decisive pairs of concepts that historically have become opposed to each other: universal and particular, for example, or subject and object. Hence the "phenomenon" around which truth as a constellation must gather is not a thing or object. Rather, it is the historically unfolding field of tension among decisive concepts—a force field (*Kraftfeld*), to use a term from Adorno's critique of Husserl (ME 79/72). Here, too, Adorno is deeply indebted to Hegel, especially Hegel's *Phenomenology of Spirit*, with its dialectical unfolding of the forms of conscious experience, and his *Science of Logic*, with its dialectical exposition of the categories of thought.

Indeed, certain conceptual polarities have special prominence in Adorno's conception of truth. In this book, I single out three: subject (*Subjekt*) and object (*Objekt*); concept (*Begriff*) and thing or subject matter (*Sache*); and historical immanence and futural transcendence. Each of these polarities intersects the other two. Moreover, as I shall argue, the polarity between history and transcendence sets a decisive direction for the other two. For Adorno, then, the idea of truth is a dynamic constellation of intersecting polarities between subject and object, concept and thing, and history and transcendence.

Of course, other polarities also play a role, and conceivably any one of these could provide an entry into Adorno's conception of truth: identity and nonidentity, for example, or universal and particular, or society and individual. Yet I believe the three I have singled out play a special role, not only in Adorno's social and philosophical critiques but also in his attempts to say what a different idea of truth would be like. They also point to both the insights and the blind spots that I consider most important for sorting out Adorno's contributions to a transformative conception of truth. Before summarizing how I plan to trace these polarities in the chapters that follow, however, I need to take up potential objections to my approach.

Hermeneutic Force Field

Other Adorno scholars might well object to my proposing a systematic reconstruction aimed at critically retrieving insights into truth as such, and their objections could have ample support in Adorno's writings. Three potential objections strike me as the most telling. They help constitute the interpretive force field within which my own approach occurs.

The first potential objection is that my approach violates the antisystematic character of Adorno's thought. The second is that it ignores Adorno's insistence on the negativity of true thought. The third potential objection is that my approach does an injustice to Adorno's emphasis on how minimal our grasp of truth is. Let me call them the antisystematic, negativist, and minimalist objections. In so labeling them, I do not suggest that the scholars who might raise these objections are themselves antisystematic thinkers or alethic negativists or alethic minimalists. Rather, I am saying that they could point to antisystematic, negativist, or minimalist features of Adorno's philosophy to question the suitability or legitimacy of my own critical hermeneutics. Each objection involves a plausible interpretation of Adorno, and each deserves a preliminary response.

Antisystem?

I have claimed that for Adorno the idea of truth is a constellation in which three conceptual polarities stand out. This suggests, contrary to the chapter's epigraph, that one can grasp both the idea of truth and Adorno's conception of it in a more than fragmentary way, in fact, that one can systematically reconstruct them. Yet Adorno prominently portrays negative dialectics as antisystematic, and his notion of a constellation resists systematization. "Constellation is not system," he writes, contrasting his dialectical method with Hegel's. When philosophy configures elements into a constellation, their configuration cannot be reduced to either the meaning of these elements or their inferential connections: "Everything does not become resolved, everything does not come out even; rather, one moment sheds light on the other, and the figures that the individual moments form together are specific signs and a legible script" (H 342/109). To narrow truth down to a nexus of three intersecting polarities would seem both to resolve what cannot be resolved and to prevent the many moments of truth from becoming a "legible script," thereby violating the antisystematic character of Adorno's thought. Wouldn't it be better to leave Adorno's conception of truth unreconstructed than to force it into a systematic straitjacket?

In response, let me say more about the sort of reconstruction I envision. It is not an attempt to show how everything Adorno has to say about truth can be derived from a few fundamental premises. One reason why Adorno describes truth as a constellation is that it is a complex idea. As a complex idea, it is not readily reduced to either a real definition or a simple summary. The reconstruction I pursue aims to retain the internal complexity of Adorno's own conception of truth. Yet such complexity should not be confused with endless variety. There are definite patterns to how Adorno's mature writings speak about truth, and one can uncover, describe, and evaluate these patterns. To do this, however, one needs to connect passages that either textually or topically lie far apart and, in this way, piece out a constellation like what Adorno claims the idea of truth to be. In that sense, what I call systematic reconstruction could be considered the mapping of a conceptual and textual constellation.

As will become apparent, my singling out three polarities is less an attempt at analytic reduction than at hermeneutic illumination. I am less interested in saying precisely what these polarities consist in than in showing how they permeate and inform Adorno's conception of truth. I also wish to understand how each polarity intersects the other two and how together, in their crosscutting tensions, they configure his conception. For the most part, I stick close to the texts of Adorno's mature writings, even as I select certain passages for special scrutiny. My reconstruction tries to preserve the textuality of Adorno's thought.

If one wants to do justice to Adorno's conception of truth, however, it is crucial not to misinterpret the antisystematic character of his thought. Although he opposes traditional attempts to derive the truth from first principles just as much as he rejects Hegelian claims to have achieved absolute knowledge of the absolute truth, that does not mean Adorno opposes logical stringency or conceptual consistency. Instead, he advocates and tries to exemplify a different sort of stringency and consistency, a way of thinking that can do justice to both the individuality and the historical interrelatedness of things. If Adorno's conception of truth also displays such individuality and interrelatedness, and if one wants to respect his way of thinking, then a hermeneutically attuned and yet systematic reconstruction of his conception does not seem inappropriate.

Alethic Negativism?

Even if one grants legitimacy to this project of reconstruction, however, another powerful objection awaits, namely, the worry that my approach ignores Adorno's insistence on the negativity of true thought. For by aiming to critically retrieve insights into truth as such from Adorno's conception, the proposed project seems to assume a positive and even holistic conception of truth. Yet Adorno seems dramatically opposed to any such conception, especially as it comes to expression in Hegel's philosophy. "The whole is the untrue," Adorno famously wrote, not only because contemporary society as it has developed is false but also because the philosophical attempt to comprehend truth as a whole both echoes and reinforces such societal falsity: " 'The whole is the untrue,' not merely because the thesis of totality is itself untruth, being the principle of domination inflated to the absolute. The idea of a positivity that can master everything that opposes it through the superior power of a comprehending spirit is the mirror image of the experience of the superior coercive force inhering in everything that exists by virtue of its consolidation under domination. This is the truth in Hegel's untruth" (H 324/87). Accordingly, it would seem perverse to try to extract positive insights into truth as such via a systematic reconstruction of Adorno's conception. For Adorno seems to say that only in rejecting falsehood, not in grasping truth as such, can thought be true.

One way to support this objection would be to argue that Adorno subscribes to a position of negativism with respect to truth itself. As described by Owen Hulatt in his fascinating book on Adorno's theory of truth, Adorno's alethic negativism would be the position "that the truth cannot be positively expressed—rather we can only outline and describe falsehoods." Adorno subscribes to such alethic negativism, Hulatt claims, because Adorno thinks society as a whole is internally contradictory, and this societal totality so thoroughly "mediates" concepts that these "are incapable of truthfully grasping their objects."[12] On Hulatt's interpretation of Adorno, even a simple predication such as "this grass is green" is necessarily false, insofar as the apparent "truth of an isolated proposition" is "made possible by a mediating holistic whole that, taken as a whole, is completely untrue."[13] At the same time, however, what Hulatt calls Adorno's "holistic theory of falsity" appears inconsistent with the many positive truth claims Adorno actually makes. Adorno thereby threatens to generate a "two-tier account of truth" that pits a momentary flash of true nondiscursive cognition against unavoidably false discursive attempts to express such truth. Hulatt tries to address these issues by arguing that Adorno resolves them in the cognitive agent's *performance* of critical reflection.[14]

Clearly an understanding of Adorno's conception of truth along such negativist lines would put in question an attempt like mine to critically retrieve Adorno's insights into truth itself. Such alethic negativism would restrict truth proper to those *nonconceptual* flashes of insight that *conceptually mediated* propositional claims and *conceptually infused* critical reflection cannot provide. Accordingly, if there were true insights to be gleaned from Adorno's writings, they too would need to be nonconceptual, and attempts to articulate them conceptually would likely run afoul of Adorno's restricting true thought to the critique of falsehood. For *conceptually* articulated insight into truth would itself be unavoidably false, and the entire project of systematic reconstruction for the sake of critical retrieval would lose its point. Indeed, it would seem to be precluded by Adorno's own writings.

Nevertheless, I am far from convinced that Adorno was an alethic negativist, nor do I think he subscribed to a holistic theory of falsity. There are enough elements of both Benjamin and Hegel in Adorno's negative dialectics to generate an internally richer conception of truth. Indeed, his comprehensive social critique necessarily appeals to the idea of truth as a whole. Here, for example, is how the passage quoted earlier about the "truth in Hegel's untruth" concludes: "By specifying, in opposition to Hegel, the negativity of the whole, philosophy satisfies, for the last time, the postulate of determinate negation that is supposed to be affirmation [*das Postulat der bestimmten Negation, welche die Position sei*]. The ray of light that reveals the whole to be untrue in all its moments is none other than utopia, the utopia of the whole truth, which is still to be realized" (H 324–25/87–88). Far from rejecting the Hegelian aspiration toward truth as a whole, Adorno claims to fulfill this aspiration more consistently than Hegel himself, by showing how society as a whole is untrue. And far from denying the possibility of there being truth as a whole, Adorno says it is this very possibility, and with it the possibility of a society that is no longer false, that "reveals" (*offenbart*) the untruth of contemporary society as a whole.

Moreover, although Adorno does not explicitly say this here, the notion of determinate negation, so decisive in his appropriation of Hegel's dialectic, would make little sense if one could not show specifically how the various "moments" (*Momenten*) of the whole are false. And to do that, Adorno implies, one needs some inkling, some "ray of light" (*Strahl*) concerning how they could be true both discretely and in combination. In other words, the untrue whole is not wholly false, and the utopian idea of truth as a whole helps reveal why and how this is so.

I have more to say about Adorno's appeal to the utopia of the whole truth in subsequent chapters. For now, however, let me highlight one dimension that too few commentators give sufficient emphasis. It is what Kaufmann calls the "redemptive" version of truth in Adorno's work. Unlike the closely interrelated version that "derives truth from the determinate negation of falsehood," the redemptive one "demands that we see what has become as a distorted version of what should be and asks us to judge the existent in terms of its distortions. Redemption—and to use its political name, Utopia—is the index of knowledge."[15] For Adorno, truth would not be possible if there were no hope for fundamental transformation of the untrue whole. As he writes in a passage from *Minima Moralia* directed against Nietzsche's *amor fati* (love your fate), "In the end hope, wrested from reality by negating it, is the only form in which truth appears. Without hope, the idea of truth would be scarcely even thinkable" (MM §61, 110/98). Moreover, as is clear from the passage already quoted from Adorno's Hegel book, the idea of truth that the hope for redemption makes thinkable is the idea of truth as a whole.

None of this resolves complex issues about how to put together the two interrelated concepts of truth that Kaufmann mentions, namely, the determinate negation of falsehood and the utopian hope for redemption. Yet it does show why Adorno should not be regarded as merely an alethic negativist. It also indicates, at least in a preliminary way, why trying to recover insights into truth as such via systematic reconstruction is not as "untrue" to Adorno's work as a negativist objection to my approach might suggest.

Alethic Minimalism?

By citing Adorno's appeal to the not-yet-realized "utopia of the whole truth," however, my response to the negativist objection might prompt a closely related worry, namely, that my approach does an injustice to how minimal Adorno thinks our grasp of truth is. I call this the *alethic* minimalist objection. One way to pose it would be along the lines of Fabian Freyenhagen's vigorous and plausible defense of what he takes to be Adorno's *ethical* minimalism.

According to Freyenhagen, Adorno holds that "there is no right life within our modern social world," yet the wrong life everyone leads *can* be lived "less wrongly."[16] This position involves a negativism about both the knowability and the actuality of the good. According to Freyenhagen, Adorno thinks "we cannot know what human potential and good is *because* this world realizes the bad and suppresses this potential."[17] And that appears to land Adorno in what Freyenhagen labels the "Problem of Normativity": because Adorno cannot appeal to the good that his normative claims unavoidably assume, it seems he "is not entitled to make the normative claims his philosophy contains."[18]

Freyenhagen rescues Adorno from this apparent dilemma by arguing that the normative claims Adorno makes are "minimalist." They are minimalist in the sense that they pertain only to what is bad, not what is good, and one does not need to "appeal to or know the good" in order for the bad to be recognized and have "normative force."[19] Understood along these lines, the utopian elements in Adorno's ethics and social critique would simply be reminders that "our radically evil social world" might not be so permanent and unchangeable as it seems. They help us recognize how bad things are, and they "make it possible for us to see that things ought to be different." But they do not "provide us with conceptions or images of the good."[20]

In a similar fashion, an *alethic* minimalist interpretation of Adorno could say his radical claim that "the whole is the untrue" does not permit a robust reading of Adorno's equally radical claim that "the utopia of the whole truth" is what "reveals the whole to be untrue" (H 325/88). Instead, a minimalist interpretation is required: Adorno simply says that the idea of truth as a whole can help us recognize how fragmentary and unsatisfactory our grasp of truth is—it does not give us access to truth as such. To the extent that a systematic reconstruction aimed at critical retrieval suggests otherwise, it fundamentally misconstrues Adorno's conception of truth.

There is something to be said in favor of such an alethic minimalist objection. No more than Kaufmann would I want to miscast Adorno in "the tub-thumping role of a utopian optimist." The regulative role of his redemptive concept of truth is critical, not straightforwardly affirmative: "The truth that the light of redemption casts reveals pained fragments, not triumphant totalities."[21] Nevertheless, what a minimalist interpretation misses is that the revelation of pained fragments occurs via a *conceptual* constellation that points *beyond* the untrue whole. It points beyond the historically developed society where our fragmentary grasp of truth occurs and where life, according to an ethically minimalist interpretation of Adorno, can only be lived less wrongly. The conceptual constellation is, as Kaufmann says, "an image of a whole that is the truth." It is "the outline of Redemption, of differences conjoined without domination."[22]

If that's right as an interpretation of Adorno's writings, then there would be more to pursuing truth and living aright under current conditions than simply criticizing falsehood and living less wrongly. Also required is an orientation toward what would be completely different, even if we cannot fully grasp under current conditions either "truth as a whole" or "the good." Contra minimalist interpretations of Adorno, one can at least ask what such an orientation looks like under current conditions and consider how this orientation should inform both truth theory and social critique. To avoid such questions would be to overlook the radical political potential of Adorno's conception of truth.

Like the antisystematic and negativist objections, the worries raised by alethic minimalism are good reminders of the anti-Hegelian side to Adorno's conception of truth. But all three sorts of objections miss just how Hegelian Adorno's critique of Hegel is, even as they soft-pedal the redemptive Benjaminian inspiration for that critique. My reconstruction aims to do justice to both sides, while asking what we can learn about truth from Adorno's unique conception.

Both as a systematic reconstruction and as a critical retrieval, then, this book aims to be true to Adorno's conception of truth. Yet no more than Adorno in his books on Husserl and Hegel do I think such an interpretation permits either slavish imitation or rigid rejection. Rather, as Adorno lucidly explains in his lectures on Immanuel Kant's First Critique, one must delve into the inner tensions that propel a philosopher's conception and thereby uncover what significant insights it has to offer. In Adorno's own words, the point is to explore what a philosopher's thought objectively expresses "of the internal history of truth, on the sundial of truth." Tellingly, Adorno uses both *constellation* and *force field* in this context to indicate what he aims to uncover in Kant. The decisive point, he says, is "the constellation of truth—and this constellation is the same as the force field I have talked about so often—that has crystallized in such a philosophy" (K 122/78).[23] In trying to reconstruct and evaluate Adorno's conception of truth, I share his concerns about how to read a philosopher's work. What I seek, and what I hope to present, is the truth content of Adorno's conception of truth.

Conceptual Polarities

As already indicated, the three most prominent conceptual polarities in Adorno's conception of truth are woven through each other. Not only does that make it difficult to disentangle them but also it reinforces the need to see how they intertwine. And it raises the question whether one of them is more crucial than the others for understanding the constellation that Adorno configures.

In my judgment, the polarity of history and transcendence is the most crucial, in three respects. First, it constitutes the most innovative departure in Adorno's truth conception from the German philosophical tradition that he reworks, especially Kant, Hegel, and Husserl. Second, it marks his most dramatic difference from the two philosophers with whom his conception of truth especially invites comparison, namely, Heidegger and Foucault. Third, the polarity of history and transcendence provides the decisive orientation for how Adorno understands the polarities of subject and object and of concept and thing.

Accordingly, my discussion begins with the history/transcendence dialectic in chapter 2, then moves to the subject/object dialectic in chapter 3 and the concept/thing dialectic in chapter 4. Yet chapter 4 also shows how differences concerning history and transcendence not only motivate Adorno's critique of Heidegger over concept and thing but also help explain Adorno's hidden affinities with Heidegger's ontological conception of truth. Then I explore how Adorno's constellation provides a counterpart to a Foucaultian politics of truth (chapter 5), show how the three polarities play out in Adorno's aesthetics (chapter 6), and consider what Adorno contributes to a transformative conception of truth (chapter 7).

To explore the history/transcendence dialectic in Adorno's conception of truth, chapter 2 focuses on the "Meditations on Metaphysics" that conclude *Negative Dialectics*. There, I argue, this dialectic propels Adorno's attempt to articulate a defensible idea of truth, despite and amid the collapse of metaphysics. First I consider the issues of absolutism and relativism raised by Adorno's insistence on the historical necessity of certain ideas and their demise. Next I show how he addresses these issues by reworking Kant's transcendental ideas of immortality, freedom, and God's existence. Then I propose a social transformationalist interpretation of the idea of truth that Adorno tries to rescue from Kant. Central to this idea is the convergence of thought and experience on what Adorno calls "the humanly promised other of history" (ND 396/404)—a society, historically not impossible, in which violence and societally induced suffering have ended.

In emphasizing such convergence, Adorno cannot be an alethic minimalist. Nevertheless, as the chapter tries to demonstrate, there is an unavoidable tension between the idea of truth Adorno has rescued and a viable account of propositional truth—the truth of propositions, assertions, and beliefs. Like Adorno, I consider propositional truth to be only part of what truth includes. Yet I question whether Adorno can actually provide an adequate account of propositional truth within his conception of truth as a whole.

Contrary to an alethic negativist interpretation, however, I believe Adorno rightly insists on the importance of propositional truth, and he defends it against both positivist trivialization and existentialist dismissal. Although it is not always clear how Adorno understands propositional truth, the polarity between epistemic subject and object plays a central role. Chapter 3 shows that, in emphasizing a dialectic between epistemic subject and object, Adorno's notion of propositional truth derives in part from his critique of Husserlian phenomenology and Heideggerian ontology for misconstruing what Adorno calls "the surplus beyond the subject" (ND 368/375).

The chapter examines three passages from Adorno's Husserl book and *Negative Dialectics* where Adorno appears intent on wresting a viable conception of propositional truth from Husserl's account of categorial intuition and Heidegger's idea of Being. While agreeing in part with Adorno's criticisms of Husserl and Heidegger, I argue that Adorno does not adequately account for the role of predication in cognition. Specifically, he cannot account for the object's predicative self-disclosure, on which correct assertions and discursive criticism depend. Consequently, he fails to offer the viable conception of propositional truth that both his critique of Heidegger and his broader idea of truth require.

Yet there is much more to Adorno's critique than a struggle over the subject/object dialectic. Chapter 4 examines the critique of Heidegger in Adorno's *Ontology and Dialectics* lectures and in part 1 ("Relation to Ontology") of *Negative Dialectics*. After reviewing relevant secondary literature, the chapter interprets Adorno's critique as a contest over the idea of truth. Here the polarity between concept and thing comes to the fore. Drawing on both Kant and Hegel, Adorno charges Heidegger with "ontologizing the ontic"

(ND 125–28/119–22; OD 109–38/73–94), in three ways: by melding the concept of Being (*Sein*) and concrete things, by absolutizing the mediation of subject and object, and by freezing actual history into an unchanging "historicity." The first of these—treating the thing as a concept—is especially significant, for it connects the critique of Heidegger with Adorno's critique of Hegel. Both of them, he says, fail to grasp how "what is, is more than it is" (ND 164/161). Instead, they try to reduce thing to concept, what is nonconceptual to the conceptual, the nonidentical (*das Nichtidentische*) to conceptual identity.

Underlying this criticism, however, is a concern Adorno dialectically shares with Heidegger over what Iain Macdonald calls "blocked possibility."[24] Adorno rejects Heidegger's blocked possibility—*beyng* (*Seyn*) beyond Being (*Sein*), another beginning before the metaphysical beginning—for the sake of a different blocked possibility—a future society in which needless suffering would end. In linking truth with a blocked possibility, Heidegger and Adorno share the claim that truth is temporal, but they disagree about how it is temporal. In this way, the history/transcendence dialectic traced in chapter 2 turns out to be a key to Adorno's debate with Heidegger as well. The chapter concludes with brief suggestions about how this debate could yield a better understanding of the temporality of truth.

Just as Adorno regarded Heidegger's ontology as an ideological response to a false "ontological need," so the dialectic between history and transcendence in Adorno's conception of truth responds to a society that, as a whole, he considered false. What makes late capitalist society false is how it allows domination to occur through the process of economic exchange. That diagnosis, going back to Max Horkheimer and Adorno's *Dialectic of Enlightenment*, raises issues like ones that arise in the genealogical writings of Michel Foucault, issues much debated in feminist critical theory. One way to sort out such issues is to examine the ideas of power and truth that figure prominently in Foucault and Adorno's critiques of Western society.

Chapter 5 focuses on the *relation* between power and truth, for here, I claim, lie both crucial insights and notable lacunae in their critiques. After introducing feminist debates about what I label interactional and macrostructural forms of power, I summarize Foucault's genealogical account of what he calls disciplinary power and state biopower. Next I contrast his account with Adorno's negative dialectical critique of domination. Based on this contrast, I then compare their understandings of how truth and power interrelate.

From this comparison two challenges of relevance to feminist critical theory emerge. One is to articulate the normative implications of how truth and power interrelate. The other is to envision genuine prospects for the transformation of society as a whole. The chapter concludes with suggestions along these lines, indicating why, in a political environment where powerful authoritarian populists not only attack the accomplishments of the feminist movement but also dismiss the importance of truth, feminist critical theory needs a new conception of truth.

The interrelation between truth and power in Adorno's social critique also helps explain the enduring relevance of his *Aesthetic Theory*. His unfinished magnum opus, which appeared in 1970, remains timely in an oddly untimely way. Chapter 6 attributes this untimely timeliness to the combination of academic askesis and modernist engagement in Adorno's *Aesthetic Theory*. Behind this combination lies a dialectical autonomism about art that is at odds with both pre- and post-1970 scholarship and that leads to an equally provocative and problematic position about art and politics: the politically important truth of art, made possible by art's societally constituted autonomy, is also politically impotent.

To sort out this position, one needs to take up the complex conception of artistic truth at the heart of Adorno's aesthetics. Chapter 6 does this in two stages. First I examine a debate between Albrecht Wellmer and J. M. Bernstein over how to interpret Adorno's autonomist conception of artistic truth. Then I reconstruct this conception in terms of the polarities traced in previous chapters. Focusing on three chapters midway through *Aesthetic Theory*, I show how these polarities surface in the dialectics of semblance and expression, of form and content, and of historical possibility that constitute Adorno's conception of artistic truth. On the basis of this reconstruction, I then reexamine Adorno's oblique approach to the politics of art, contrasting it with both politically engaged and apolitical approaches, and I propose a new way to think about how artistic truth contributes to political struggles for justice and freedom.

Weaving together the threads of the previous chapters, chapter 7 asks what remains important and valid in Adorno's conception of truth. It argues that Adorno offers a crucial alternative to the mainstreams of both analytic and continental philosophy. At the same time, however, significant blockages occur in his conception of truth, and these need to be addressed. They have to do with the nature of propositional truth, its relation to truth as a whole, and the tasks of a truth-oriented social critique.

Addressing such issues is not simply a matter of concern to professional philosophers. Truth, as Adorno understood, lies at the center of politics, art, and scholarship. That is why this book reconstructs and critically examines his conception, teasing out hidden affinities with both Heidegger and Foucault. Despite the cynicism of post-truth politics and the skepticism of many scholars, truth continues to be one of the most important philosophical ideas. And Adorno's conception of truth remains highly relevant for both philosophy and public life.

2

The Humanly Promised Other of History

> The ray of light that reveals the whole to be untrue in all its moments is none other than utopia, the utopia of the whole truth, which is still to be realized.
>
> —Theodor W. Adorno (H 325/88)

Theodor W. Adorno's *Negative Dialectics* appeared in 1966, when he was at the height of his intellectual presence as a professor, author, cultural critic, and administrator. A second edition was published a year later. Along with Adorno's unfinished *Aesthetic Theory*, which appeared one year after his death in 1969, *Negative Dialectics* marks the brilliant culmination to his philosophical work. It also gives an uncompromising summation of Critical Theory in its first generation. As Adorno states upfront, he wants to "lay his cards on the table" (ND 9/xix), and he stands ready for the attacks this book will invite in both the west and the east ["hüben und drüben" (ND 11/xxi)—a Cold War phrase used to indicate both sides of the "Iron Curtain"]. Aside from some of Adorno's students and close colleagues, however, few critics at the time engaged thoroughly enough with his magnum opus to figure out exactly why and how to attack it. Serious reception in the wider philosophical world has experienced a long delay.

Nevertheless, *Negative Dialectics* provides a virtual compendium of everything Adorno has to offer contemporary philosophy and social critique. The long introduction (ND 13–66/1–57), nearly a small book in itself, reveals the inner dynamics of what Adorno calls negative dialectics and positions it in the history of Western thought. Next, part 1 of the book

(ND 67–136/59–131) explains how Adorno's negative-dialectical philosophy relates to existential ontology, launching a critique of Heidegger that complements Adorno's more overtly polemical *The Jargon of Authenticity* (1964). Part 2, titled "Negative Dialectics: Concept and Categories" (ND 137–207/133–207), explicates the most important ideas and arguments of Adorno's philosophy, with an emphasis on questions of epistemology and social philosophy. There is no better statement of how Adorno not only continues but also challenges the legacies of Kant, Hegel, and Marx, with an eye to the problems posed by both existentialism and logical positivism.

Part 3, comprising nearly half the book (ND 209–400/209–408), makes good on the introduction's claim that a comprehensive and socially critical philosophy needs to construct "thought models" in which theory and experience interact (ND 39–42/28–31). The three models Adorno constructs seek to illuminate contested ideas by engaging critically with their most important philosophical articulations. In effect, each is a metacritique, reminiscent, in this regard, of *Hegel: Three Studies* (1963) and Adorno's earlier book on Husserl titled *Toward a Metacritique of Epistemology* (1956) (inaccurately translated as *Against Epistemology: A Metacritique*). The first model, "Freedom: On the Metacritique of Practical Reason," takes up central issues raised by Kant's moral philosophy (ND 211–94/211–99). The second, "World Spirit and Natural History: An Excursus on Hegel," deals with questions concerning the ideas of rationality and progress in Hegel and Marx (ND 295–353/300–360). The third model, which also concludes the book, offers twelve "Meditations on Metaphysics" (ND 354–400/361–408).

Given the ambitions and complexity of *Negative Dialectics*, there are many ways to enter it for the first time. Yet I think no one should exit it without grappling with these concluding meditations, especially with the idea of truth that they disclose. That is the focus of this chapter.

Truth and Metaphysics

Truth, Adorno writes, is the most important (*die oberste*) among metaphysical ideas (ND 394/401). "Meditations on Metaphysics" can be read as his attempt to articulate a defensible idea of truth, despite and amid the collapse of metaphysics.[1] Moreover, as Adorno wrote in a letter to Gershom Scholem dated March 14, 1967, "The wish to salvage metaphysics is in fact central to *Negative Dialectics*."[2] This wish to rescue metaphysics is closely connected to Adorno's "inverse theology," which some have linked to his "allegiance" to Kierkegaard and "the philosophy of existence,"[3] and others have anchored in his Hegelian Marxist emphasis on "determinate negation."[4] To the extent that the key to Adorno's negative dialectics lies in his "Meditations on Metaphysics," the attempt there to articulate what truth is and why it matters is crucial for his contributions to contemporary philosophy.

Many readers of Adorno, attentive to his insisting in part 2 of *Negative Dialectics* on the preponderance or priority of the object (*Vorrang des Objekts*, ND 184–87/183–86),[5] regard the mediation between subject and object as central to his negative-dialectical conception of truth. One sees this, for example, in Brian O'Connor's focus on "the priority of the object" and "the role of subjectivity" in Adorno's epistemology,[6] and in Andrew Bowie's discussion of Adorno's critical appropriation of Kant and Hegel.[7] At strategic spots Bowie refers to Axel Honneth's critical retrieval of the notion of reification from the subject/object dialectic established by Georg Lukács and partially retained by Adorno.[8] Honneth proposes to redescribe reification as a forgetting of the *intersubjective* recognition that ontogenetically and conceptually precedes object-oriented cognition—a redescription he derives, in part, from Adorno. Although Honneth does not spell out the implications of an emphasis on intersubjective recognition for a conception of truth, it points to one in which subject/object mediation is secondary rather than primary. Honneth's own interpretation of *Negative Dialectics* implies this shift in priority, it seems to me.[9]

I have sympathies both with an emphasis on subject/object mediation in interpreting Adorno's approach to truth and with attempts to expand his approach to include intersubjective recognition. For example, I have portrayed Adorno's appeal to emphatic experience as a dialectical counterpart to Heidegger's emphasis on authenticity in *Being and Time*, arguing that both Adorno and Heidegger provide problematic accounts for what I call the public authentication of truth.[10] And the next chapter will examine selected passages where, employing a subject/object dialectic, Adorno tries to extract a viable conception of propositional truth from Husserlian phenomenology and Heideggerian ontology.

In the current chapter, however, I focus on passages from Adorno's "Meditations on Metaphysics" where he tries to rescue the idea of truth from the collapse of metaphysics. Of primary importance in this rescue effort is not the mediation between subject and object, I argue, but rather the polarity between history and transcendence. First, commenting on Meditations 1–4, I consider the issues raised by Adorno's insistence on the historical necessity of certain ideas and their demise. Next, reviewing portions of Meditations

6–9, I show how Adorno addresses these issues via a critical retrieval of Kant's transcendental ideas of immortality, freedom, and God's existence. Then, turning to Meditations 11–12, I propose a social transformationalist interpretation of the idea of truth that, via this critical retrieval, Adorno tries to rescue. I conclude by demonstrating an unavoidable tension between the idea Adorno has rescued and what a viable conception of propositional truth would require.

Historical Necessity and Possibility

From the outset, in the meditation titled "After Auschwitz" (ND 354–58/361–65), Adorno's meditations on metaphysics insist that philosophy needs a different conception (*Begriff*) of truth in order to be true to what life after Auschwitz demands. With this different conception, metaphysics might succeed by becoming materialist and by thinking against thought. Central to the change Adorno envisions lies the claim that truth, like other crucial metaphysical ideas, would not simply transcend what is transient. Rather, truth would also be temporal and historical through and through.

On Adorno's conception, the historical character of truth has two dimensions. One is the necessity of historical development. The other is the historical possibility of transcendence. Let me discuss historical necessity first.

As is well known, Adorno is sharply critical of Hegelian speculations about the universal history of spirit, and he takes distance from Marxian constructions of a progressive dialectic between forces and relations of production. Yet he does not hesitate to claim that history, as it has unfolded, requires certain ideas and undermines others. In this sense, historical development necessarily makes certain ideas true and others false.

For example, when Adorno announces a new categorical imperative in the meditation titled "Metaphysics and Culture" (ND 358–61/365–68), he suggests this imperative is imposed by what happened under Hitler's regime. He also says that the "course of history" compels metaphysical reflections to embrace, as the true basis of morality, the "unvarnished materialist motive" of corporeally abhorring the infliction of "unbearable physical pain" on any individual (ND 358/365). In at least one sense, then, he claims that his materialist turn is true insofar as it is historically required. This suggests that if, as Adorno says in the introduction to *Negative Dialectics*, the need to let suffering speak is a condition of all truth (ND 29/17–18), then the historical conditions under which suffering occurs and is voiced govern the truth of such expression. Moreover, this historical necessity, as Adorno recognizes, governs the truth of his own philosophy.

Adorno's insistence on historical necessity exposes his truth conception to two worries. One is that his conception—indeed, his entire philosophy—relies so heavily on a historical metanarrative—namely, the dialectic of enlightenment—that the truth of particular assertions and claims cannot be tested. Instead, every particular assertion or claim is so thoroughly embedded in the historical metanarrative that the only way to either confirm or challenge it would be to accept or reject Adorno's entire philosophy of history. The other worry is that, despite Adorno's repeated warnings against collapsing validity and genesis—against judging the validity of an idea solely on the basis of how and where it originated—he may have turned historical forces (origins) into guarantees for the truth (validity) of his own ideas. Here the worry is that Adorno regards his philosophical responses to his historical context as true just by virtue of being products of that context—and, more generally, that he regards the truth of all philosophical ideas as similarly tied to the historical contexts in which they arise. The first worry pertains to a kind of historical absolutism; the second, to a kind of historical relativism. I shall return to these worries in a moment.

The dialectical counterpart to historical necessity in Adorno's conception of truth lies in the possibility of transcendence. He introduces this possibility in the very next meditation, titled "Dying Today" (ND 361–66/368–73). The issue here is whether contemporary experience provides any basis for hope in life after death of the sort seemingly attached to traditional metaphysical ideas about the immortality of the soul. Although Adorno thinks capitalist society after Auschwitz severely impedes the requisite metaphysical experience, he also asserts it is philosophically impossible to regard death as "simply and purely ultimate [*das schlechthin Letzte*]." The reason he gives for this impossibility is that to regard death as absolute would undermine any and every truth claim. Amid truth's temporality, truth must endure, he says; if truth did not endure, its final trace would be swallowed up in the victory of death (ND 364/371). Here Adorno employs the same verb—*verschlingen*—used by Martin Luther to translate two biblical passages about death being "swallowed up": swallowed up by "the Lord of hosts" in Isaiah 25:7, and swallowed up "in victory" in I Corinthians 15:54. I do not believe Adorno's usage is a coincidence: the text in I Corinthians punctuates a passage about the perishable body's putting on immortality—the body, not the soul—and this resonates with Adorno's subsequent claim that "hope means corporeal resurrection," something he says Christian dogmatic theology understood better than speculative metaphysics did (ND 393/401).

Similarly, in the following meditation, titled "Happiness and Waiting in Vain" (ND 366–68/373–75), Adorno suggests that anticipating unique and irreplaceable happiness (*Glück*), even while one waits in vain for the happiness promised, is intrinsic to the experience of truth. Truth has to do with the possibility that there is something more to life than the death that surrounds us. Just as every trace of truth would vanish if death were absolute, so anything we could experience "as truly living [*als wahrhaft Lebendiges*]" would also promise "something that transcends life [*ein dem Leben Transzendentes*]" (ND 368/375).

This possibility is not simply a logical possibility; rather, it is both historical and anthropological. The promised transcendent both "is and is not," Adorno says (ND 368/375): the very course of history that points toward it also blocks its arrival, and our experience of what's promised, although real, is fragile. The mixture of historical and anthropological possibility is especially striking in Adorno's lectures on metaphysics where, in the lecture "Dying Today" (a precursor and parallel to Meditation 3, ND 361–66/368–73), Adorno suggests that "only if the infinite possibility . . . radically contained in every human life . . . were reached . . . might we have the possibility of being reconciled to death." The context makes clear that Adorno regards this "infinite possibility" as not only historically enabled and blocked but also anthropologically universal: it is a potential that, if actualized, would mean we are "really identical to that which we are not but which we deeply know we could become, though we may want to believe the contrary."[11]

The manner in which this possibility is historical differs from a Hegelian understanding that subordinates possibility to actuality, however. As Iain Macdonald shows, the historical possibility that carries most weight for Adorno is one that historical actuality has blocked but that nevertheless remains both possible and preferable to the "real possibilities" afforded by "real historical actuality."[12] Yet it remains crucial that historical actuality *points toward* the possibility it also blocks. This is why Adorno claims happiness simultaneously inhabits objects and is remote from them. It is also why he says "objective" theological and metaphysical categories simultaneously encapsulate a "hardened society" and the "priority of the object" (ND 367/374).

Consequently, as a parallel passage in Adorno's lectures on metaphysics states, metaphysical experience, to the extent it is still possible, occurs in a nearly instantaneous configuration between "flashes of fallible consciousness" and "the primacy of the object."[13] *Negative Dialectics* translates this depiction of metaphysical experience into the following description of truth: "The surplus beyond the subject, however, which subjective metaphysical experience does not want to surrender, and the truth-moment in what is thing-like [*das Wahrheitsmoment am Dinghaften*] are extremes that touch in the idea of truth. For [truth] could not exist without the subject that wrestles free from illusion [*Schein*] any more than [it could exist] without that which is not the subject and in which truth has its prototype [*Urbild*]" (ND 368/375). To wrestle free from societally imposed illusion, and to be touched by the nonidentical, by what in the object escapes the subject's concepts, are the key to metaphysical experience. Together, they are what the experience of truth comes to for Adorno, and their conjoint occurrence is a historically and anthropologically available possibility.

Adorno's pointing to the possibility of transcendence goes some distance to allay the worries about absolutism and relativism raised by his emphasis on the necessity of historical development. Despite and amid the pervasiveness of his historical metanarrative, he emphasizes the openness and fallibility of philosophical experience. This emphasis raises the possibility that the truth of particular assertions and claims can be tested in experience and not simply deferred along an endless chain of interlinked assertions. Although, as I have argued elsewhere, Adorno problematically makes philosophical experience self-authenticating,[14] nevertheless the appeal to experience provides an important counterweight to his historical metanarrative—one that Habermasian critics, who charge Adorno with having an "esoteric" conception of truth, have been reluctant to acknowledge.

So too, by indicating that historico-anthropological transcendence is not impossible—that the sociohistorically comprehensive context of illusion (*Verblendungszusammenhang*) does not have the final word—Adorno alleviates the worry that historical forces would be thought to guarantee the truth of his ideas. Given his own conception of truth, whether or not his ideas are true depends, in the end, on the extent to which they align with the possibility of something else and something more than the historical forces that require him to articulate these ideas. These forces might necessitate the articulation, but they do not guarantee the truth of his ideas.

Now, however, other concerns arise. For to test truth claims in experience requires that the right sort of experience be historically available and not simply historically possible. Moreover, to appeal to the possibility of historico-anthropological transcendence presupposes that this possibility actually obtains and is not simply the figment of a historically desperate imagination. Is the right sort of experience historically available? Does the possibility of transcendence actually obtain? To address these concerns, we need to look at Adorno's critical retrieval of Immanuel Kant's transcendental ideas in Meditations 6–9.

Critical Self-Negation and Mimetic Self-Disclosure

Like Hegel, Adorno criticizes Kant for having an unduly restricted conception of truth, one that makes a certain model of scientific rationality the standard for all knowledge. This scientistic and restricted conception of knowledge is at odds, however, with what Adorno calls the "pathos of the infinite" (ND 377/384) in Kant's account of practical reason, which is supposed to have primacy over theoretical reason. As a result, the (infinite) truth toward which Kant aspires in his practical philosophy cannot be assigned to what he regards as finite knowledge. Unlike Hegel, who resolves this tension in an absolute knowledge of the absolute, Adorno reconfigures it via a novel reconstruction of Kant's transcendental ideas. As Martin Shuster suggests, this reconstruction of transcendental ideas belongs to the effort in Adorno's mature work to negotiate between the dialectic of enlightenment, which threatens to dissolve agency, and the "rational theology" Kant articulates in order to support rational autonomy.[15]

There are three such ideas in Kant's Critiques. Kant construes all three as pointing to matters that can be thought but cannot be known: the immortal soul, an intelligible world in which humans can be free moral agents, and God as the Supreme Being. In the Second Critique, Kant treats the soul's immortality, human freedom, and God's existence as "postulates of pure practical reason": these ideas are subjectively necessary in order for people to be moral and to pursue the highest good.[16] In this way, as Adorno says, Kant retains traditional metaphysical ideas and even gives them a crucial role. Yet Kant refuses to conclude from the practical necessity of our having these ideas that therefore their objects must exist—for such we cannot know, given Kant's restricted conception of knowledge (ND 378/385).

What Kant attributes to the inherent limitations of human knowledge, Adorno ascribes instead to the barriers imposed by the societal (and historically changeable) preformation of knowledge. Capitalist society privileges science over other modes of experience, Adorno claims, and it imprisons people in the pursuit of self-preservation and production for its own sake; Kantian restrictions on knowledge both ratify and arise from such societal preformation (ND 379–82/386–90). As an alternative, Adorno once again points to the historical possibility of wrestling free from illusion and giving priority to the object: "The moment of independence, of irreducibility in spirit [*Geist*] might very well accord with the priority of the object. Where spirit becomes autonomous [*selbständig*] here and now, as soon as it names the fetters in which it lands by fettering others, it, not entangled praxis, anticipates freedom" (ND 382/390).

This independence in spirit, this wrestling free from illusion, is precisely what Adorno finds in Kant's transcendental ideas. Taken collectively as what Adorno calls "the concept of the intelligible" (*der Begriff des Intelligibeln*), they must be thought in a negative fashion, he says, as the "self-negation of finite spirit" (ND 384/392). In this self-negation is registered not only the insufficiency of spirit—caught, as it is, in the partially self-spun webs of societally truncated life—but also the insufficiency of finite existence itself. At the same time, however, the finite existence that spirit tries to comprehend and, in comprehending, tries to dominate, receives an opportunity to show itself as being more than what it is under the distorting conditions of societal domination. Accordingly, the object of the transcendental ideas—what the concept of the intelligible is about—is, in Adorno's memorable formulation, that which what is concealed to finite spirit discloses [*zukehrt*] to finite spirit and which finite spirit is compelled to think—but which finite spirit also deforms, due to its own finitude, its own societal preformation ("was das dem endlichen Geist Verborgene diesem zukehrt, was er zu denken gezwungen ist und vermöge der eigenen Endlichkeit deformiert," ND 384/392). In other words, the transcendental ideas—immortality, freedom, God—are about the nonidentical—about that which both invites and resists conceptual thought—and they are a "moment of transcendent objectivity" in spirit. They are about "something that does not exist and yet is not simply nonexistent [*etwas, was nicht ist und doch nicht nur nicht ist*]" (ND 385/392–93).

As responses to the concerns I raised earlier, these formulations suggest that the right sort of experience for testing truth claims is indeed historically available, and that the possibility of historico-anthropological transcendence actually obtains. On the one hand, what Adorno calls the "self-negation of finite spirit" is itself made possible by the historical dialectic of enlightenment. On the other hand, the self-disclosure of that which resists and exceeds the grasp of finite spirit does not completely depend on the operations of finite spirit: spirit's self-negation helps create the opportunity for the nonidentical's self-disclosure, but this self-disclosure is not constituted by the operations of finite spirit. There is, one could say, a precarious yet historically rooted oscillation between finite spirit's self-negation and the nonidentical's self-disclosure.

Because this oscillation is both precarious and historical, Adorno describes the transcendental ideas as a necessary illusion or necessary semblance (*Schein*). Their objects are neither real nor imaginary (ND 384/391) yet, as a historically rooted semblance of transcendence, the transcendental ideas are necessary. That is why the redemption of illusion, which Adorno makes central to aesthetics, has "incomparable metaphysical relevance," he says (ND 386/393).

Here still other questions arise. It is one thing to claim that the experience needed to test truth claims is historically available and that the possibility of historico-anthropological transcendence actually obtains. It is something different, however, to suggest that the historically necessary illusion that epitomizes such experience and such transcendence can be redeemed. What makes the redemption of illusion possible, and in what does it consist? In other words, what is truth?

Convergence and Hope

At this point, readers of Adorno face a fork in the hermeneutical road. Some interpreters, such as Habermas, read Adorno as having become so entrapped in his own historical metanarrative that only (modern) art and aesthetic theory could provide the escape hatch he both seeks and needs: only in aesthetics could he rescue the semblance of transcendence. Habermas's interpretation presupposes that Adorno and Horkheimer regard reason as being only instrumental both in modernity and throughout human history.[17] Unlike Habermas's influential interpretation, others read the occasional references to art and aesthetics in Adorno's "Meditations on Metaphysics" as emblematic, not definitive, of the semblance of transcendence and its rescue. For such interpreters, the most fundamental redemption of illusion would not occur in art and aesthetics but in a structural transformation of society as a whole. Let me distinguish these two lines of interpretation as the aestheticist and the social transformationalist readings of Adorno's metacritique of metaphysics. I count myself among the social transformationalist interpreters.

Meditation 11, titled "Semblance of the Other [*Schein des Anderen*]" (ND 394–97/402–5), bears out a social transformationalist interpretation. One could call this meditation Adorno's negative eschatology. Not surprisingly, it begins with Hegel, whose metaphysical construction of world history is the antipode to Adorno's historical construction of metaphysical experience. According to Adorno, Hegel problematically resurrects ontological proofs for God's existence when he makes the concept the guarantor of the nonconceptual, thereby abolishing transcendence. After that, transcendence crumbled at the hands of societal and cultural enlightenment and became increasingly arcane [*zum Verborgenen wird—das Verborgene* being the same term Adorno used in Meditation 8 (ND 384/392) to talk about the object of the transcendental ideas]. This arcanization was registered, Adorno suggests, in dialectical theologies of the "wholly other" (e.g., Karl Barth and Rudolf Bultmann) (ND 394/402). So questions about the historical possibility and availability of transcendence have intensified.

In response, Adorno appeals to something that resists being demythologized. What resists being demythologized, he says, is a metaphysical experience, namely, the experience that thought that "does not decapitate itself" flows into transcendence. It flows all the way into the idea of a world where "not only extant suffering would be abolished but also suffering that is irrevocably past would be revoked." It is the experience of having all thoughts converge in the concept of "something that would be different" from the current unspeakable world (ND 395/403). It is, one could say, the thought expressed by Max Horkheimer in "The Longing for the Wholly Other," his remarkable interview in *Der Spiegel* magazine one year after Adorno's death. There Horkheimer suggests that in the end, despite all the injustice and violence both experienced in the past and continuing today, injustice will not prevail—a thought Horkheimer describes as a "theology," a "hope," and a "longing": "Theology is . . . the hope that the injustice that marks the world would not prevail, that injustice would not have the final word. . . . [Theology is] the expression of a longing, a longing that the murderer would not triumph over the innocent victim."[18]

Adorno calls this the "concept" (*Begriff*) and the "experience" of convergence (*Erfahrung von Konvergenz*) (ND 395–96/403–4). The experience of convergence does not ignore sociohistorical reality. Yet it resists any claim that this reality is all there is, that no better future is possible. The basis for such resistance lies in the traces we experience of something other within the "disturbed and damaged" course of the world, the broken promises of something other within the breeches to total identity, the fragments of happiness (*Glück*) that people have while they both deny and are denied complete happiness (ND 395–96/403–4). Adorno calls such convergence "the humanly promised other of history" (ND 396/404), and he says it points to that transcendence which (Heideggerian) ontology illegitimately locates before or outside history. The humanly promised other of history points to a historically not impossible society in which violence and suffering have ended.

Unlike ontological proofs for God's existence, Adorno's negative eschatology does not claim that this utopian condition is real or actual (*wirklich*) just because certain sociohistorical traces and fragments point to it. Yet he does claim that the concept of convergence could not be conceived if something actual (*in der Sache*) did not press toward it (ND 396/404). Just as he had said earlier that the object of the transcendental ideas discloses itself to finite spirit and compels finite spirit to think it, so now he claims that something within the sociohistorical world elicits and compels the thought of convergence.

Here we have answers to the questions posed earlier about the redemption of illusion. The redemption of illusion is made possible by the convergence of experience on the humanly promised other of history, and such redemption consists in the persistent refusal to give up on what is humanly and historically promised. In other words, truth is the undying and critically articulable hope for complete social transformation. Art is emblematic in this regard, not because it is the only bastion left where truth can occur, but because it amplifies both the refusal and the promise.

This, it seems to me, is how we should read the eloquent passage that concludes Meditation 11. Let me quote parts of it before I comment on it:

> Thought that does not capitulate before wretched existence comes to naught before its criteria, truth becomes untruth, philosophy becomes folly. And yet philosophy cannot give up, lest idiocy triumph in actualized unreason [*Widervernunft*]. . . . Folly is truth in the shape that human beings must accept whenever, amid the untrue, they do not give up on truth. Art, even at its highest peaks, is semblance [*Schein*]; but art receives the semblance . . . from nonsemblance [*vom Scheinlosen*]. By refraining from judgment, [art] says . . . everything would not be just nothing. Otherwise, everything that is would be pale, colorless, indifferent. No light falls on people and things in which transcendence would not appear [*widerschiene*]. Indelible in resistance to the fungible world of exchange is the resistance of the eye that does not want the world's colors to be destroyed. In semblance nonsemblance is promised. (ND 396–97/404–5)

In this passage, art is emblematic of anything in society and experience that resists the "fungible world of exchange," but art is not exhaustive in this regard. Adorno also mentions "philosophy" and "human beings" as being capable of not capitulating "before wretched existence" and not giving up truth. Moreover, he does not restrict the light falling on people and things to either art or philosophy. As Adorno suggests earlier in this meditation, transcendence can appear wherever people experience fragments of happiness or, as he says in the passage just quoted, whenever the eye "does not want the world's colors to be destroyed." Truth is a persistent hope for complete social transformation; in principle, access to it cannot be limited.

Looking back, we can see more clearly why Adorno regards truth as the most important "metaphysical" idea. It is most important because no resistance to "wretched existence," including the resistance within Adorno's own negative dialectics, would have a purpose or a point if there were no hope that existence could be otherwise. Further, the idea of truth is metaphysical because, in the end, the only way for this hope to show up is by breaking through the finitude and fallibility of necessary illusion. If there were no hope for complete social transformation, then "actualized unreason" would have the final word, and Adorno would have to surrender his claims to speak truth about "wretched existence." It is by rescuing a negatively eschatological idea of truth from Kant's critique of metaphysics that Adorno shows "solidarity with metaphysics in the moment of its collapse" (ND 400/408). The entire point of what Adorno calls the migration of metaphysics into "micrology" is to assemble existence into a "legible constellation" (ND 399/407) where, despite and within the wretchedness, the historically not impossible possibility of social transformation shines through.

Predicative Self-Disclosure and Hopeful Critique

The unprecedented mixture of history and transcendence in Adorno's conception of truth makes it susceptible to criticisms from many different angles. I too have raised some of these criticisms, arguing, for example, that Adorno fails to find an adequate basis for transformative hope.[19] Here, however, I want to explore what is right about Adorno's idea of truth as a whole and then consider how it relates to a conception of propositional truth. Paradoxically, as I shall show, Adorno's most important contributions on the topic of truth as a whole undermine his potential contributions to a conception of propositional truth. Conversely, what Adorno's *Negative*

Dialectics could offer a theory of propositional truth conflicts with his conception of truth as a whole.

Like Adorno, and unlike most contemporary truth theorists, I regard propositional truth as only one dimension of truth as a whole—an important dimension, to be sure, but not all-important. Once one distinguishes propositional truth from truth as a whole, however, one also needs to account for their relation. Like Heidegger, albeit in strikingly different ways, Adorno fails to give an adequate account of this relation. Soon I shall explain why. But first let me say what Adorno has contributed to our understanding of truth as a whole. Two contributions stand out: the nexus of hope and critique, and a negative cognitive relation.

To begin, Adorno's conception of truth calls attention to a nexus of social hope and social critique that receives short shrift in most philosophical conceptions of truth. Moreover, Adorno accomplishes this without turning the object of hope into an ahistorical unknown. We might not know precisely what a wholly transformed society would be like, but we can know it would be one where violence and suffering do not prevail. Further, we have sufficient indications in our experience—ciphers of promise, as it were—to believe hope for such a society need not be misplaced. At the same time, precisely because social hope need not be misplaced, it makes sense to undertake a thoroughgoing critique of the historical societal formation we inhabit. It makes sense, as Adorno famously put it at the end of *Minima Moralia*, to try "to contemplate all things as they would present themselves from the standpoint of redemption" (MM 283/247). Truth is the idea in which social hope and social critique interlink. If Adorno is right, we cannot have one without the other, and without truth as a whole we would not have either hope or critique.

So too, Adorno's conception of truth calls attention to the negative side of a cognitive relation that most truth theorists either dismiss or treat in an exclusively positive manner. The relation in question holds between the subject and the object of knowledge, between what I label the epistemic subject and the epistemic object. Contemporary truth theorists primarily discuss this as the relation (if any) between "truth bearers" and "truth makers" (if any), a discussion that is central to debates between alethic realists and alethic antirealists. Alethic realists and antirealists share an underlying assumption, however, namely, that if there is a truth-making relation between, say, propositions and facts, then this would be a positive relation: a correspondence or correlation or congruence, for example.

Adorno explodes this assumption. He introduces the notion of a precarious, historically rooted oscillation between critical self-negation on the part of the epistemic subject ("finite spirit") and mimetic self-disclosure on the part of the epistemic object *in its nonidentity* with the epistemic subject's concepts. According to this notion, the truth of knowledge would primarily consist not in a positive relation between epistemic subject and object (e.g., correspondence) but in a negative relation. It would consist in the epistemic subject's *not* imposing conceptual identity on the object and in the epistemic object's *not* aligning with the subject's conceptual identifications. Moreover, such nonalignment would occur when the epistemic subject criticizes its own identifications and thereby allows the epistemic object to show itself to be more than it is thought to be. Unlike most contemporary truth theorists, then, Adorno makes subjective self-critique and objective otherness central to the truth of knowledge. This, in turn, implies that social critique and social hope are intrinsic to the acquisition and confirmation of true knowledge—yet another insight one seeks in vain among most contemporary truth theorists.

Nevertheless, both of Adorno's contributions concerning truth as a whole—truth as a nexus of hope and critique, and negativity as central to the truth of knowledge—make it difficult for him to give an adequate account of propositional truth—the truth that accrues to beliefs, assertions, propositions, and the like. I believe Adorno recognized this difficulty. Moreover, precisely because he recognized it, he labored mightily to distinguish his negative dialectics from Heideggerian ontology, where a similar disconnection occurs between propositional truth and truth as a whole, but for different reasons. Whereas Heidegger's disconnection occurs because his account of Dasein's disclosedness (*Erschlossenheit*) leaves too few ways to distinguish true assertions from false ones,[20] Adorno's disconnection occurs because his emphasis on the nonidentical prevents him from giving an adequate account of the epistemic object's *predicative* self-disclosure. Let me explain.

Adorno's idea of the nonidentical (*das Nichtidentische*) is a protean notion, and it can be applied to many different matters.[21] Insofar as it pertains to the epistemic object, however, *the nonidentical* indicates something more to the object than the identity it has under existing (societally preformed) predications. In order for this "something moreness" to become available for predication, two things must happen on the epistemic subject's side. First, existing ways of predication that miss—indeed, suppress—the object in its nonidentity must be overturned. That is the role of self-negation and self-critique. Second, other ways of relating to the object, ways that are open to the object's being something more, must come into play. That is what Adorno indicates with the concept of mimesis: an archaic mode of conduct that can persist even in the outer reaches of abstract thought. What I discussed earlier as the nonidentical's self-disclosure takes place via mimesis.

Predication, however, occurs in ordinary language usage and, as Adorno himself recognizes, language usage is highly variable. For the requisite self-critique to be on target, there must be a way to specify which predications concerning an object are better or worse with respect to the object's identity. Further, in order for there to be better and worse predications in this respect, the object's own identity must offer itself for predication in better and worse ways. But the object can offer itself in better and worse ways only if it already has an identity that exceeds any that the subject asserts about it. This implies in turn that objects must be capable of self-disclosure *not only in their nonidentity* vis-à-vis the subject's existing predications but also—and importantly—*in their identity prior to the subject's predicating* and *in openness to being predicated*. In addition to *mimetic* self-disclosure, then, the epistemic object must be capable of *predicative* self-disclosure. It must be able to offer itself to propositional cognition in such a way that the object's availability for practices of predication aligns well with relevant ways in which the object is available for nonpredicative practices.

Adorno cannot countenance predicative self-disclosure, however, because, as Espen Hammer has argued, Adorno's conception of propositional truth rests on a fundamental failure "to distinguish properly between predication and identification."[22] Adorno tightly associates the ordinary *use of predicates* to identify something in a certain respect with the (dominating) *imposition of identity* on something as such. Because of this, he cannot see that ordinary predication neither attempts nor accomplishes an imposition of identity. When I say, "This house is green," for example, I do not violently subsume a particular house under universal greenness. Nor do I thereby violate either the full-blown object (a particular house) or my robust experience of it. I simply call attention to one specific aspect of the object's identity, an aspect it shares with other objects but displays in its own unique way, and an aspect that is only one among many aspects it displays. Because Adorno tends to equate predication with impositional identification, he needs, as an alternative, to appeal to a Benjaminian notion of nonintentional truth—accessible via mimetic conduct, artworks, and dialectical self-critique—as what allows the particular "to identify itself as what it is independently of all human strategies or procedures for identification."[23] For Adorno, the only self-disclosure available from the epistemic object is mimetic, not predicative. In taking this position Adorno shows what Hammer describes as an indebtedness to "two radically diverging philosophical visions," a Kant/Hegel idealist emphasis on the conceptual mediation of experience, which Adorno appropriates in a primarily negative direction, and a Schelling/Benjamin metaphysically realist emphasis on nondiscursive access to "transcendent objecthood."[24] Or, as I said in the previous chapter, Adorno appropriates Hegel's idea of truth in a Benjamin-inspired way.

Hence Adorno cannot really account for what I call the epistemic object's predicative self-disclosure. He cannot account for this because he ties predication so closely to the societally preformed and conceptual imposition of identity upon the epistemic object. Indeed, this tendency to equate predication with the imposition of identity is what leads Owen Hulatt, in his detailed account of "the interpenetration of concepts and society" in Adorno's conception of truth, to argue that Adorno's embraces a type of "negativism" with respect to propositional truth.[25] In an odd way, the deception of constitutive subjectivity, which Adorno's *Negative Dialectics* rightly aims to shatter (ND 10/xx), returns in his failure to recognize the object's availability for accurate predication.

Now one could try to defend Adorno by arguing, as Philip Hogh suggests, that Adorno does not conflate predication and identification. For Adorno, one could say, there is always more to the concept than its being a "unit of properties" (*Merkmalseinheit*): it has both an ethical and an aesthetic "surplus."[26] Similarly, there is always more to predicative judgments than their being conceptual identifications, for they always also give expression to subjective experiences and sociohistorical contexts.[27] The problem with such a defense, however, is that it accepts Adorno's claim that, under current sociohistorical conditions, the primary usage of concepts—as units of properties—and predicative judgments—as conceptual identifications—is to *impose* a universal identity on objects and thereby to do an injustice to particular objects in their particularity. Adorno's mistake, in my view, lies precisely here, in his thinking that ordinary predications "only determine that moment of an object that marks it as a specimen of a universal concept" and that therefore we need other means—negation, conceptual constellations, and the like—to redirect concepts "towards the nonidentical by their ethical surplus."[28] It may be so that, for Adorno, "the relationship between the concept as a unit of properties and its ethical surplus . . . is the leading concern in approaching predicative judgments."[29] The reason why this would be his leading concern, however, is because Adorno has misconstrued concepts and predications as impositions of universal identity in the first place.

Contra Adorno, it is because epistemic objects are always already available for linguistic reference and predication that we can make assertions about them. And it is because such predicative availability on the part of objects can align with their other, nonlinguistic modes of availability that our assertions can be more or less correct. In other words, so-called propositional truth requires not only that the object of knowledge have its own prior identity, as Adorno rightly insists, but also that this identity can disclose itself *when predication occurs* and that it is *not imposed* by the epistemic subject's predication.

In the context of propositional truth, this prior identity of the object vis-à-vis predication is the true priority of the object, it seems to me, and it is one that Adorno's worries about the societal preformation of knowledge prevent him from spelling out. Because of this, Adorno fails to offer an adequate account of predicative self-disclosure, as I show at greater length in the next chapter. Adorno thereby also fails to provide an adequate account of propositional truth within his conception of truth as a whole.

At this point, a loyal defender of Adorno's negative dialectics might be tempted to retort, "So much the worse for propositional truth." I am not such a defender. Yet, in expecting Adorno to give an adequate account of propositional truth, I believe I remain faithful to the spirit of his philosophy. And here I agree with Peter Gordon, who, while demonstrating "the hidden and not-so-hidden points of contact between Adorno and existentialism," nevertheless distinguishes Adorno from irrationalist critics of modernity: Adorno's negativity "still glows, however faintly, with a rationalist's hope for a better world."[30] To distort the facts, embrace the lie, and spout destructive ideology cannot be in line with a world without violence and suffering. To say why this is so, philosophers need to account for propositional truth. Yet, as Adorno understood, their account also needs to align with a vision of hopeful critique.

3

Surplus beyond the Subject

> The surplus beyond the subject . . . and the truth-moment in what is thing-like are extremes that touch in the idea of truth.
>
> —Theodor W. Adorno (ND 375/368)

Theodor Adorno's conception of truth is an intricate force field (*Kraftfeld*) where dialectical polarities intersect. Perhaps the most prominent dialectical tension in his conception—or at least the one most frequently commented on—lies in the mediation between subject and object.[1] It is also the focal point for criticisms of Adorno among his successors. Jürgen Habermas, for example, thinks that Adorno's alleged inability to break with "the modern philosophy of the subject" and with a "philosophy of consciousness" is a fundamental failure, one Habermas aims to correct by proposing a philosophy of communicative action.[2]

As Brian O'Connor[3] and others have shown, Adorno's understanding of subject/object mediation stems primarily from his complex reworking of both Kant and Hegel. Less well recognized, however, is that this understanding is implicitly predicated upon Adorno's critique of Edmund Husserl's conception of categorial intuition, with a view to Martin Heidegger's conception of Being. For Adorno, Husserl's account of categorial intuition in *Logical Investigations* not only demonstrates the irresolvable antinomies in Husserlian phenomenology but also paves the way for Martin Heidegger's flawed ontology. At the same time, Adorno's own conception of truth—as evinced in the epigraph above—carries the imprint of this critique, as he tries to provide an immanently critical alternative to the accounts of truth in Husserl's *Logical Investigations* and Heidegger's *Being and Time*.[4]

In this chapter I examine three passages where Adorno appears intent on wresting a viable conception of propositional truth from Husserlian phenomenology and Heideggerian ontology. The first passage is a discussion of categorial intuition from chapter 4 of *Zur Metakritik der Erkenntnistheorie*, Adorno's book on Husserl. The second and third passages concern the relation between Adorno's own negative dialectics and Heideggerian ontology, and they come from the "On Categorial Intuition" and "Copula" sections in part 1 of *Negative Dialectics*. After examining these passages, I consider the issues they raise for Adorno's own conception of propositional truth.

Husserl's Categorial Intuition

In *Zur Metakritik der Erkenntnistheorie*, Adorno reads the account of categorial intuition (*kategoriale Anschauung*) in Husserl's *Logical Investigations*, volume 2, as extending the "logical absolutism" of the "Prolegomena to Pure Logic" in volume 1. According to Adorno, Husserl's prolegomenon challenges the relativism in psychologizing accounts of propositional truth by insisting on the complete independence of "propositions in themselves." Adorno claims that Husserl's subsequent discussion of categorial intuition in the Sixth Investigation tries to secure the pure yet experienced facts to which pure propositions must correspond. Husserl says these facts, which he calls "states of affairs" (*Sachverhalte*), are intentionally given in categorial intuition. Husserl's discussion of categorial intuition thereby permits an apparent reconciliation between his "rationalist" tendency to insist on absolute "truths of reason" (*vérités de raison*) and his "positivist" tendency to insist on the givenness of facts. Yet the reconciliation is only apparent, Adorno says, and the paradoxes in Husserl's account of categorial intuition hide a dialectic that unfolds over Husserl's head (ME 204–5/201–2). Adorno's goal is to demonstrate the paradoxes and uncover this dialectic.[5]

I, by contrast, read the discussion of categorial intuition in chapter 6 of Investigation 6 from *Logical Investigations* as an attempt to fill a significant gap in Husserl's accounts of intentional experience (Investigation 5), phenomenology of knowledge (Investigation 6), and truth (chapter 5 of Investigation 6). According to Husserl, knowledge and truth require that the meaning intentions expressed in judgments and assertions be fulfilled in the acts of intuition (either perception or imagination or both) whereby intuited objects are given for intentional experience. Yet whatever fulfills the meaning expressed using words such as "a," "some," "not," and "or"—including the copula "is"—cannot be given to sensuous perception or imagination. Husserl's categorial intuition is an attempt to account for the fulfillment of such "formal moments" in what he calls signitive acts.

For Husserl, then, the main issue in this context is not to secure the truth of propositions in themselves but rather to complete his phenomenological account of experience, knowledge, and truth. He thus postulates a supersensuous kind of intuition that can be just as fulfilling as sensuous perception and sensuous imagination are. This is what Husserl calls "categorial intuition," and the matters given to categorial intuition are what he calls "states of affairs." For example, if I express my act of perceptual judgment by asserting "this house is green," and my assertion is correct, the "is" of my assertion is fulfilled by a categorial intuition to which "predicative being" (*prädikatives Sein*) is given as a state of affairs, just as the house and its color are given to sensuous intuition—specifically to sensuous perception.[6]

Adorno, however, finds this notion of "predicative being" highly problematic. It arises because Husserl's phenomenology of knowledge wrongly assumes a thoroughgoing parallelism between signitive acts, such as judging and asserting, and their intuitive fulfillment. This assumption misleads Husserl into claiming that the formal moments in signitive acts must be intuitively fulfilled via categorial intuition.[7] But Husserl's claim is fundamentally mistaken, according to Adorno: even Husserl must realize that one cannot grasp such formal "moments of thought" as "copies [*Abbilder*] of a nonsensuous, transsubjective being, since there is no way to determine the nonsensuous moments other than indeed as moments of thought" (ME 206/203). Despite Husserl's own attack on a copy theory of knowledge, his "fundamental thesis of propositions in themselves" forces him to adopt a picture theory of categorial intuition, such that the formal moments in signitive acts copy and "correspond" to some "objective-ideal being" that is categorial-intuitively given (ME 207/204).

Here we have the core of Adorno's Hegelian objections both to Husserl's account of categorial intuition and to Heidegger's understanding of Being (*Sein*): both of them turn the conceptual into the nonconceptual and the mediated into the unmediated.[8] Yet Adorno's objections also raise questions about his own conception of propositional truth. For his claim that the nonsensuous moments of thought can be grasped only as moments of thought fails to address two questions of concern for both Husserl and Heidegger. First, what do these nonsensuous moments include? Specifically, is what Husserl calls "predicative being" nothing more than what Adorno calls "a moment of thought"? Second, how are Adorno's moments of thought fulfilled? Specifically, how do we account for the fact that predicating does real, cognitive work in our judging and asserting, such that the results of this process—judgments, assertions, and propositions—can be true? One does not need to subscribe to a "copy theory" of knowledge or a correspondence theory of truth in order to think such questions are legitimate.

PROCESS OF JUDGING

Although Adorno does not pose these questions, he indirectly addresses them when he argues that so-called categorial intuition is simply part of the whole process of knowledge that amounts to "grounded judgment" (*begründetes Urteil*) (ME 208/205). Adorno makes this argument by unpacking a purported ambiguity in Husserl's claim that we immediately "become aware" (*Gewahrwerden*) of "states of affairs" in categorial intuition. Adorno suggests that the immediacy of our becoming aware of a state of affairs—which Husserl attributes to categorial intuition—is simply the immediacy of the process of judging something (*die Unmittelbarkeit des Urteilsvollzugs*): judging something is the same thing as becoming aware of the state of affairs judged. We do not need a special categorial intuition in order to become aware of a state of affairs; we can simply pass judgment. After the process of judging is completed and we reflect on the truth or legitimacy of the completed judgment, we might become aware of a "state of affairs," but this state of affairs would be the completed judgment and not some "predicative being." Husserl's account of categorial intuition confuses the synthesis completed in the *process* of judging with the evidence we can achieve in reflection upon the *results* of this process (ME 208–9/205–6).

Despite the initial plausibility of Adorno's argument, on closer inspection we must wonder whether Adorno rather than Husserl is the one confused. For in early Husserl's account of knowledge and truth, the synthesis completed in conjunction with the act of judging always involves both a coincidence between signitive and intuitive acts and an objective identity between the object as signitively meant and the object as intuitively given.[9] This multidimensional account of cognitive synthesis gives rise to Husserl's account of categorial intuition. Adorno tries to undermine Husserl's account by appealing to the "synthesis" that occurs in the process of judgment (*Urteilsvollzug*). Yet Adorno's undefined notion of a "process of judging" is just as ambiguous as he claims Husserl's notion of "becoming aware" (*Gewahrwerden*) to be. On the one hand, the process of judging can be the entire multidimensional cognitive process within which we form judgments and make assertions. Typically, such a process includes what Husserl calls intuitive acts, which go beyond signitive acts such as judging and asserting. Hence the question arises of how, say, (signitive) judging and (intuitive) perceiving line up—of how they are synthesized—when we achieve knowledge. That, in part, is the question Husserl's notion of categorial intuition aims to answer. On the other hand, Adorno's term "process of judging" might, strictly speaking, refer only to a signitive act or practice within the cognitive process, such as the act of asserting something, and any "synthesis" achieved within this more delimited and one-dimensional signitive act would be inherently conceptual and nonintuitive.

Adorno appeals to the first, multidimensional sense of "process of judging" when he claims that judging something is the same thing as becoming aware of a state of affairs. If he were to analyze this process, or at least if he rendered Husserl's analysis accurately, Adorno would need to indicate that the so-called process of judging is not simply an act or practice of judging; it is also, in Husserl's terms, an act or practice of intuiting, as well as an aligning of these two qualitatively distinct acts or practices—judging and intuiting—within a cognitive synthesis. Adorno would also need to distinguish the object as signified, intuited, and synthetically known from what, in Husserl's terms, is a state of affairs. If Adorno did all of this, he could not so casually equate "becoming aware" (of a state of affairs) in Husserl's sense with "the original [signitive] intending of something judged, the process of judging as an act, the synthesis that simultaneously reaches and establishes [*trifft und schafft*] the state of affairs that is judged" (ME 208/206). And just as Adorno could no longer equate judging with knowing, neither could he so easily reduce the object about which one makes a judgment ("something judged") to a state of affairs ("the state of affairs that is judged").

Adorno appeals to the second, one-dimensional sense of "process of judging"—that is, judging as a qualitatively distinct act or practice, not as the synthetic process of knowing—when he claims that the result of our judging can become a "state of affairs" as we reflect on this result and try to establish whether the original judgment is true. For the result of our judging is indeed a signitive judgment or assertion, not a percept or image, and also not a synthetic cognition. Moreover, when we critically reflect on this result, we need to link it with other judgments, as Adorno rightly suggests: "[Reflection] relates the judged state of affairs to other states of affairs: its own result is a new categorization" (ME 209/206).

But while Adorno uses "state of affairs" to mean something like the propositional content of an accomplished judgment, this is not what Husserl means when he says we become aware of "states of affairs" in categorial intuition, any more than he means that we become categorial-intuitively aware of the *entire* object about which the judgment is made. For Husserl, a "state of affairs" is neither the propositional content nor the entire object of a judgment. Although Adorno is right to worry about the "immediacy" that Husserl seems to attribute to becoming categorial-intuitively aware of "states of affairs," his criticisms fundamentally misconstrue what Husserl has in mind. Husserl is not saying that categorial intuition renders our judgments infallible. Rather, without categorial intuition our judgments could not be fully fallible: they would neither have a purchase nor fail to have a purchase on certain ways in which objects are predicatively available.

Indeed, Adorno's insistence that neither the "process of judging" in the multidimensional sense nor the reflection on accomplished judgments can be "interpreted as categorial intuition" (ME 209/206) is a red herring: Husserl never says that they *can* be interpreted as categorial intuition. Rather, Husserl claims that the formal elements in signitive acts and in their results must reach fulfillment via nonsignitive acts, and this happens when categorial intuition gives us access to states of affairs *in Husserl's sense*. Otherwise the synthesis of knowing would be incomplete at best, and there would be no way to account fully for our ability to achieve assertoric correctness and propositional accuracy within the larger process of knowledge. Or, to use a phrase familiar from Adorno's own writings, if the object is to have "priority" in epistemology, then there must also be a priority of the object *in its predicative availability*.

Predicative Being

Adorno, however, would be wary about any notion of predicative availability. It is too redolent of Husserl's notion of "predicative being" (*prädikatives Sein*), which Adorno regards as the camel's nose that lifts the tent flap to Heidegger's ontological house of Being, where the concept of "being" inflates into a metaphysical hyperreality. Husserl introduces the notion of predicative being in opposition to empiricists such as John Locke who say we arrive at categories like being and nonbeing or unity and plurality by reflecting on certain mental acts such as judgments. Husserl, by contrast, insists in section 44 of the Sixth Investigation that the true source of such categories lies in the objects of these acts, not in the acts themselves. So, for example, the concept of "being," in the sense of the predicative being at the basis of saying "*x* is *y*," can arise only if some state of affairs is given to us—and this, according to Husserl, occurs in categorial intuition.[10]

Quoting from this passage, Adorno accuses Husserl of equivocating between highly mediated, abstract "being" (*Sein*) and immediately intuitable "beings" (*Seiendes*)—an equivocation that, Adorno claims, contaminates all of existential philosophy. He further accuses Husserl of ignoring Hegel's insight into how the concept of being in its immediacy is simply part of the process of conceptual mediation in which it arises. As a consequence, Adorno charges, Husserl tries to move the concept of being beyond the reach of critical epistemological reflection (ME 210–11/207–9)—an odd, if not inflammatory charge to make, given Husserl's efforts to wrest the concept of being from empiricist and neo-Kantian neglect and to return it to epistemological salience.

Upon inspection of part 1 from *Negative Dialectics* (especially the sections titled "On Categorial Intuition" and "Copula"), it becomes clear that Adorno's real target here in *Zur Metakritik der Erkenntnistheorie* is not Husserlian phenomenology but rather Heideggerian ontology, not the camel's nose but rather the entire house of Being. It is so, of course, that Adorno's initial target in *Zur Metakritik der Erkenntnistheorie* is Husserl's "Idealism," especially Husserl's failure to break decisively with neo-Kantian problematics. Yet the book's introduction signals that the ultimate object of Adorno's criticisms is Heidegger's ontological appropriation of Husserlian phenomenology, an appropriation that "speaks the jargon of authenticity." According to Adorno, the "turn to ontology that Husserl hesitatingly began and quickly recanted" leads to a Heideggerian ontology that "acts as if it found itself in a glass house with impenetrable but transparent walls and espied the truth outside like an inaccessible fixed star. . . . The new ontology returns penitently to the beginning of Hegel's *Logic* [i.e., to the concept of being] and expires in the abstract identity with which the whole game began" (ME 40–42/33–35). Hence it is not surprising that *Negative Dialectics*, when it mounts the sustained critique of Heidegger's ontology that I examine at greater length in the next chapter, returns to themes in Adorno's earlier criticisms of Husserl's "Idealism."

In "On Categorial Intuition" (ND 87–90/80–83), Adorno describes categorial intuition as a reminder that some nonsubjective moment must correspond to synthetic and categorically constituted states of affairs. For example, the "synthesis of numbers" presupposed by a valid simple equation (e.g., *7 + 5 = 12*) would be impossible unless a relationship between the elements corresponded to this synthesis. Husserl and Heidegger, however, isolate "the moment of state of affairs" from the synthetic moment and thereby reify it. Adorno's alternative here is to approach "states of affairs" as sedimented products of a historical process that thought can reconstruct and release. Because the states of affairs are constituted by the historical process to which they belong, they permit something like a direct intuiting of their "essence," within the medium of what Adorno calls "exemplary thought" (*Medium exemplarischen Denkens*). Husserl and Heidegger, by contrast, regard such products as static self-presentations, Adorno argues, and they treat the concept of being as the supreme "allegedly pure self-presenting categorial state of affairs" (ND 89/81).

Two things become clear from this section in *Negative Dialectics*. First, Adorno replaces Husserl's "categorial intuition" with his own notion of "exemplary thought." Exemplary thought brings together not only the universal and the particular but also the conceptual and the nonconceptual, and it does so without freeze-framing the historical character of its subject matter.[11] Second, and correlatively, Adorno's notion of a "state of affairs" is much more fluid and open-ended than Husserl's. For Adorno, the "moment of state of affairs" amounts to the historically mediated subject matter that cognition tries to grasp. For early Husserl, by contrast, states of affairs are formal elements in intuitively given objects, and such elements fulfill the formal moments in signitive acts such as judgments and assertions. Husserl might allow that historically mediated subject matter presents such formal elements, and that a cognitive grasp of historically mediated subject matter requires such formal elements to fulfill the formal moments in our judgments and assertions. But he would reject Adorno's inflating of states of affairs into subject matter as such. Husserl also would resist Adorno's tendency to equate signitive acts such as judging and asserting with cognition as a whole. Whereas Adorno considers Husserl's "categorial intuition" too static and "positivist," Husserl would regard Adorno's "exemplary thinking" as too fluid and imprecise.

Heidegger's Being

Heidegger, by contrast, would see both approaches as overly invested in a subject/object model of knowledge and truth. But Adorno claims that Heidegger, with his emphasis on Being, tries to usurp a standpoint beyond the difference between subject and object, and this attempt must fail:

"Thought cannot seize any position where the separation of subject and object, which lies in every thought, in thinking itself, would immediately disappear" (ND 90/85). In Adorno's interpretation, Heidegger reaches this impossible standpoint by inflating Husserl's notion of predicative being as a categorially intuitable state of affairs.

Copula

That is why *Negative Dialectics* devotes an entire section (ND 107–11/100–104) to discussing the copula, the "is" in every existential judgment such as "This house is green."[12] Without mentioning Husserl, the section essentially argues that the "is" in an existential judgment does not need to be intuitively fulfilled. So there is no need to posit "being"—whether predicative or otherwise—as a categorial-intuitively given state of affairs to fulfill it. Let me reconstruct Adorno's actual argument, which he directs not at Husserl's "predicative being" but at Heidegger's "cult of Being."

According to Adorno, the copula plays two roles. On the one hand, it establishes a connection (*Zusammenhang*) between the judgment's grammatical subject and its predicate—between "this house" and "green," for example, in the judgment "This house is green." In this role, the predicative "is" suggests something ontic, something that actually exists or could actually exist. What the ontic "is" means depends on which specific connections are being made. On the other hand, taken simply as a copula, as the logical connective in all existential judgments, the "is" indicates the logical connection required in any judgment of the form "x is y." In this logical role it points, Adorno says, to the "universal categorial fact [*Sachverhalt*] of a synthesis" (ND 107/100). No matter which specific existential judgment has been reached, to say something in the form of "x is y" is to claim that there is a logical connection between x and y. In this logical role, the copula does not represent something ontic.

Hence "is" has both particular (ontic) and universal (logical) meanings. Heidegger, however, conflates these meanings, Adorno claims. Heidegger derives a purely ontological "Being" from the copula in its universal logical meaning. Then he assigns it the sort of ontic givenness suggested by "is" in its more particular, judgment-specific role. He thereby hypostasizes the "categorial achievement of synthesis as something given [*Gegebenheit*]" (ND 107/100–101), as a state of affairs. The net result is the supposed givenness of pure Being.

Now Adorno does not deny that a "state of affairs" corresponds to the predicative "is" or that this "is" has a meaning (*Bedeutung*), just as the grammatical subject and predicate do. Yet this state of affairs "is intentional, not ontic," he says, and the copula achieves meaning only within the relation between grammatical subject and predicate (ND 107–8/101).[13] Because the copula does not exist independently from this grammatical relation, what it means is not being in itself. Predication is not a third thing added to the subject and predicate; it is simply how they are connected.

In other words, Adorno claims that Heidegger tries to derive "Being" as an essence from the copula. By doing so, however, Heidegger conflates the two meanings of the copula, namely, its universal logical meaning as "the constant grammatical coinage" for any judgment's synthesis—a meaning derived from the copula's second, logical role—and the specific meaning that "is" achieves in each particular judgment (ND 108/101)—a type/token conflation, we could say. By eliding the difference between the copula as a universal logical category and the predicative "is" that carries import in each particular judgment, Heidegger "transforms the ontic achievement of the 'is' into something ontological, [into] an ontological mode of Being [*eine Seinsweise von Sein*]" (ND 108/102).

Unlike Heidegger, Adorno regards "being" as primarily and perhaps exclusively a concept. But what sort of concept is the concept of being? Adorno's course lectures on *Ontology and Dialectics* refer in this connection to "The Amphiboly of Concepts of Reflection" in Kant's *Critique of Pure Reason*, an appendix to the "Transcendental Analytic" that anticipates the "Transcendental Dialectic" it precedes.[14] The concept of being is a concept of reflection (*Reflexionsbegriff*) in Kant's sense, Adorno argues, and therefore it should not be treated "as an expression of true Being as such" (OD 47/28). Kant describes transcendental reflection (*Überlegung, Reflexion*) as the act of sorting out which cognitive powers concepts belong to, whether to pure understanding or to sensible intuition. This requires reflection on which cognitive powers—understanding or sensibility—have access to the objects that the concepts are about and thereby on whether the objects themselves are noumena—which can only be conceived—or phenomena—which can be perceived and known. When concepts are not properly sorted out in this way, a transcendental amphiboly, "a confusion of the pure object of the understanding with the appearance," is likely to arise.[15]

Although, *pace* Adorno, the amphiboly chapter does not identify "being" as a concept of reflection,[16] Kant does use a similar strategy when, near the end of the "Transcendental Dialectic," he reflects on the concept of "being" in order to demolish ontological proofs for the existence of God.[17] Recalling his general argument that analytic judgments are not synthetic judgments, and vice versa, Kant argues that "logical predicates" should not be confused with "real predicates." Whereas a logical predicate is already contained in the concept of a judgment's grammatical subject, a real predicate, as "the determination of a thing," goes "beyond the concept of the [grammatical] subject and enlarges it. Thus it may not be included in it already." Then follows Kant's ontological-proof-smashing punchline: "*Being* is obviously not a real predicate, i.e., a concept of something that could add to the concept of a thing. It is merely the positing of a thing. . . . In the logical use it is merely the copula of a judgment." Hence, if one asserts that God exists—that God is or that there is a God—one adds "no new predicate to the concept of God" but simply says the idea of God is logically possible or that it is possible to make predications about God.[18] To say more than that—for example, to claim that God really does exist—one would need to have experiential access to the object of this concept: God would need to be an object of sensible intuition, something that Kant denies. Being as such—that something is—is no more than a logical predicate.

By calling the concept of being a concept of reflection, Adorno means to deny that it has a direct purchase on things or matters as such. Instead, it points to the conceptual mediation of anything and everything about which judgments and assertions can be made. Even though he rejects what he regards as Kant's rigid bifurcation between concepts and intuitions and between thought and sensibility, Adorno, as we have seen, appeals to a distinction between the logical "is" and the ontic "is." This distinction closely resembles the one between logical predicates and real predicates in Kant's demolition of ontological proofs for God's existence. Just as these proofs try to derive God's real existence from a logical possibility, so, according to Adorno, Heidegger tries to derive a purely ontological but immediately given Being from an amphiboly of the copula: he trades on the grammatical ambiguity of "is" in ordinary existential judgments to create the illusion of a cogent conception of Being.

Reconstruing Kant

Ironically, in appealing to Kant, despite his own Hegelian misgivings about Kantian epistemology, Adorno misses an opportunity to engage Heidegger on common terrain. For Heidegger was not unaware of Kant's approach to the concept of being, having examined it in *Kant and the Problem of Metaphysics* (1929)[19] and then returning to it more than thirty years later in the essay "Kant's Thesis about Being."[20] Like Adorno, Heidegger connects

Kant's critique of ontological proofs for the existence of God with the earlier passage on "The Amphiboly of Concepts of Reflection." Unlike Adorno, however, Heidegger devotes most of his attention to the thesis in Kant's critique of the ontological proofs that "being" is not a real predicate but simply the positing of something. On the one hand, Heidegger suggests, by rejecting "being" as a real predicate, Kant decisively breaks with the "onto-theo-logical" tradition that asks, à la Anselm, about the Being of beings in order to ask about the ultimate being (i.e., God). On the other hand, by treating "being" as nothing substantial but simply something conceptually posited, Kant prepares the way for Hegel's "speculative-dialectical interpretation of [B]eing as Absolute Concept."[21]

According to Heidegger, a key to this transition from, say, Anselm to Hegel, lies in precisely that double usage of the copula which, Adorno has claimed, empowers Heidegger's own ontological sleight of hand. Implicitly, at least, Kant's thesis distinguishes between the "logical" and the "ontic" uses of "being" or "is," Heidegger claims. Logically, when we say *x is y* we simply say the grammatical subject and predicate are related. Ontically, however, we posit a relation between the subject and object of cognition and claim that in some sense the object exists: "In the ontic use of being—this stone is ('exists')—it is a matter of the positing of the relation between I-subject and object—this, however, in such a way that the subject-predicate relation cuts across, as it were, the subject-object relation. The significance of this is that the 'is' as copula in the statement of an objective cognition has a different and richer sense than the merely logical sense. But . . . Kant arrived at this insight only after long reflection and did not even express it until the second edition of the *Critique of Pure Reason*."[22]

Specifically, in the restatement of the "Transcendental Deduction of the Pure Concepts of the Understanding" inserted into the second edition, Kant takes issue with the restricted logician's understanding of the judgment as merely a relation between concepts (i.e., between grammatical subject and predicate). Beyond that, Kant says, the copula is used to claim that this relation is grounded in the object referred to by the grammatical subject: "A judgment is nothing other than the way to bring cognitions to the *objective* unity of apperception. That is the aim of the copula *is* in them: to distinguish the objective unity of given representations from the subjective."[23] Or, as Heidegger glosses Kant's point a little later, the copula in a judgment or assertion bespeaks "a connecting of subject and predicate of the sentence in the object."[24] And this connection is anchored in the transcendental unity of apperception that makes any understanding possible.

Accordingly, says Heidegger, Kant transfers the traditional Being of beings into "the objectivity of the object of experience,"[25] and he elaborates this conception of Being in the "postulates of empirical thought in general," which distinguish the modality of cognitive judgments (possible, actual, or necessary) in terms not of what the object is but rather of how it relates to the faculty of cognition.[26] Hence for Kant, Heidegger claims, "Being, as being possible, being actual, being necessary, is not . . . a real (ontic) predicate, but it is a transcendental (ontological) predicate."[27] Yet the ontological predicates of "Being"—possibility, actuality, and necessity—have their origins in thought itself, Kant suggests, and not in the object per se. This subjective origin to "Being" as a transcendental predicate in thought is reinforced by Kant's "On the Amphiboly of Concepts." There, Heidegger says, "the ultimate determination of [B]eing as positing is accomplished for Kant in a reflection on reflection"—that is, in a transcendental reflection on which cognitive faculties various representations belong to.[28]

Although, as is clear from the questioning with which Heidegger concludes his essay, he does not agree with Kant's thesis on being, it carries two insights that Heidegger does endorse, namely, that "Being cannot be"—in other words, Being is not a being (*ein Seiendes*)—and that Being involves positing—not as something thought posits, however, but as "that which grants presence" (*das Anwesenheit Gewährende*). On this creative reconstrual of Kant's thesis about being, the positedness or objectivity of objects would prove to be "a modification of presence," an insight missing (*ungedacht*), Heidegger suggests, from pre-Kantian metaphysics.[29] Thus Heidegger's interpretation of Kant looks for a way to avoid either onticizing or logicizing the ontological—that is, either treating Being as a being, à la Anselm, or turning Being into an absolute concept, à la Hegel—but without subjectivizing it à la Kant.

From the fact that both Adorno and Heidegger find something of worth in Kant's thesis about being—namely, that it is not a real predicate but a positing of something—it becomes clear both why Adorno accuses Heidegger of ontologizing the ontic and why Heidegger refuses to onticize the ontological. Although Adorno does not see this, they agree with Kant that Being is not a being: Being does not "exist" in the sense that an object or person might exist. Yet they disagree with each other about what this nonexistence of Being comes to. For Adorno, it means that "Being" cannot be anything other than a concept. For Heidegger, by contrast, "Being" must be more than a concept if the being or "existence" of objects and the like is to make sense. And that means, contra Adorno, that Being is not simply a concept of reflection in Kant's sense.

Objectivity and Synthesis

Despite their disagreement over the implications of Kant's thesis, Adorno does acknowledge an insight in Heidegger's alleged ontologizing of the ontic. What Heidegger recognizes but distorts, Adorno claims, is "the objective moment that conditions the synthesis in every predicative judgment," a moment that nevertheless first crystallizes in that synthesis (ND 109/102). This objective moment, this "state of affairs in the judgment," is not independent, however. The grammatical subject and predicate are not only mutually mediated but also irreducible one to the other, he says, as are the epistemological subject and object. Yet their mediation is not something in addition to what is mediated any more than their irreducibility is anything outside of these relations. To say that the "is" in an existential judgment is neither a subjective thought nor an objective entity is not to say this "is" (or what it means) is something else: a third thing, or pure Being. Every attempt simply to think the "is" necessarily "leads to the existent [*Seiendes*] here and concepts there. The constellation of moments cannot be turned into [*aufbringen*] a singular essence; it is inhabited by what itself is not essence" (ND 111/104).

Regardless of the vigor to Adorno's argument, there is something unsettled in it, almost as if he repeatedly hits a slippery patch and tries to skate around it. His phrases "objective moment that conditions the synthesis in every predicative judgment" and "state of affairs in the judgment" seem deliberately vague. What exactly does Adorno mean by "the objective moment"? How precisely can a state of affairs be *in* a judgment? Perhaps Adorno recognizes the slippery patch. Perhaps, too, that is why the "Copula" section devotes a long footnote to sorting out distinctions and intersections between (1) the grammatical subject/predicate relation and (2) the "epistemological-material" subject/object relation (ND 109–10/103), and why he returns to this topic at the beginning of the next section, titled "No Transcendence of Being" (ND 111–14/105–8).

The long footnote describes the grammatical "subject" as the basis of predication (*das zugrunde Gelegte, von dem etwas prädiziert wird*) and as a sort of "objectivity" vis-à-vis both "the act of judging [*Urteilsakt*]" and "what is judged in the synthesis of judgment [*Urteilssynthesis*]." It is that on which thought gets deployed. Epistemologically, by contrast, the "subject" is the function of thought or the thinker-as-such. Nevertheless, the two distinct matters labeled "subject" are interrelated. Adorno describes this interrelationship using two terms: recall (*mahnen an*) and abstraction (*Abstraktion*). From one angle, the relation between the judged *Sachverhalt* (i.e., the grammatical subject or "what is judged as such") and the intrajudgmental synthesis (which both rests on and produces this *Sachverhalt*) recalls the epistemological, reciprocal, and "material" relation between object and subject. From a different angle, one can say the logical or intrajudgmental relation between synthesis and *Sachverhalt* is "an abstraction from the subject/object relation." Not even the purest logical judgment can dispense with a reminder of that material subject/object relation: it will always be a judgment *about something*, and this "something" is a reminder of the epistemological and material object, "the trace of what exists [*die Spur des Seienden*]" (ND 109–10/103).

Similarly, when the subsequent section argues that "Being" is not transcendent to the epistemological subject and object but simply indicative of their mutual mediation and the "imbrication" (*Verflochtenheit*) of everything with everything else, Adorno grants Heidegger the point that the "is" in a judgment is not something ontic or objective (*keine Seiendes, keine Objektivität*). The reason for this, however, is not that the "is" indicates Being as a third. Rather, the "is" indicates a synthesis and, in the absence of this synthesis, it would have "no substrate" (ND 111–12/105–6).

If I understand him correctly, Adorno wishes to distinguish between the objectivity within a judgment and the objectivity that has epistemological priority. The first pertains to the grammatical subject upon which something is predicated. The second pertains to whatever we can know when we experience objects and make judgments about them. Correlatively, Adorno appears to distinguish between two types of synthesis: the intrajudgmental synthesis that unites grammatical subject and predicate, and the wider cognitive synthesis that occurs within our experience when we make judgments and assertions.[30]

Accordingly, "the objective moment that conditions the synthesis in every predicative judgment" is simply the grammatical subject. And, as the grammatical subject, it can be called the "state of affairs in the judgment." Yet Adorno does not explain how the epistemological and material object informs or impinges on this "state of affairs in the judgment." Nor does he explore at any satisfactory length how the synthesis we presumably achieve in cognition informs or impinges on "the synthesis in every predicative judgment." By failing to address these issues in the passages we have considered, Adorno passes up an opportunity to explore not only how Husserl and Heidegger might have pitched the wrong (ontological) tent but also how the tent they pitched might hold valuable insights for an Adornian metacritique of epistemology.

Metacritique

Earlier I claimed that the critique of categorial intuition in Adorno's *Zur Metakritik der Erkenntnistheorie* fails to address two questions about propositional truth of concern to both Husserl and Heidegger. First, is so-called predicative being nothing more than a "moment of thought"? Second, how does predicating do real cognitive work, such that judgments, assertions, and propositions can be true? The two sections we have reviewed in *Negative Dialectics*, while not ignoring these questions, do not provide satisfactory answers. To give a satisfactory answer to the first question, Adorno would need to explicate the relation between grammatical subject and material object. To give a satisfactory answer to the second question, he would need to account for the relation between judgment-internal synthesis and cognitive synthesis. I shall discuss these two issues in turn.

Grammatical Subject and Practical Object

First, to explicate the relation between grammatical subject and material object, Adorno would need a more robust account of what I call *predicative availability*. Predicative availability is among the various ways in which everyday matters offer themselves for human practices. Let me call these matters *practical objects*. Among the differentiated ways in which practical objects can offer themselves is their offering themselves for linguistic practices. Among these linguistic practices are those of reference and predication. The grammatical subjects of sentences, judgments, and assertions are referring terms. They are the linguistic means by which we pick out whatever we wish to talk about. When we talk about practical objects, these objects let us refer to them in language. Practical objects also allow us to make predications about them, to specify what they are or how they are in one respect or another. We can say "This house is green," "The water is too cold," or "The traffic is terrible today," and what we refer to allows us to specify in language what or how it is with respect to color or temperature or congestion. The predicative availability of practical objects is how, under linguistic reference, they allow themselves to be linguistically specified.

This account of predicative availability implies that the primary relation between grammatical subject and practical object is one of linguistic reference and referability. So too the primary relation between grammatical predicate and practical object is one of linguistic specification and specifiability. What Adorno describes as a sort of "objectivity" or "objective moment" within judgments pertains to the relation between the linguistic referring and predicating that we accomplish in our judgments, on the one hand, and the referability and predicability of the practical objects about which we make these judgments, on the other.

Adorno, however, would worry that my account of predicative availability tries to sneak in Husserlian "predicative being" through a Heideggerian back door. For the notion of "availability" derives from Heidegger's concept of *Zuhandenheit* ("handiness"). Indeed, "predicative availability" echoes the account in *Sein und Zeit* of the "discoveredness" (*Entdecktheit*) of that which is judged or asserted.[31] Accordingly, we must ask: Does the notion of predicative availability assume that "being" must be given to us in nonpredicative ways (e.g., via categorial intuition) in order to "fulfill" the "is" that connects referring and predicating terms in an assertion? Or, to raise a similar question in more Adornian language, must an *extra*judgmental *Sachverhalt* (state of affairs) impinge on the *intra*judgmental synthesis in order for a judgment to be correct?

Predicative and Cognitive Syntheses

In a very loose sense, I want to answer yes to both questions. Yes, in a sense, "being" must be given in nonpredicative ways; and yes, in a sense, an "external" *Sachverhalt* must impinge on the predicative synthesis. Moreover, I think Adorno's reluctance to address the question of how predicating does real cognitive work points to a weakness in his account. He does not adequately explain the relation between cognitive synthesis and predicative or intrajudgmental synthesis. Nevertheless, I share Adorno's reservations about the Husserlian notion of predicative being. When we say "*x* is *y*," we do not need the *being* of the "is" to fulfill our predication or to help make our judgment correct. What we do need, for the most part, is for the "is *y*" asserted concerning *x* to be disclosed to us in more than predicative ways. The "is" is simply a linguistic device for asserting such identity—it is "intentional, not ontic," as Adorno says (ND 108/101).

Yet the asserted identity is not simply linguistic; and the predicative use of "is" presupposes, for the most part, that the asserted identity goes beyond the linguistic referability and predicability of the practical object about which an assertion is made. This, in turn, requires the object's predicative availability to align properly with other ways in which the object is available. Such alignment is not an independent "being"; nonetheless, in each case it is how an object (potentially) *is* and not simply how it is *asserted to be*.

Accordingly, Adorno's denial that *being* corresponds to the predicative "is," while correct, should not lead us to think the meaning of the "is" simply resides in the relation between grammatical subject and predicate. The meaning of the "is" equally resides in an alignment, on the part of the object, between its availability for predication and its availability for some other practice(s)—an alignment I have labeled *predicative self-disclosure*. Further, this more-than-predicative meaning can be established only within the multidimensional relationship between epistemological subject and epistemological object or, better, between epistemic subject and object—a relationship in which logical and linguistic practices such as judging and asserting mesh with other practices, and in which the predicative availability of the practical object meshes with other ways in which the object is available.

In this sense, the relation between what is judged and intrajudgmental synthesis does not simply *recall* the epistemological subject/object relation, as Adorno suggests. Rather, it *belongs to* this subject/object relation, and it would be hard to imagine any such epistemological relation where predicative practices and predicative availability are completely absent. At the same time, however, both on the subject side and on the object side, there is always more to knowledge and truth than predication—more, too, than the propositional content of judgments and assertions.

In fact, I believe Adorno writes the following passage from his "Meditations on Metaphysics," already quoted in the previous chapter, to provide insight into the scope of this "more"—an insight, I might add, that he shares with Husserl and Heidegger: "The surplus beyond the subject, however, which subjective metaphysical experience does not want to surrender, and the truth-moment in what is thing-like [*das Wahrheitsmoment am Dinghaften*] are extremes that touch in the idea of truth. For [truth] could not exist without the subject that wrestles free from illusion [*Schein*] any more than [it could exist] without that which is not the subject and in which truth has its prototype [*Urbild*]" (ND 368/375). To get to this "more," however—to acknowledge those sides of truth that cannot be reduced to the correctness of assertions and the accuracy of propositions—a philosophical idea of truth needs to include a viable conception of propositional truth. Despite Adorno's attempts to wrest such a viable conception from Husserlian phenomenology and Heideggerian ontology, his concerns about "being," whether predicative (Husserl) or ontological (Heidegger), keep him from offering a satisfactory account of how practical objects lend themselves to predicative practices. Only such an account could demonstrate how propositional truth, too, requires the truth-in-things to touch "the subject that wrestles free from illusion."

4

What Is, Is More Than It Is

> It can no longer be maintained that the immutable is truth and . . . the transient is illusion [*Schein*].
>
> —Theodor W. Adorno (ND 355/361)

Adorno's Heidegger Critique

Theodor W. Adorno and Martin Heidegger acted as if they had little in common. As a young scholar in the early 1930s, Adorno set out, in the words of his friend Walter Benjamin, to "annihilate" Heidegger's philosophy.[1] Forty years later, shortly after Adorno's death in 1969, the nearly eighty-year-old Heidegger laconically reported he had never read anything by Adorno. This, despite the urging of Hermann Mörchen, one of Heidegger's first doctoral students, who, like Adorno, lived in Frankfurt during the postwar years.[2]

So far as we know, Adorno met Heidegger just once, on January 24, 1929, two years after Heidegger published *Sein und Zeit*, and two years before Adorno launched his first public criticisms of Heidegger's philosophy, in an inaugural lecture titled "The Actuality of Philosophy." According to Mörchen, this brief meeting between the twenty-five-year-old Adorno and thirty-nine-year-old Heidegger took place in Frankfurt at the home of university rector Kurt Riezler, who had invited Heidegger to deliver a lecture titled "Philosophical Anthropology and the Metaphysics of Dasein." Adorno and Heidegger did not converse at length.[3]

After Heidegger's death in 1977, Mörchen published two books on Adorno and Heidegger, arguing that, despite their failure or refusal to communicate (*Kommunikationsverweigerung*), they shared fundamental concerns, most notably their resistance to power or domination, their critique of constitutive subjectivity, their rejection of scientism, their emphasis on the disclosive capacities of language, and their insistence on the temporal character of thought and its objects. Moreover, these shared concerns lay at the heart of the conflict between them, Mörchen claimed.[4] Whether and how that is so remain open questions.

History of Interpretation

Despite Mörchen's valiant efforts, for the next two decades few philosophers paid much attention to Adorno's lifelong critique of Heidegger's work. In the mid-1980s, Jürgen Habermas criticized both of them for allegedly undermining enlightenment rationality while, paradoxically, remaining trapped in a "philosophy of the subject."[5] Fred Dallmayr, by contrast, moving away from Habermas, tried to find a valuable rapport between Adorno and Heidegger in what he called "critical ontology." During the 1980s and 1990s, a number of commentators also made comparisons in philosophy of art and the critique of modernity.[6] And some, especially German scholars, began to piece out possibly hidden connections between Adornian dialectics and Heideggerian ontology.[7] Only after 2000, however, did engagements with Adorno's critique of Heidegger begin in earnest, prompted in part by three events: commemorations of Adorno on the 2003 centennial of his birth;[8] the publication of four lecture courses that Adorno held in the early 1960s when he was writing *Negative Dialektik*;[9] and gatherings in 2016 to mark the fiftieth anniversary of that book's publication.[10] Not only have analyses of his Heidegger critique become more common[11] but also discussions of Heidegger have become de rigueur in synoptic studies of Adorno's work.[12]

To these Adorno-related events one could add the outbreak of new conflicts over Heidegger's proximity to Nazism, fueled by the 2005 French publication of Emmanuel Faye's book on this topic[13] and the subsequent publication of Heidegger's explicitly antisemitic *Black Notebooks* from the 1930s and 1940s.[14] Although many participants in these debates oddly overlook Adorno's work, anyone who has read his critique of Heidegger will know that, long before Emmanuel Faye linked Heidegger with Nazism, and Victor Farias and Pierre Bourdieu before him,[15] Adorno had repeatedly challenged what Adam Knowles calls Heidegger's "fascist affinities."[16] Moreover, Adorno had identified these at the core of Heidegger's thought—and not simply in his actions and informal writings.

Adorno's critique of Heidegger developed over four decades. It began in the early 1930s with two lectures and a set of theses[17] as well as a book on Kierkegaard;[18] proceeded through subsequent studies on Husserlian phenomenology;[19] gathered momentum during lecture courses in the 1950s and 1960s;[20] and culminated in *The Jargon of Authenticity* (1964)[21] and *Negative Dialectics* (1966). Among all of these sources, the most thorough and systematic criticisms of Heidegger occur in the lecture course *Ontology and Dialectics 1960/61* and in part 1 of *Negative Dialectics*, titled "Relation to Ontology" (ND 67–136/59–131). These two texts are closely related: approximately three quarters of *Negative Dialectics* part 1 (specifically, ND 83–136/76–131) stem from lectures 19–22A in *Ontology and Dialectics* (specifically, OD 277–325/197–235). Those lectures in turn mostly replicate the texts for the first two of three lectures that Adorno delivered in March 1961 at the Collège de France in Paris.[22]

Both texts—both the more extemporaneous course lectures and the more rigorous book chapters—come across as vigorously engaged, notably selective, and sometimes sloppy readings of Heidegger. The vigor of Adorno's engagement is unmistakable: clearly he regards Heidegger's work as socially significant, politically dangerous, and fundamentally mistaken. Although not obvious at first, the selectivity of his engagement becomes apparent when one notes the narrow range of passages and works that Adorno actually cites.[23] In both publications, nearly all citations of Heidegger's more than four-hundred-page *Sein und Zeit* come from the book's forty-page introduction; in *Negative Dialectics*, nearly half of the endnoted Heidegger citations come from just one publication, the 1946 "Brief über den Humanismus" ("Letter on 'Humanism'") that Heidegger addressed to the French philosopher Jean Beaufret and then published, together with an essay on Plato.[24] Further, these citations provide a sign of sloppiness in Adorno's reading, for he regularly cites the humanism letter as if it were the Plato essay, as the editor Rolf Tiedemann indicates in a note to *Ontology and Dialectics*.[25] Unfortunately, exactly the same mistake occurs, even more frequently, in *Negative Dialectics*.[26]

Wie zu lesen sei?

The polemically charged history of interpretation (*Rezeptionsgeschichte*) so briefly reviewed here raises the question Adorno famously posed about

Hegel: *Wie zu lesen sei?*[27] How should Adorno's lectures and book chapters on Heidegger be read? Adorno himself recommends an approach to Hegel that he calls immanent critique: experimenting with possible interpretations until they begin to make sense, the reader should aim to find the truth content in Hegel's writings by evaluating whether they live up to their own claims. When, according to Adorno, Hegel "violates his own concept of the dialectic" by not doing justice to that which is particular and nonconceptual (to "the nonidentical"), the path of immanent critique leads Adorno to defend this concept against Hegel—in what Adorno calls a negative dialectic (H 373–75/145–48).

Adorno claims that his own course lectures and book chapters on Heidegger take the same approach. The very first lecture announces that he plans to follow "the path of immanent criticism." Beginning with legitimate and illegitimate aspects to the then current "need for ontology," he sets out to measure Heidegger's ontology "against its own claim," show that "it fails to redeem this claim," and then indicate how this immanent critique leads to Adorno's own dialectical alternative as "the self-reflection of ontology" (OD 12–13/3–4).[28] The eighth lecture explains that critique asks whether something measures up "to its concept" (i.e., whether something is what it purports to be) and asserts that, in this sense, "Heidegger's philosophy in its entirety is essentially anti-critical" (OD 116–17/78–79). (Presumably, this assertion emerges from comparing Heidegger's philosophy with its concept!) In the last two lectures, Adorno once again insists on the immanence of his critique: his approach has allowed "the motifs of dialectical thinking" to emerge from "the ontological problematic" and from "the questions that arise with regard to its own truth" (OD 325/235). Moreover, by pursuing these ontologically emergent dialectical motifs in the last few lectures, he has taken immanent critique to "its limit" (OD 341/249).

Similarly, the preface to *Negative Dialectics* says part 1 aims to understand Heideggerian ontology from the "problematic need" for it and to criticize it "immanently," before Adorno proceeds from the results of this immanent critique to "the idea of a negative dialectics" in part 2 (ND 10/xx). The second chapter ("Being and Existence") of part 1 reinforces this emphasis, titling its first section "Immanent Critique of Ontology" and beginning as follows: "Critique of the ontological need impels the immanent critique of ontology. Nothing that repels ontology [*Seinsphilosophie*] generally, from the outside, instead of taking it up in its own fabric . . . has any power over it" (ND 104/97).

One approach to reading Adorno, then, would be to ask whether his texts on Heidegger live up to their claim to offer an immanent critique—that is, to take Adorno's claim at its word in an immanently critical fashion. But soon we would discover, as Gordon Finlayson points out, that Adorno's criticisms of Heidegger are rarely immanent.²⁹ Responding to Peter Gordon's description of *Negative Dialectics* as "a masterpiece of immanent criticism,"³⁰ Finlayson writes, "The trouble is that Adorno . . . signally fails to engage with Heidegger's philosophy in the nuanced and patient manner that an immanent criticism requires. Instead of attempting to understand what Heidegger is trying to do, Adorno declares his whole philosophy a failure. Instead of surgically inserting the scalpel, he detonates hand grenades in adjacent territory. . . . Adorno is ready to dish out sarcasm, moral invective, and even *ad hominem* criticism whenever it suits, which is nearly always where Heidegger is concerned. Criticism it definitely is. Immanent criticism, it is not." Yet Finlayson also rightly notes that the many "different ways of criticism" Adorno deploys against Heidegger "often hit their target."³¹ For that reason, to get at the real issues between them, and to uncover the "truth content" in Adorno's texts about Heidegger, immanent criticisms of Adorno's only purportedly immanent critique will not suffice. For it is obvious that to read him as an immanent critic of Heidegger would be to miss what Adorno is really up to.

Instead, I propose to pursue a central topic that comes up sideways in *Ontology and Dialectics* and in *Negative Dialectics* part 1, namely, the temporality of truth. This approach has three advantages: it addresses a theme that clearly matters to both Adorno and Heidegger; it considers a topic highlighted by other studies that situate their writings in the history of continental philosophy;³² and it builds on Iain Macdonald's book *What Would Be Different*, one of the most astute recent comparisons of Heidegger and Adorno. I hope to show how, in the words of Dieter Thomä, the philosophies of Adorno and Heidegger are radical competitors: they pursue the same matter, but they head in fundamentally different directions.³³

The temporality of truth comes up sideways because Adorno, in the writings under consideration, does not take direct aim at Heidegger's understanding of truth. Instead, he focuses on Heidegger's conception of Being (*Sein*), asking first about the "ontological need" (*Bedürfnis*) that helps explain its origin and appeal and then problematizing it in relation to beings (*das Seiende*), especially the existence of human beings (*Dasein*). Yet truth (*Wahrheit*), for Heidegger, is intrinsic to this Being/beings relation, and so is the temporal character of Being, as the title *Sein und Zeit* already suggests. Moreover, the mostly Hegelian ideas deployed in Adorno's critique of Heidegger—especially the mediation (*Vermittlung*) of concept (*Begriff*) and thing (*Sache*) and of subject (*Subjekt*) and object (*Objekt*)—are the same ones Adorno uses to articulate his own conception of truth's temporal character. Hence, without thematizing Heidegger's understanding of truth, Adorno's critique can be read as a contestation over truth's temporal character. Put simply: in opposition to much of the Western philosophical tradition[34] and indeed much of contemporary analytic philosophy,[35] Adorno and Heidegger agree that truth is temporal. They disagree, however, about what truth and its temporality come to. To demonstrate this, let me comment first on Adorno's discussion of the ontological need, before we turn to his critique of Heidegger in the chapter "Being and Existence" (ND 104–36/97–131) for "ontologizing the ontic."

The Ontological Need

Both the *Ontology and Dialectics* lectures and the chapter titled "The Ontological Need" (ND 69–103/61–96) provide multiple overlapping descriptions of the need to which Adorno thinks Heidegger's ontology responds. Some of these are broadly sociohistorical: a desire for substantial individuality within a completely functionalized society (ND 73–74/65–67); a reaction to how capitalist society has undermined the supposed sovereignty of the human subject (ND 74–76/66–68); the genuinely critical need to ask, amid a distracting culture, about the point and purpose of it all (ND 93/85–86); and a desire to restore the order and authority that the secularizing process of enlightenment destroyed (ND 94–96/87–89). Other descriptions point to matters more specifically philosophical and academic: a longing in post-Kantian German philosophy for direct or immediate knowledge of the Absolute (ND 69–71/61–63); a dissatisfaction with the failures of traditional metaphysics (ND 78–79/70–72); a move to eliminate the supposed scientism in Husserlian phenomenology (ND 76–78/69–70); and a desire for concrete knowledge of substantial matters beyond the abstractions of science (ND 80–83/72–76). Additional descriptions combine broadly sociohistorical and more specifically philosophical matters: the need for thought to reach its other, combined with anxiety about doing exactly that (ND 85–86/77–78); the attempt to break through ossified socioconceptual constructs, and out of the immanence of consciousness, to the things themselves (ND 86–87/78–80, 90–92/83–85); a desire for immediate insight into intellectually or culturally mediated matters (*geistige Sachverhalte*, ND 87–90/80–83); and a need to resist societally imposed reification (ND 96–99/89–92).

Perhaps we can label these descriptions the sociohistorical, the academic, and the sociophilosophical manifestations of the ontological need, and summarize them as follows: the sociohistorical desire for normatively oriented agency; the academic absence of holistic and concrete knowledge; and the sociophilosophical need to resist reification. Clearly all three point to prominent concerns within Adorno's own philosophy, such as human autonomy, mimetic knowledge, and social critique. In that sense they do not simply describe a need to which Heidegger's ontology responds. They also lay out issues Adorno takes up in his negative dialectics—in his ontology of the "false condition" or "the wrong state of things" (*Ontologie des falschen Zustandes*, ND 22/11).

Because he regards Heidegger's response as fundamentally mistaken, however, and because, within a false society, no need, no matter how urgent and compelling, can be simply and straightforwardly true, Adorno concludes his description of the ontological need by calling the need "false" (ND 99–100/92–93).[36] To understand why, we must turn to the passage at the end of "Protest against Reification," the immediately preceding section, where Adorno sets up this conclusion. There he accuses Heidegger of untruthfully removing reification from the society that creates it and shoving it back into Being and the history of Being as a fateful forgetting of Being (*Seinsvergessenheit*). Adorno says Heidegger thereby registers the hope that fundamental subject/object, essence/appearance, and concept/fact dualisms need not be absolute, that they could be reconciled. The problem, however, is that Heidegger projects such reconciliation backward as an "irrecoverable origin" and thus sabotages the possibility of reconciliation in the future. Because, as we have seen in previous chapters, Adorno clings to a future-oriented hope for reconciliation, this problem lies at the heart of his critique: Heidegger's "funeral song over the forgetting of Being [*Seinsvergessenheit*] sabotages reconciliation; the mythically impenetrable history of Being [*Seinsgeschichte*] . . . denies hope" (ND 98–99/91–92; cf. OD 297–98/212–13).

Accordingly, Adorno aims to break through the "fatality" of Heidegger's history of Being, to expose it as an elaborate ideology, as what he calls a context of delusion or illusion (*Zusammenhang von Verblendung*, ND 99/92). Precisely for this reason the next section calls the ontological need false. Yet it is not only false: the need to which Heidegger's ontology responds, albeit ideological, is real, Adorno says. It is real insofar as society keeps human beings from understanding the destructive societal patterns that control them. But the need is ideological because it wrongly longs for something "self-aware subjects would not need" and thus "compromises every possible fulfillment" (ND 99/92). So the problem with Heidegger's ontology is not that it responds to an intellectual need: "Needs are a conglomerate of the true and false; true thought would wish for what is right" (ND 100/93). Rather the problem is that, instead of wishing for a society where genuine needs are truly met, Heidegger's ontology hankers after a false substitute, an ersatz satisfaction. It wrongly longs for "something solid," for "invariant structures" within which life would be secure. What should be hoped for instead, Adorno strongly suggests, is a society that, by satisfying real material needs, no longer perpetuates the threat of "total destruction" (ND 100/93).

In the next section—the chapter's last section, titled "Weakness and Support" (*Schwäche und Halt*)—Adorno links the yearning for invariant structures with conservative cultural criticism and the "hatred for radical modern art, in which restorative conservatism and fascism always blissfully chime together" (ND 102/95). He says the culture-conservative lament over a loss of cohesive styles and binding forms, although misdirected, points to how the really dominant form—the all-pervasive principle of exchange—levels "all qualitative determinations" and undermines human autonomy (*Mündigkeit*, ND 101/94). False consciousness latches on to invariant structures because the attempt to free society from false forms has failed.[37] Since it is reified, such consciousness cannot explode the invariants that imprison it. It accepts them instead, while mourning the absence of invariant structures. The ontological need is the metaphysics of reified consciousness. To the extent that an emphasis on invariant structures "eternalizes how little has changed," the ontological need, desiring something stable and solid, "is false." A liberated consciousness, being autonomous, would not need invariant props (ND 102–3/95–96).

If there is a thread to lead us through the labyrinth of Adorno's critique, perhaps we can discover it via the polarities posited in his discussion of the ontological need. They occur between stability and transience, between an irrecoverable origin and a hoped-for reconciliation, between reified consciousness and social freedom. Implicit in each polarity is the contrast that Iain Macdonald draws between two visions of blocked possibility: Heidegger's, which locates the blocked possibility in an "other beginning," and Adorno's, which finds it in a different and better future.[38] In describing and criticizing the need that purportedly helps explain Heidegger's ontology, Adorno has already signaled that to seek a different beginning in a forgotten Being, rather than holding open the possibility of a better future, is fundamentally false. Moreover, future-oriented hope is central to the conception of truth that informs Adorno's critique of Heidegger for "ontologizing the ontic." And that, as I hope to show, means Adorno and Heidegger have fundamentally opposed approaches to the temporality of truth.

In what follows, I first explore the concept/thing dialectic in Adorno's critique of Heidegger's conception of Being (*Sein*). Next, and more briefly, I uncover the subject/object dialectic in his critique of Heidegger's ontology of human existence (*Dasein*). Then I show that Adorno's criticisms about Being and Dasein revolve around a concern about blocked possibility that he shares with Heidegger but understands in a radically different way.

Ontologizing the Ontic

Adorno's critique of Heidegger's conceptions of *Sein* and *Dasein* provides a set of variations on a single complex theme. The chapter "Being and Existence" argues in ever new guises that Heidegger's conception of Being "ontologizes the ontic"—both despite and via Heidegger's insistence on what his writings after *Being and Time* call "the ontological difference." Adorno understands the ontological difference as one that obtains between Being (*Sein*) and beings (*das Seiende*). He also thinks Heidegger's account of this difference necessarily gives priority to Being over beings.

Archaic Being

One can see how Adorno arrives at this interpretation of the ontological difference in the first two lectures of *Ontology and Dialectics*. First, in a misreading of *Sein und Zeit*, Adorno claims that Heidegger regards Being as "the *meaning of beings* [*Sinn des Seienden*]" (OD 18/8). This claim stems from Adorno's misquoting the text. Where Heidegger parenthetically describes the book's topic as "the *Being* of beings [*Sein des Seienden*], or the *meaning of Being* [*Sinn des Seins*] in general" (SZ 27), Adorno misquotes him to be defining ontology as "the 'explicit theoretical questioning concerning the meaning of *beings*" (OD 18/7, emphasis added)—a phrase ("the meaning of beings") Heidegger never uses.[39] The misquotation then leads to a further complication, for Adorno claims not only that Heidegger distinguishes the question of "*the meaning of Being itself*" from "the question regarding the

Being of beings" but also that Heidegger gives priority to the first question (OD 23–24/11).

Accordingly, Adorno uncovers a supposed hierarchy in Heidegger's ontology, an order of priority from the meaning of Being as the meaning of beings to the Being of beings and on to beings themselves.[40] As Adorno interprets Heidegger, Being has priority over beings, in the manner of an "utterly true and primal" origin, an *archē* that "is truer and better and deeper than anything which issues from it" (OD 31–32/17). This also means, as subsequent lectures argue, that Heidegger mistakenly regards Being as *separate* and *independent from* beings as well as *superior to* them.[41] And here, Adorno immediately indicates, lies "the really decisive difference" between Heideggerian ontology, as he understands it, and his own negative dialectics: such a politically laden "priority of the First . . . cannot be accepted in the way it is proposed by ontology" (OD 32/17).

It could be argued that by interpreting Heidegger in this way, Adorno attributes to him precisely the Western metaphysical error that Heidegger vigorously aims to avoid, namely, to treat Being as if it were a being, indeed, an ultimate being. Whereas Adorno criticizes Heidegger for allegedly ontologizing the ontic, Heidegger himself, at least in *Sein und Zeit*, rejects any onticizing of the ontological: he rejects the notion of a supreme being. There his leading question concerns the meaning of Being, and it pertains to whatever makes beings intelligible as beings; whatever that is, it cannot itself be a being.[42] Heidegger's preliminary conception of Being has more to do with the notion of transcendentals in medieval philosophy than with the pre-Socratic notion of an *archē*. Be that as it may—and here we barely touch the tip of a huge iceberg in Heidegger scholarship—Adorno always comes back to the archaic or mythological character of Heidegger's conception of Being, which either results from or propels Heidegger's alleged ontologizing of the ontic.[43]

The section titled "Copula," already discussed in the preceding chapter, sets up this interpretation of Heidegger's "Being" as an *archē*. After Adorno calls for an immanent critique, and then promptly portrays Heidegger's *Seinsphilosophie* as an elaborate ideology (ND 104–7/97–100),[44] the "Copula" section (ND 107–11/100–104) in the second chapter of *Negative Dialectics* part 1 does in fact attempt something like an immanent critique. Adorno tries to show that Heidegger's conception of Being trades on an ambiguity in how we use "being" (*Sein*) or "to be" (*sein*) and related words to form sentences, make assertions, and formulate judgments—in what one could call the propositional use of "is." The ambiguity stems from the fact that the propositional "is" has both a particular "ontic" and a universal "logical" meaning. According to Adorno, Heidegger trades on this ambiguity to transform "the ontic achievement of the 'is' into . . . an ontological mode of Being [*eine Seinsweise von Sein*]" (ND 108/102). Moreover, this provides the key to Heidegger's sleight of hand, as Adorno labels it elsewhere, to his alleged ontologizing of the ontic.[45]

Of course, this is not entirely sleight of hand. What Heidegger's "Being" recognizes but misconstrues, according to Adorno, is that every particular entity (*ein jegliches Seiendes*) is more than it is: it is always already related to something else, or, in the Hegelian language Adorno prefers, it is mediated (ND 109/102). To the extent that Heidegger recognizes how everything is mediated, he verges on "the dialectical insight into the nonidentity in identity" (ND 110/104)—a central insight for Adorno's own negative dialectics. Unfortunately, however, Heidegger absolutizes mediation as such, Adorno claims, as if it were a third and higher matter (i.e., Being) beyond whatever is mediated, beyond whatever points beyond itself to something else (i.e., beyond beings). As the parallel passage puts this in *Ontology and Dialectics*, "Heidegger's concept of Being . . . is really nothing other than the absolutization of mediation, without regard to what it mediates" (OD 305/218).

Two mediations or relations are central to Adorno's critique of Heidegger for ontologizing the ontic, namely, the polarity between concept (*Begriff*) and thing or subject matter (*Sache*), and that between epistemic subject and object. In each case Adorno acknowledges that Heidegger does not completely obscure the distinction and relation between the two poles. Instead of working out how each pole mediates the other, however, Heidegger posits a relatedness, so to speak, an absolute mediation that would be neither one nor the other but would be beyond both, namely, Being, as neither concept nor thing and neither subject nor object. As we shall see, Adorno especially locates the distortion of the first polarity in how Heidegger conceptualizes Being; the second, in how Heidegger inflates the existence of Dasein. The first of these polarities is especially important because it links Adorno's critique of Heidegger with the critique of Hegel at the heart of Adorno's negative dialectics.

CONCEPTUALIZING BEING

As was shown in the previous chapter, Adorno primarily regards "Being" as a concept of reflection in a Kantian sense, one that Heidegger inflates into a nonconceptual *archē*. Yet the concept of Being is not only a concept of reflection, a concept useful for sorting out other concepts. Adorno also regards it as the most abstract concept, in Hegel's sense of its being the most indeterminate concept. In the hands of Adorno's critique, such indeterminacy becomes a two-edged sword. On the one hand, Adorno appeals to Hegel's insight into the indeterminacy of "Being" in order to reject what, following Günther Anders, Adorno calls the "pseudo-concreteness" of Heidegger's fundamental ontology. According to Adorno, Heidegger uses the concept of Being to cover up and exploit how pure particularity and pure universality are both indeterminate. Heidegger thereby turns indeterminacy "into a mythical Panzer." He does this by stripping every being of its particularity, raising it "to Being, its own pure concept," while simultaneously presenting Being, which is completely indeterminate ("absent any delimiting content") as not a concept but as something particular and "concrete." According to Adorno, this *quid pro quo*, which trades on indeterminacy, is a "central feature of Heidegger's philosophy" (ND 82–83/75–76; cf. OD 255–61/180–85).[46]

On the other hand, Adorno also objects to how Hegel begins his logic with "Being" rather than with "something." Hegel treats "something" as the result of an abstract dialectic between Being and Nothing that yields Becoming, now qualitatively specified as Being Determinate, as something that has come to be.[47] To see how this critique of Hegel goes, we need to turn to the section titled "Ontologizing the Ontic" in *Negative Dialectics*. Unlike the two lectures so titled in *Ontology and Dialectics* (OD 109–38/73–94), the section by that title in *Negative Dialectics* deals primarily with *Hegel* rather than Heidegger. It has no equivalent passage in Adorno's course lectures: understandably so, since perhaps more than any other section in part 1, "Ontologizing the Ontic" (ND 125–28/119–22) forces one to "cross the icy wasteland of abstraction," to borrow the phrase from Walter Benjamin quoted in Adorno's preface (ND 9/xix).

Preparing to criticize Heidegger's conception of human existence as *Dasein*, Adorno takes Hegel to task for equating the *concept* of indeterminacy with *that which is indeterminate*, with that which the concept of indeterminacy is *about*. Whereas, according to Adorno, Heidegger treats the concept of Being—the most indeterminate concept—as if it were not even a concept, Hegel treats whatever is not a concept as if it were reducible to the concept. Hegel can do this because the only way conceptually to talk about that which is nonconceptual, about that which is conceptually indeterminate, is, obviously, conceptual. Yet, Adorno objects, the indeterminate, nonconceptual, and nonidentical is not itself a concept. While it is so that we can think about it only by using concepts and, in this sense, the nonidentical is conceptually mediated, this does not mean one can equate that which is nonidentical with the concept of nonidentity.

Nevertheless, that essentially is what Hegel does. Whereas, according to Adorno, all conceptual identity depends on that which is nonidentical, Hegel totalizes conceptual identity by elevating "the mediatedness of the nonidentical to its absolute conceptual Being." Instead of bringing the nonidentical to appropriate conceptual articulation, Hegel subsumes it under a "universal concept" (ND 126/120). Although Hegel's logic correctly identifies Being as the most indeterminate concept, which can move toward determinacy only through the concept of Becoming, by *beginning* with Being Hegel takes a fateful step toward running roughshod over anything that, in its nonconceptual particularity, is indeterminate. The first concept *of* Being becomes the concept *as* first Being, such that all beings have their being in being conceivable. Accordingly, Hegel practices openly what Heidegger tries to conceal: the ontologizing of the ontic (ND 127/121).[48] In different ways, both of them fail to work out properly the mediation between concept and thing.

Deflating Dasein

According to Adorno, Heidegger's ontologizing the ontic permeates his conception of Dasein as human existence (*Existenz*). Adorno repeatedly rejects what he regards as Heidegger's attempt to inflate the ontic individual subject's existence, emphasized by Kierkegaard, into Dasein as an ontological mode of Being. For Adorno, nothing particular or individual—no being (*Seiendes*) in Heidegger's terms—can be ontological, for Being is always only a copula or a concept, never a fact (*Tatsache*) or thing (*Sache*): "No something, only propositions, could ever be ontological" (ND 131/125). By inflating the ontic individual into ontological Dasein, Heidegger ignores how rooted all thought, including ontological consciousness, remains in the individual who thinks, itself mediated by the society it inhabits. Heidegger's account of Dasein as existence may have appealed to many because it seemed to unite the transcendental and the empirical subject, to use Kantian language: the subject that universally constitutes knowledge and its objects, on the one hand, and the concrete individual's experience, on the other (ND 129–30/123–24). But Adorno claims the account ignores the extent to which Being itself, of which Dasein's existence supposedly is an ontological mode, contains both the constituting subject—for Being is a concept constituted by the subject—and individual consciousness, such that the ontological is itself ontic (ND 131/125).

Here, in Adorno's critique of Dasein, the second polarity, that between subject and object, comes to the fore. It shows up in two guises: the sociohistorical role played by the concept of existence (ND 128–30/122–24; cf. OD 319/230–31), and the allegedly authoritarian character of Heidegger's emphasis on authenticity (ND 132–34/127–28; cf. OD 321–23/232–33). Tracing Heidegger's concept of existence back to Kierkegaard, Adorno says there is something right about the protest this concept registers against reification in society and science. The emphasis on *Existenz* challenges a condition that represses "unregimented experience" and virtually expels "the subject as a moment of knowledge." In French existentialism (e.g., Jean-Paul Sartre), however, the subject is "hypostatized," as if it were not itself mediated by the society that weakens and disempowers it (ND 129/123). Moreover, this hypostatization, which draws on Heidegger's account of Dasein as existence, leads to misplaced philosophical-anthropological attempts to spell out the concrete universal essence of human existence.[49] Like Heidegger's analytic of Dasein, these attempts do not see that what universally characterizes human existence is itself societally mediated and, for the most part, makes it unfree, burdened by millennia of societal "disfigurements." To decipher the essence of humanity from its contemporary existence would be to sabotage the future "possibility" of true humanity (ND 129–30/123–24). In other words, the account of Dasein as existence fails to account for the mediation of subject and object: the actual mediation of the individual subject by the societal object, and the possible mediation of the societal object by the human subject.

Just as Heidegger's ontologizing of the ontic ignores the societal mediation of individual existence, sabotaging the possibility of true humanity, so his related emphasis on authenticity ignores the objective mediation of subjective thought, thwarting thought's "utopian potential" (ND 134/128). Adorno recognizes, of course, that *Sein und Zeit* not only distinguishes the (ontic) *existentiell* from the (ontological) *existential* but also, in the discussion of truth and authenticity, mostly focuses on what Heidegger calls "existentials" such as understanding (*Verstehen*) and attunement (*Befindlichkeit*). In that sense Heidegger does not subscribe to the Kierkegaardian premise that subjectivity (i.e., how the individual is and acts) is the measure of truth, rather than objectivity of some sort. Yet Adorno claims that this premise of truth's subjectivity resonates throughout Heidegger's analytic of Dasein (ND 132–33/127).

Citing Karl Jaspers, but clearly targeting Heidegger, Adorno raises both ideological and systematic objections. Ideologically, the appeal to the truth of subjectivity reinforces the reactionary jargon of authenticity (ND 133/127).⁵⁰ By appealing to its own "truth" without connection to anything beyond itself, subjective existence validates mere decrees "in an authoritarian way, just as, in political praxis, a dictator validates current ideology" (ND 133–34/128).

Systematically, the premise of truth as subjectivity distorts truth itself. For truth, Adorno insists, is "the constellation of subject and object in which both interpenetrate." It cannot be reduced to subjectivity, no more than truth can be reduced to Being, "whose dialectical relation to subjectivity Heidegger tries to erase" (ND 133/127). Truth in the subject needs its other—the object—in order to unfold. Without this relation to the object, the subject's thought would be worthless (*nichtig*): thought would stop in its tracks, and subjectivity would shrivel up (ND 133–34/127–28).

What Adorno points to, instead of subjective truth, is "the utopian potential of thought": when mediated by the reason "embodied in individual subjects," thought has the potential to break through the "regressive consciousness" of thinkers who simply stick to their own "reified" and "well-trod" subjective "ground of truth." This utopian potential is the "best strength" thought has "to surpass weak and fallible thinkers," a strength the "existentiell concept of truth [*existentieller Wahrheitsbegriff*]" paralyzes (ND 134/128).⁵¹ In other words, the historically unfolding polarity between subject and object should not be suppressed, nor should it be subsumed into a prior Being. It should be carried out with a view to what might possibly lie beyond it. And for that, one needs a proper understanding of the temporality of truth.

History, Time, and Truth

In the last section of part 1, titled "'Historicity'" (ND 134–36/128–31; cf. OD 323–25/233–35), the objections to Heidegger's ontologizing the ontic culminate in what has impelled Adorno's critique all along, namely, the concern that Heidegger's fundamental ontology freezes actual history into a permanent and unchanging structure.⁵² Here it becomes apparent that a third polarity—between history and transcendence—plays through the concept/thing and subject/object mediations that also inform Adorno's critique and, as was already indicated in chapter 2, sets the direction for Adorno's own conception of truth.

History and Historicity

What Adorno has in mind, although he provides only one direct citation, are the last two chapters in *Being and Time*, at the conclusion of division 2 ("Dasein and Temporality"). There Heidegger argues, against what he calls the "vulgar" conceptions of history and time, that actual history as studied by historians is rooted in Dasein's more primordial temporality (*Zeitlichkeit*). Moreover, such temporality is the ontological meaning (*Sinn*) of Dasein's care (*Sorge*), and care is the Being (*Sein*) of Dasein. Hence, if Heidegger does provide an answer to the question of the meaning of Being in *Sein und Zeit*,[53] it is that temporality is the meaning of Dasein's Being. Accordingly, he analyzes Dasein's historicity (*Geschichtlichkeit*) in order to show that Dasein "is not 'temporal' because it 'is in history,' but [that], on the contrary, [Dasein] exists and can exist historically only because it is temporal in the ground of its Being" (SZ 376, original in italics).

Adorno ignores such complications, however, and cuts to the chase. He raises two objections. First, by transposing what is historical into an ontological structure, Heidegger's concept of historicity "freezes history into what is unhistorical, heedless of the historical conditions that govern the inner composition and the constellation of subject and object" (ND 134/129). Heidegger thereby ignores how real history accumulates within the objects of knowledge and needs to be recognized. Second, by ontologizing history, "historicity" accords inordinate ontological power (*Seinsmächtigkeit*) to real historical forces, thereby justifying blind submission to historical situations "as if they were commanded by Being itself." As a result, political actors can either ignore or deify history as needed (ND 135/130).

Similar objections apply to the conception of temporality (*Zeitlichkeit*) that undergirds Heidegger's concept of historicity. Heidegger both absolutizes and transfigures time (*Zeit*) and transience (*Vergängnis*), Adorno holds. Heidegger thereby embraces the "most catastrophic" myth from the history of philosophy, namely, the Platonic prejudice "that the imperishable [*das Unvergängliche*] must be the good" (ND 136/131). For Adorno, this is equivalent to claiming that whatever prevails is best, that might makes right. Whereas Plato tempered such fatalism by appealing to the eternal idea of justice, however, Heidegger's "existence" has no such exit: "Nothing remains of the eternal idea . . . but the naked affirmation of what in any case is: the affirmation of power" (ND 136/131). In the concept of historicity, then, Heidegger's ontology shows itself to be ontic, all too ontic: a German ideology.

Adorno himself, of course, does not affirm "the eternal idea," whether that idea be of justice or goodness or truth. Rather, what he objects to is an account of history that allows no transcendence and an account of Being that erases all transience. This becomes clear from other passages where Adorno discusses Heidegger's "historicity." Already in the early 1930s, Adorno's inaugural lecture had juxtaposed Heidegger's "ontologizing of time itself" and his "ontologizing history as totality in the form of mere 'historicity'" on the one hand, to Adorno's own emphasis on the dialectical interpretation of "historical images" as possible configurations of truth, on the other.[54] The next year his lecture on "The Idea of Natural History" described Heidegger's conception of historicity as correctly eliminating the "pure antithesis" between history and ontology in Max Scheler's work and radically demonstrating their "insuperable interwovenness."[55] But this happens at the expense of Heidegger's subsuming all contingent historical phenomena under the "subjective category of historicity" in a totalizing way,[56] or, to use Adorno's later terminology, Heidegger's ontologizing the ontic. What "historicity" lacks, and what Adorno sets out to provide, in his own terms, is a "concrete unity of nature and history" derived from actual beings in their "concrete inner-historical determinacy [*Bestimmtheit*]."[57] Moreover, as the rest of the lecture lays out, this can be understood only as a dialectical unity where the deepest point of convergence lies in what Walter Benjamin called "transience" (*Vergängnis*) and where even the most calcified myth holds a transcendent "promise of reconciliation."[58]

As Rolf Tiedemann indicates, the same line of critique returns in Adorno's unpublished 1957 lectures on the philosophy of history, where Adorno says the concept of historicity effectively abolishes "the concept of history" and "ends up by converting history itself, change in time, into a constant."[59] In *History and Freedom*, from the mid-1960s, the second of two lectures titled "Naturgeschichte"[60] suggests that Heidegger's concept of historicity eternalizes change just like a nature religion from whose constant cycle there is no escape. By ontologically inflating history, Heidegger not only conjures away the concept of history but also eliminates anything that would resist conceptual domination.[61]

So too, in "History and Metaphysics," the very last section of the model "World Spirit and Natural History" in *Negative Dialectics*—a section whose text the 1965 lecture just cited nearly replicates[62]—Adorno, without naming or quoting Heidegger, claims Heidegger's "unhistorical concept of history" enables the arbitrary transposition of what is historically contingent into something permanent, just as if historical relations were "natural" (ND 352/358). Yet it would be equally mistaken to seek some absolute first principle in "nature." Instead, Adorno appeals once more to Benjamin's notion of transience as the "moment in which nature and history become mutually commensurable" (ND 353/359). In contrast to "historicity" in Heidegger's "falsely resurrected metaphysics" (ND 352/358), "transience" transmutes metaphysics into history, while simultaneously enabling the meditations on metaphysics that immediately follow in *Negative Dialectics*: "No recollection of transcendence is possible any longer, except by virtue of transience; eternity does not appear as such but [as] refracted through what is most transient" (ND 353/360). Whereas, according to Adorno, Heidegger's "historicity" eliminates any possibility of fundamental change in human history, Adorno's emphasis on transience clings to transcendence, to the possibility that everything could be different.

Thus we arrive at a difference between Heidegger and Adorno that really does make a difference: their contrasting visions, in Macdonald's words, of what would be different. For within Adorno's critique of Heidegger's ontology lies a struggle over the priority of possibility and its temporal direction. This struggle has everything to do with how each of them understands the temporal character of truth.

Blocked Possibilities

Iain Macdonald has shown that Adorno and Heidegger take "divergent paths" on the basis of a "shared premise." Although easily missed within the fireworks of Adorno's critique, he shares with Heidegger an attempt to reverse the "priority of actuality over possibility" in traditional metaphysics, for the sake of an emphatic but blocked possibility that does not fit the Hegelian distinction between formal and real possibility.[63] Macdonald explains that when Hegel drew this distinction, he gave priority to real possibility, especially in his critique of Kantian morality. Hegel regards a Kantian ought as a type of formal possibility: what the categorical imperative enjoins may be possible, but finite humans cannot attain it. In this sense, it is non-actual, a merely formal possibility: "For Hegel, the ought names a renunciation of actuality in the form of clinging to something that actuality cannot produce."[64] Hegel prefers real possibility, what actuality in its complexity indeed makes possible. Consequently, a Hegelian critique of society would not ask in the abstract what society should be like. Rather, perhaps in the manner of Marx, it would ask what, concretely and historically, society can become: What real possibilities does society actually contain?

Despite his indebtedness to Hegel, Adorno resists this either/or. For Adorno, society could be altogether different, and that is a genuine possibility, not because society as it has developed positively makes it possible but because this possibility lies blocked within society as it has developed. The possibility of a society that, as a whole, would not be false is neither formal nor real, neither a mere ought nor an actual possibility. Rather, it is what Macdonald calls a "real ought" or a "blocked possibility." It is a "historically developed yet sadly suppressed, liberating [potentiality] by which society can and ought to transform itself," a "redemptive possibility hobbled and shunted into unreality by real actuality."[65]

Although Adorno's critique of "Being," "Dasein," and "historicity" occludes his close proximity to Heidegger concerning the priority of possibility, there is a strong case to be made—and Macdonald makes it—that from 1927 onward, if not earlier, Heidegger's entire project also aimed to overturn the priority of actuality over possibility in Western metaphysics, in favor of a possibility not captured in the Hegelian contrast between formal and real possibility. Quite simply, Dasein, whose existence is a key to the meaning of Being in *Sein und Zeit*, is defined primarily not by what it is but what it can be. At the very outset, Heidegger asserts that Dasein essentially *is* its possibility: "The being which is concerned in its Being about its Being is related to its Being as its truest possibility" (SZ 42). Indeed, Dasein is "primarily Being-possible [*Möglichsein*]," and "possibility . . . is the most primordial and the ultimate positive ontological determination of Dasein" (SZ 143–44). Later, discussing Dasein's temporality, Heidegger indicates that Dasein exists primarily in the mode of futural temporality, ever "projecting toward a potentiality-of-Being [*Seinkönnen*] for the sake of which Dasein always exists" (SZ 336, italics in original).[66]

Moreover, there are many indications that Heidegger thought Being itself should be understood primarily in terms of possibility rather than actuality. Indeed, by the time of his *Beiträge zur Philosophie (Vom Ereignis)*, written a decade or so after *Sein und Zeit* appeared, Heidegger, to distinguish Being from any actual being, was ready to say that what he now calls *beyng* or be-ing (*Seyn*) "is possibility."[67] The whole point of his talking about the ontological difference between Being and beings, Heidegger claims, was to open the possibility of an alternative to the entire Western metaphysical tradition, the possibility of an "other beginning": ontological difference "is something transitional in the transition from the end of metaphysics to the other beginning."[68]

Like the potential for a true society in Adorno's negative dialectics, Heidegger's "other beginning" is a blocked possibility. Although Heidegger seems to locate this possibility in a prehistoric past—in original *beyng* prior to the metaphysical Being that has governed all of Western thought and society—nevertheless he, like Adorno, views the blocked possibility as real. It is real precisely because it does *not* align with the fundamentally mistaken priority of actuality over possibility in Western metaphysics. For Heidegger, the Greek origins of the West are "not the only possible beginning." And the other possible beginning he envisions would be "more true to the original impetus, if not the historical results, of Western thought."[69] Resonating in the history of metaphysical Being, yet repeatedly missed, is "the truth *behind* the [Being] of revealed beings." Yet it resonates there, as Macdonald puts it, "as a blocked possibility—a possibility that remains 'real,' but only in the form of a future that is incompatible with the actuality . . . so prized in the history of [metaphysics]. According to Heidegger, this blockage is due to the fact that beings and *Dasein* itself cover over and dissemble the ground of their own possibility, turning it into a repressed and therefore hidden ground (*Ab-grund*)."[70]

Adorno, of course, had no access to the book where Heidegger makes his most emphatic claims about the "other beginning." Although written in 1936–38, Heidegger's *Beiträge*, regarded by many as his most important work after *Sein und Zeit*, was not published until 1989, twenty years after Adorno's death. Yet the moves Heidegger makes there with respect to Being and *beyng* are visible in other writings that Adorno does cite. Moreover, from the very outset, Adorno was hypersensitive to what he perceived as Heidegger's archaism, his turn to a mythical origin. What has become apparent, however, thanks to Macdonald's work, is that Adorno opposes Heidegger for the sake of a dialectically shared concern. Adorno rejects Heidegger's blocked possibility—*beyng* beyond Being, so to speak, a beginning before the metaphysical beginning—for the sake of a different blocked possibility—the possibility of a future society in which needless suffering would end. As Macdonald puts it, the point of Adorno's Heidegger critique "is that the truth lies not in a return to an archaic or mythological past—be it a ground beyond or beneath all metaphysical grounds—but in transforming the world on the basis of what society denies us in the name of the social continuum rather than human well-being."[71]

Unfolding Truth

The struggle over blocked possibility is also a contestation over truth, in at least three ways. First, as we have seen, Adorno considers Heidegger's ontology societally false: it is an ideological response to a partially false need. Second, Adorno also regards it as philosophically false: it is a mistaken attempt to circumvent the historically developed polarities between concept and thing and between subject and object that, for Adorno, help constitute the constellation of truth. Third, and perhaps most fundamentally, Adorno also implicitly takes issue with Heidegger's conception of truth. Whereas Heidegger understands truth as a process of concealment and unconcealment issuing forth from the blocked possibility of an other beginning,[72] Adorno ties truth in its most comprehensive sense to the blocked but "humanly promised other of history," which Heidegger's ontology "illegitimately settles before history or exempts from history" (ND 396/404). This humanly promised other would be a society, historically not impossible, that puts an end to needless violence and suffering, which late capitalist society both epitomizes and occludes. Truth in this sense issues forth from the blocked possibility of a different future. As I put it in chapter 2, truth in Adorno's conception is the undying and critically articulable hope for complete social transformation.

Accordingly, both Heidegger and Adorno link truth with a blocked possibility that, although neither formal nor actual in Hegel's sense, is temporal and real. And by insisting on truth's temporality, they agree with Hegel, for whom "becoming is the first adequate vehicle of truth."[73] For both Heidegger and Adorno, truth itself is temporal and, indeed, historical: it unfolds in time and, despite Heidegger's alleged archaism, within human history. Heidegger holds that truth unfolds via attunement to the possibility of an (ab)original call—it is the truth of *beyng*. Adorno, by contrast, holds that truth unfolds via the dialectic of enlightenment and its possible transcendence. Hence, despite Adorno's sharp criticisms of Heidegger's concepts of temporality and historicity, the claim that truth is temporal and historical is not really in dispute. What is in dispute, however, is what truth and its temporality come to.

Yet this dispute remains mostly implicit in Adorno's critique of Heidegger's ontology. Perhaps that fact points, in turn, to another apparently blocked possibility: If put into genuine debate, rather than left suspended in what Mörchen called a *Kommunikationsverweigerung* (failure or refusal to communicate), would their overtly opposed but silently connected conceptions of truth yield a more adequate understanding of the temporality of truth? A more adequate conception, as both Heidegger and Adorno would agree, would reject the "eternalism" that has haunted truth theories since Parmenides and Plato. Unlike contemporary "temporalist" positions, however, it would also refuse to restrict truth to its propositional forms.[74] Instead, such a conception would recognize both the prior calling and the future hope that make all truth possible, whether propositional or not. Yet, as I envision it, a more adequate conception would not draw a hard link from either the call or the hope to a blocked possibility. For, contra Heidegger, the ever-unfolding call to truth does not issue from a nearly inaccessible source. Nor, contra Adorno, need the hope for a better future lie blocked in society as it has historically developed.

Despite the damage wrought by Western metaphysics and the stranglehold exercised by global capitalism, possibilities of truth—neither formal nor actual, but also not merely blocked—lie embedded and embodied in the practices and institutions of social life. It remains historically possible to be true to societal principles, themselves historically unfolding, such as solidarity and justice. It also remains historically possible to follow such principles in ways that societally foster the interconnected flourishing of Earth's inhabitants. Adorno's critique of Heidegger poses the challenge of envisioning such historical possibilities, unblocking them where necessary, and pursuing them whenever possible. Truth unfolds in historical time. An adequate conception would show why and how this is so.[75]

5

Politics of Truth

Adorno, Foucault, and Feminist Critical Theory

> But the absolute that metaphysics has in mind would be the nonidentical that would emerge only after the identity-compulsion dissolved.
>
> —Theodor W. Adorno (ND 398/406)

Having explored the constellation of truth and its intersecting polarities in Adorno's meditations on metaphysics and critique of Heidegger, we can consider the contemporary relevance of Adorno's conception of truth. First, in the current chapter, I discuss its relevance for what Michel Foucault has called the politics of truth,[1] with a view to debates in feminist critical theory. In chapter 6, I consider the import of Adorno's conception of truth for debates about the politics of art. Then chapter 7 explores its significance for contemporary philosophy.

So far as we know, Theodor Adorno (1903–1969) and Michel Foucault (1926–1984) never met. Nor, for the most part, did they read each other's work. Yet their critiques of Western society are strikingly similar—so similar, in fact, that they have drawn comparable criticisms from Jürgen Habermas and Axel Honneth. They have also received analogous defenses from feminist Critical Theorists, such as Amy Allen and Deborah Cook, who challenge Habermas and Honneth's criticisms.

Central to these disputes lie issues concerning rationality, normativity, and the prospects for social transformation. Habermas takes Adorno and Foucault to task for so totalizing their critiques of modern rationality that no normative basis remains for their critiques.² Likewise, Honneth criticizes both of them for neglecting the normative implications of social practices and social struggle.³ By contrast, Amy Allen, addressing the concerns of post- and decolonial theory, turns to Foucault and Adorno for worthy alternatives to the Eurocentric progressivism of Habermas and Honneth. According to Allen, Foucault and Adorno call "those who have inherited the project of Enlightenment to live up more fully to its normative ideals of freedom, inclusion, and respect for the other."⁴ So too, in response to Habermas's criticisms, Deborah Cook argues that both Adorno and Foucault have sufficient normative grounding for their social critiques—Adorno, in the process of determinate negation; Foucault, in the history of resistance; and both of them, in a commitment to autonomy. According to Cook, such grounding makes them more astute critics than Habermas is of a society where economic exchange and political power predominate, and it lets them hold open the possibility of radical social transformation.⁵

Complex issues are at stake in these responses to Foucault and Adorno. There is no way to sort all of them out in one chapter. Nor do I intend to review the extensive literature on debates between Habermasians and Foucaultians concerning rationality, normativity, and social transformation.⁶ Instead, let me focus on two concepts at the heart of these debates, ones that contemporary feminists need to revisit, namely, the ideas of power and truth. The concept of power has played a central role in feminist theories; the concept of truth, not so much.⁷ Yet I shall argue that *both* concepts should be central to feminist critical theory.

I am especially concerned about the *relation* between power and truth, for here, it seems to me, lie both important insights and disturbing blind spots in Foucault and Adorno's critiques. Moreover, even when this relation is not explicitly thematized, it engenders many of the disputes about Foucault and Adorno in feminism and critical theory. My aim is not to resolve such disputes. Yet I do want to find a better way to think about power, truth, and their relation—better both conceptually and with respect to a contemporary political environment where powerful authoritarian populists not only try to undo the accomplishments of the feminist movement but also dismiss the importance of truth.

My discussion has three stages. First I compare Adorno and Foucault's conceptions of power, with an emphasis on the connection between interactional and macrostructural forms of power. Next I compare their conceptions of truth, with a focus on the interrelation between truth and power. Then, aiming to retrieve insights relevant for contemporary feminism, I offer critical reflections on their conceptions of truth and power and argue that feminist critical theory needs to develop both a new conception of truth and a sufficiently normative critique of power.

Power Dynamics

Feminism and Forms of Power

Power is a protean concept, and it is the topic of countless contentions among feminist theorists. Amy Allen maps many of these feminist disputes in an illuminating article titled "Feminist Perspectives on Power."[8] In the first place, she says, disagreements arise over whether power is best regarded as influence ("power-over") or agency ("power-to").[9] These disagreements spill over into disputes about whether, in my own vocabulary, power is primarily interactional (i.e., occurring in the interrelations, practices, and institutions that configure human agency and influence) or primarily macrostructural (i.e., occurring in or via the large-scale structures that organize social life—today, arguably, civil society and economic and political systems). Whereas liberal feminists and care theorists tend to emphasize agency and interactional power, feminists who are critical theorists in the broad sense tend to emphasize influence and macrostructural power.[10] Moreover, what Allen calls "phenomenological feminist approaches" (e.g., Iris Young) and "analytic feminist approaches" (e.g., Ann Cudd) often emphasize both interactional and macrostructural power, as indicated, for example, by Sally Haslanger's calling attention to both "agent oppression" and "structural oppression."[11]

Even if one acknowledges both interactional and macrostructural forms of power, however, questions remain about how these two forms interconnect—whether, for example, one form has precedence over the other, and whether their interconnection undergoes sociohistorical shifts. For, like race and class, issues of gender transect what I have distinguished as macrostructural and interactional forms of power. That is why, for example, Nancy Fraser rightly argues that the injustices suffered by women and people of color in the contemporary West can be adequately addressed only by a politics that properly combines striving for socioeconomic equality with struggles for cultural recognition. Gender and race are what she calls "paradigmatic bivalent collectivities." They encompass both "political-economic dimensions and cultural-valuational dimensions." For such bivalent collectivities, "both socioeconomic maldistribution and cultural misrecognition . . . are primary and co-original."¹² In other words, the injustices the members of these collectivities suffer arise from power dynamics in both the macrostructures of society (especially the capitalist economy and the administrative state) and the patterns of social interaction (i.e., in interrelations, practices, and institutions) and, as Fraser argues, they require a suitably "bivalent" response.

Because both Adorno and Foucault, each in his own way, thematize the interconnection between interactional and macrostructural power, their social critiques remain relevant for feminist theory and politics. Even though neither one focused on issues of gender, by highlighting questions about how interactional and macrostructural power interconnect and making them central to a critique of Western society, Adorno and Foucault make indispensable contributions to feminist critical theory, as well as to other modes of critical theory such as queer theory, postcolonial theory, and critical race theory. Yet they have different conceptions of both interactional and macrostructural power. In these differences one can discern conceptual problems that, I argue, feminists should not perpetuate. These problems become especially pressing when one considers how power and truth interrelate.

FOUCAULT: DISCIPLINARY POWER AND BIOPOLITICS

The most prominent concepts of power in Foucault's work, and certainly the ones that have attracted the most discussion and debate, occur in genealogical writings from the mid-1970s. These include *Surveiller et punir* (1975)¹³ and *La Volenté de savoir* (1976, the first volume in *The History of Sexuality*)¹⁴ as well as essays, interviews, and lectures from the same time. Deborah Cook and Amy Allen rightly point out that these writings deploy two closely related concepts of power, namely, disciplinary power and state biopower.¹⁵ Foucault claims that these are distinctly modern forms of power. They have developed since the end of eighteenth century, and they have gradually supplanted earlier forms of power.

That is why common social-critical concepts of power such as repression and domination, which Foucault himself had used in earlier writings, fail to capture how power operates in contemporary society. Hence, for example, he rejects what he calls "the repressive hypothesis" with respect to modern sexuality—the hypothesis "that modern industrial societies ushered in an age of increased sexual repression."¹⁶ He also insists that a "juridical" or "sovereign" theory of power, one which posits a sovereign ruler wielding control over social subjects by enforcing the rule of law, is inappropriate for understanding modern society (TP 121–25), where power primarily flows through disciplinary practices and institutions and via state-sanctioned biopolitics.

Foucault regards modern power as a relation rather than either a substance or a nonrelational property. More specifically, as Allen suggests, it is a strategic relation in which opposing forces struggle to get the other to do what each wants.[17] It is also productive, rather than repressive, aiming for results, rather than mere control: modern power "traverses and produces things, it induces pleasure, forms knowledge, produces discourse" (TP 119). In contrast to the juridical or sovereign theory of power, then, what Allen calls Foucault's "strategic model" sees modern power as dispersed across society rather than concentrated in one institutional complex or macrostructure, as generated in myriad interrelations, practices, and institutions, and as aimed at results over which individual subjects might have little or no control.

Indeed, rather than think of individual subjects as "having" power, we should regard them as effects and conduits of power, Foucault says: "One of the first effects of power is that it allows bodies, gestures, discourses, and desires to be identified and constituted as something individual. The individual is not . . . power's opposite number; the individual is one of power's first effects. The individual is in fact a power-effect, and . . . , to the extent that he is a power-effect, the individual is a relay: power passes through the individuals it has constituted."[18] Hence, one general effect of power in modern society is the subjection (*assujettisement*) of individuals, in a double sense: they are subject to relations of power, and they are constituted as subjects by the effects of power.

Although this does not mean that individuals are no more than the effects of power, it does mean that resistance to modern power must take the form of a struggle against subjection, a process Foucault calls "desubjection" (*désassujettisement*). This struggle involves both critical reflection on how power constitutes the subject and deliberate refashioning of the subject, using what Foucault calls technologies of the self. The freedom of individuals, then, lies not in an escape from power but in "strategically reworking the power relations to which we are subjected."[19] In the first instance, these are relations of disciplinary power.

Disciplinary Power

Foucault explains the disciplinary model of power in *"Society Must Be Defended,"* lectures he gave in 1976, around the time of the "Truth and Power" interview I have already cited. Contrary to liberal and Marxist misconceptions, he says, disciplinary power is not a contractually negotiable private possession, nor is it simply political power aimed at economic ends. Instead, it is "exercised . . . in action" and is "primarily . . . a relationship of force."[20] But how is power exercised? Not as oppression (which would presuppose a contractual model of legitimacy), nor as repression or top-down domination. Rather, disciplinary power operates by producing multiple "discourses of truth" that have "powerful effects." And such operation is not peripheral or optional: our society needs power-produced truth "in order to function."[21]

Moreover, that is precisely how contemporary power flows—not from a central authority or a predominant macrostructure (e.g., State or economy) but via a wide diversity of practices and institutions to which individuals are subject. This implies, in turn, that, far from *possessing* power, individuals always simultaneously *submit to* and *exercise* power, and such power flows from the tiniest mechanisms into "increasingly general mechanisms" and even into "forms of overall domination."[22]

Indeed, the circulation of disciplinary power does not so much rely on ideological constructs as on instruments for creating and accumulating knowledge: "the observational methods, the recording techniques, the investigative research procedures, the verification mechanisms."[23] This sort of power makes possible the extraction of time and labor from human bodies; it is "exercised through constant surveillance" (in what Foucault describes as a *surveillance society*);[24] and it operates via the discourses of the human sciences, especially those tied to clinical knowledge (e.g., psychology, sociology, and the medical sciences). These disciplinary discourses do not seek to sort out what is legally or morally legitimate or right. Instead, they aim to establish and enforce what is normal, thereby leading to what Foucault calls a *normalizing society*.[25]

For Foucault, the only viable and worthwhile alternative to such normalizing disciplinary power would not be an absence of power, and it certainly would not be reversion to the outdated sort of sovereign power from which the normative concepts of legitimacy and right stem. Instead, it would be a "nondisciplinary"—but also nonsovereign—form of power, tied to a new "antidisciplinary"—but also nonsovereign—form of right.[26]

State Biopower

Although Foucault emphasizes the interactional form of power he calls disciplinary, he does not deny that power also takes a macrostructural form in the modern West. This is what he labels *biopower*, and he locates it primarily in how the administrative state intersects a capitalist economy. Foucault insists, however, that state biopower relies heavily on the operations of disciplinary power. Whereas disciplinary power targets individuals—as students, workers, prisoners, patients, and the like—biopower aims at entire populations and sometimes even at the human species as a whole.

Together, these two interlinked forms of power—disciplinary power and state biopower—make up a characteristically modern mode of power that, as Allen puts it, is "simultaneously individualizing and totalizing."[27] The first volume to *The History of Sexuality* describes this modern mode as a "power over life" having two interlinked "poles of development." The first pole centers on disciplining the individual body, optimizing its capability, making it more useful and docile, and integrating it into systems of control. Foucault calls such disciplinary power over life, exercised in schools, armies, prisons, and other institutions, an *"anatomo-politics of the human body."* The second pole of development focuses on what Foucault labels "the species body" as the basis for human survival and biological reproduction. It involves state supervision of entire populations, of births and deaths, public health, and the like. Foucault calls such state biopower over life a *"bio-politics of the population."*[28]

According to Foucault, the development of sexuality was one of the most important ways in which these two forms of power over life conjoined in the nineteenth century. Also important, however, was how capitalism developed. On the one hand, the techniques of disciplinary power across diverse institutions such as the family, schooling, and medicine prepared a ready work force. On the other hand, techniques of state biopower made it possible to connect population growth with "the expansion of productive forces and the differential allocation of profit."[29] Similar observations can be made about the domains of law and politics.

The main point, however, is that we cannot properly resist contemporary forms of subjection if we do not understand how both interactional (disciplinary) and macrostructural (state supervised) forms of power have developed and have become tightly intermeshed. That is why, on its own, neither a Freud-inspired diagnosis of sexual "repression" nor a roughly Marx-inspired diagnosis of economic "exploitation" or "oppression" will suffice for the purposes of Foucaultian social critique. That is also why feminist critical theorists, who tend to emphasize both influence and macrostructural power, find Foucault's work so important. Their challenge, as it was for Foucault, is to envision normative pathways along which the subjection of women can be not only resisted but also transformed, a topic I return to below.

Adorno: Three Modes of Domination

When Jacques Derrida accepted the City of Frankfurt's Theodor W. Adorno Prize in September 2001, he called himself an "heir to the Frankfurt School" for whom Adorno was an "adoptive father." Derrida thereby presented himself as a sibling rival to Jürgen Habermas. If Derrida could thus pose as Adorno's "other son," then both the similarities between Foucaultian and Adornian critiques of modernity and the striving between Foucault and Habermas over the legacy of the Enlightenment suggest, as Allen indicates, that we should regard Foucault as Adorno's "other 'other son.' "[30] This is especially so with regard to what Honneth has labeled the critique of power.

Yet there are also significant differences, as I hope to show, and they point to underlying issues that neither Foucault nor Adorno could adequately address. These differences are suggested by the title of the book by Adorno and Max Horkheimer to which Foucault shows the greatest affinities[31] and that Habermas most vigorously criticizes:[32] *Dialectic of Enlightenment.* For although, like Adorno and Horkheimer, Foucault conducts a genealogy of the imbrication of power and rationality, unlike them, he does not construe this as a universal-historical dialectic. Nor does Foucault hold out the hope, however dim, that such imbrication could be loosened or overcome. Unlike Foucault, as Peter Dews puts it, "Horkheimer and Adorno envisage a genuine dialectic of Enlightenment."[33] These differences are reflected in the term Adorno prefers when he talks about power, namely, domination (*Herrschaft*). Adornian social critique unfolds as a critical reflection of the dialectic of domination, within the utopian horizon of possible liberation. What makes late capitalist society in its entirety false, Adorno says, is how it lets domination occur through the process of economic exchange, a process that leaves no gender, class, or race unscathed.

A frequently cited passage from *Negative Dialectics* in the model on "World Spirit and Natural History" captures the gist of Adorno's social critique. In this passage Adorno responds to the Hegelian concept of universal history as a continuous, dialectical, and progressive unfolding of spirit (*Geist*). Let me quote it at length and then comment:

> Universal history must be [both] constructed and denied. After [recent] catastrophes and in view of future ones, it would be cynical to assert a self-manifesting and all-encompassing world plan for the better. This, however, is no reason to deny the unity that welds together the discontinuous, chaotically splin-

> tered moments and phases of history—the unity of control over nature [*Naturbeherrschung*], progressing into domination [*Herrschaft*] over human beings and finally over inner nature. No universal history leads from savagery to humanity, but one does indeed lead from the slingshot to the megaton bomb. It culminates in the total threat of organized humankind against organized human beings, in the epitome of discontinuity. Hegel is thereby horribly verified and stood on his head. . . . History is the unity of continuity and discontinuity. Society preserves itself not despite its antagonism but by means of it: objectively, the profit motive [*Profitinteresse*] and hence the class relation are the motor of the process of production on which everyone's life depends and whose primacy portends the death of all. And this implies what is reconciling in the irreconcilable: because it alone lets people live, a changed life would not even be possible without it. What historically created that possibility can just as well destroy it. (ND 314/320)

In other words, human history is a dialectical process of ever more expansive domination that simultaneously creates both the real threat of Earth's complete destruction and the conditions for a possibly postdominative future.

When compared with Foucault's accounts of disciplinary power and state biopower, three features stand out in this passage. First, if, as Foucault claims, there is a distinctly modern mode of power, then Adorno would want to emphasize how this develops *from* earlier modes of power. Whereas Foucault locates historical discontinuity in irreversible shifts from one "regime of truth" to the next (e.g., in his terms, from the classical to the modern), Adorno locates historical discontinuity in the antagonism that drives historical development *across* different "moments and phases," an antagonism that now threatens to destroy everyone and thereby bring history to an end, in "the epitome of discontinuity."

Second, whereas Foucault disavows or downplays continuity across different regimes of truth and historical modes of power, Adorno emphatically asserts such continuity. It occurs, he says, in the unfolding of domination within three mutually intertwined modes, which we can distinguish as subjugation (of nature), exploitation (of some human beings by others), and repression (of nature within human existence). These three modes of domination take different shapes in different historical settings. Yet their mutual entwinement is, if you will, a historical constant. And at its core that constant is one of antagonism, antagonism between humans and nature, among humans, and within human existence. In this sense history is, as Adorno says, "the unity of continuity and discontinuity."

Third, whereas Foucault stresses the dispersion of modern power across interrelations, practices, and institutions, such that not even state biopower can properly be called "domination," Adorno forthrightly continues a Marxian emphasis on the capitalist economic system, with its class conflicts and private ownership of the means of production, as the key to modern modes of domination. As Deborah Cook shows, this emphasis on the economic macrostructure does not combine easily with a Foucaultian emphasis on diverse power relations and the subjection of individuals to them. Whereas Adorno would want to say the forms of modern power that Foucault diagnoses are anchored in the late capitalist economy, to which the administrative state is also subordinate, Foucault repeatedly stresses that capitalism itself relies heavily on the modern development of disciplinary power and state biopower.[34]

Given Adorno's emphasis on the antagonistic unity of domination as anchored in the capitalist economic system, two other differences from Foucault emerge, in sentences I omitted from the passage cited. First, the primary motivation for Adorno's critique of domination does not lie in a desire for individual freedom but rather in the need to remove suffering. This motivation lies at the heart of Adorno's critique of Hegel, who, Adorno says, transfigured "historical suffering" into a conduit for the world spirit's progress rather than recognizing how suffering has persisted, albeit "with breathing spells," throughout human history until now (ND 314/320). A really transformed society would be one where suffering is mitigated or removed. Although Cook occasionally suggests that Foucault shares Adorno's concerns in this regard, I do not find suffering to be a primary motivation for Foucault's critique of power. Rather, individual desubjection is.[35]

So too, whereas Foucault is wary about specifying a general pattern or principle that governs all the diverse power relations in modern society, Adorno has no such qualms. The principle that governs all three modes of domination as well as everyone and everything subject to them is what Adorno calls the "all-subjugating principle of identity" (*alles unterjochenden Identitätspinzip*). This principle turns the nonidentical—whatever resists imposed identity and instrumental rationality—into something to be feared (ND 314–15/320). To the extent that the historical process of enlightenment follows the principle of identity and serves blind domination, it is, in Horkheimer and Adorno's memorable phrase, "mythical fear radicalized" (DA 32/11).

This suggests, however, that the principle of identity is not in fact "all-subjugating," and the process of domination is not all-powerful. There is more to people and things than the identity they acquire under late-capitalist conditions, and there are forms of resistance not even blind domination can wipe out. Hence an Adornian social critique would point to this "more," without subsuming it under the principle of identity, and it would enact such resistance, without reinforcing patterns of domination. Although some of this will involve the sorts of individual change that Foucault calls desubjection, the context for such self-transformation lies in the historically evolved structure of a society where a capitalist economy dominates other macrostructures, social interrelations, and individual lives. Moreover, as we shall see, both a social critique of domination and resistance to it require a different conception of truth.

Truth Matters

FEMINIST CONTENTIONS

In a debate with Judith Butler during the early 1990s over the implications of postmodernism for feminist theory and politics, Seyla Benhabib worried that postmodernism had produced a "retreat from utopia within feminist theory." Recalling the phrase Max Horkheimer used in a telling interview one year after Adorno died,[36] Benhabib describes utopian thinking as "the longing for the 'wholly other' (*das ganz Andere*), for that which is not yet," without which, she says, "not only morality but also radical transformation is unthinkable." Absent this "regulative principle of hope," she suggests, postmodernism will seduce feminists into contentedly and self-destructively "singing the swan song of normative thinking in general."[37] Although Benhabib mentions Lyotard in this context, Butler's appropriation of *Foucault's* critique of power lies at the center of her worry.

Butler, for her part, prefers to speak of poststructuralism rather than postmodernism, and she says the "fine point" poststructuralism makes is that "power pervades the very conceptual apparatus" that tries to sort out how power works, "including the subject position of the critic." Moreover, "this implication of the terms of criticism in the field of power is *not* the advent of a nihilistic relativism incapable of furnishing norms, but, rather, the very precondition of a politically engaged critique. To establish a set of norms that are beyond power or force is itself a powerful and forceful conceptual practice that sublimates, disguises, and extends its own power play through recourse to tropes of normative universality."[38] With that move Butler turns the debate into one about the entanglement of power and validity as well as both the possibility and the desirability of a normative social critique[39]—and not about utopian thinking.

Indeed, Benhabib's worry about a retreat from utopia gets lost in her exchange with Butler—her own response to Butler says "issues of subjectivity, selfhood, and agency" (implicitly, not utopia) lie at the core of their disagreement.[40] When the theme of utopian thinking does return, in Drucilla Cornell's contributions, it receives mostly dismissive responses: Benhabib objects to Cornell's wishing to reinscribe "a utopian female sexuality";[41] Butler questions how to understand "the deconstructive notion of 'the constitutive outside' ";[42] and Nancy Fraser worries that Cornell's "quasi-Lacanian/Derridean framework" does not adequately "permit us to . . . infuse all of our work with a normative critique of domination and injustice."[43] The actual role of utopian hope in feminist theory and politics—which Cornell's response to Benhabib emphasizes, appealing to Adorno and Benjamin[44]—is left unaddressed.

This lack is doubly unfortunate. First, it weakens feminist critiques of power. Second, it keeps feminist critical theorists from reimagining the idea of truth that their critiques silently presuppose—silently, because questions about truth come up only obliquely in *Feminist Contentions* and do not receive direct attention. In the social critiques that Foucault and Adorno offer, by contrast, questions concerning truth and its interrelation with power are front and center. At the same time, as we shall see, the differences in how they understand these matters raise central issues for feminists to address, not least of which is the role of hope in feminist theory and politics.[45]

Foucault: Regimes of Truth

Foucault explains how power and truth interrelate in a wide-ranging and well-known 1976 interview titled "Truth and Power," first published in 1977. The interview proposes that scholars and professionals should understand their political role in postwar France as being "specific intellectuals" who take up struggles over disciplinary power in the interactional sectors where they live or work, such as "housing, the hospital, the asylum, the laboratory, the university, family and sexual relations" (TP 126). These are sites of power. They are simultaneously sites of truth. And, to sustain sector-specific political struggles, scholars and professionals must understand the interrelation between truth and power. For, Foucault says, "truth isn't outside power, or lacking in power. . . . Truth is a thing of this world: it is produced only by virtue of multiple forms of constraint. And it induces regular effects of power" (TP 131). Hence truth is not an alternative to power, nor is it a sacred space from which to critique and resist power. Rather, truth—specifically, social-scientific truth—is how power—specifically, disciplinary power—operates.

To capture such interlinkage, Foucault introduces the notion of a *regime of truth*. The term *regime* implies that a nexus of truth *and* power emerges historically and can undergo "a global modification" (TP 113). A regime of truth is the dynamic, historically conditioned pattern that governs which sorts of statements and claims are acceptable and authorized, along with the discursive means and methods valorized and "the status of those who are charged with saying what counts as true" (TP 131). Because authority, sanctions, and valorization are built in, a regime of truth regulates how power is exercised in a society. It constrains social conduct, and it helps produce the practices and institutions that organize social life.

According to Foucault, the modern regime of truth places scientific discourse and organizations at the center, in conjunction with ongoing economic and political demands for scientifically established truth. That means institutions of education and information, where truth claims attract widespread contestation, have an especially prominent role in the modern circulation of truth, and these are themselves under the control of major political and economic "apparatuses" (e.g., universities and media). Because of the modern emphasis on scientific discourse and the role of scientific discourse in political and economic systems, intellectuals need not only to engage in sector-specific struggles over truth but also take on the entire modern regime of truth, in "a battle about the status of truth and the economic and political role it plays." For Foucault, the aim of what he calls "a new politics of truth" would not be to free truth from power as such. Rather, the aim would be to detach "the power of truth from the forms of hegemony . . . within which it operates at the present time" (TP 132).

Foucault leaves little doubt that truth is a central concern within his critique of the modern West. As he says in another interview from around the same time, he regards the "problem of truth" as "the most general of political problems."[46] Less apparent, however, is exactly what he thinks truth and its interlinkage with power involve. This is exacerbated by Foucault's strong tendency to use general concepts such as power and truth as no more than historically specific categories. Nevertheless, in order, for example, to draw a distinction between premodern "juridical" power, on the one hand, and modern "disciplinary" power, on the other, Foucault must presuppose that they belong to the same conceptual field—that both categories are in fact concepts of power and hence have something significant in common.

What they have in common, in the first instance, is that they are about relations and processes, and not about either substances or nonrelational properties. As we have seen, power, for Foucault—and not only disciplinary power—is a relational concept. It primarily pertains to the social relations whereby certain social forces influence human identities, lives, and conduct. Secondarily, it also pertains to the social relations within which human agents respond to such influences. Depending on the historical era and societal structure, such relations can be top down, bottom up, or side-to-side, and that is a matter for genealogical investigation. But in any case, power is a relational concept.

So is Foucault's mostly implicit general concept of truth. Reconstructed from other publications both earlier and later than the "Truth and Power" interview, his concept regards truth as a complex, conceptually articulated, and methodically secured relation between epistemic subjects and the objects of their search for knowledge (which objects, in the social sciences, include epistemic subjects).[47] Although he does not restrict truth to what the sciences, especially the social sciences, aim to achieve, Foucault's concept of truth is a version of what some would delimit as scientific truth, as distinct, for example, from artistic truth or religious truth.

When Foucault speaks of a regime of truth, then, he claims that, to understand how power works in modern society, we must understand the relation between two relational concepts. Further, the relation between power and truth is such that we cannot have one without the other. In that sense, power and truth are *inter*relational concepts. On the one hand, as a specific sort of relation between the subjects and objects of knowledge (objects that can include subjects), truth is a necessary condition for the exercise of power in modern society. If, as Foucault says in a later interview, relations of power are ways of influencing the actions of "acting subjects,"[48] then such influence usually requires the influencing agency to strive for truth-claiming knowledge about the acting subject and its actions. That's what is implied, in part, by calling a dominant form of modern power "disciplinary": it depends upon the deployment of knowledge achieved in scientific or scientifically informed disciplines.

On the other hand, as a relation of social influence and response, power is a necessary condition for pursuing and achieving truth as a specific epistemic subject/object relation. For this relation is not one that occurs in the abstract. In the modern West (roughly from the late eighteenth century onward), Foucault points out, we have increasingly relied on scientific and professional discourses to establish what is true, have employed scientific procedures and instrumentation to distinguish between true and false statements, and have authorized scientists and professionals to say what counts as true. Despite the dismissal of science and the celebration of "alternative facts" among contemporary authoritarian populists, a Foucaultian might say they have not provided any genuine alternative to the truth-producing discourses, truth-sorting mechanisms, and truth-claiming authorities within the modern regime of truth. And these discourses, mechanisms, and authorities are themselves ways in which power is exercised, ways in which how people live, act, and understand themselves are influenced, for good or ill.

Yet this last phrase—"for good or ill"—introduces an issue that Foucault never resolves—indeed, barely addresses. For he fails to think through the normative implications of power and truth as *relational* concepts. To posit truth as a specific sort of epistemic subject/object relation is to broach the question whether there are better and worse forms of this relation. So too, to regard power as a relation between social forces and human agents is to suggest that there might be better and worse forms of this relation for society and human life. Moreover, if these concepts are *interrelational*, if they are mutually necessary (but not sufficient) conditions for each other, then the question arises whether certain forms of the epistemic relation are more or less conducive to better forms of power and whether, conversely, certain forms of the social influence/response relation are more likely to support the sorts of knowledge needed or desired. These are questions for which, so far as I can tell, Foucault has no response.[49]

Adorno: Truth as Constellation

Similar questions arise in Adorno's dialectical critique of domination. Unlike Foucault, however, Adorno does not ignore or avoid them. Rather, he makes them central to what, countering Hegel, he calls negative dialectics. Indeed, they are the underlying topic in "Self-Reflection of Dialectics" (ND

397–400/405–8), the last of the "Meditations on Metaphysics" that conclude *Negative Dialectics*. There Adorno asks whether metaphysics, understood as knowledge of the absolute (*Wissen vom Absoluten*), can avoid the horns of a dilemma bequeathed by Hegel's dialectic: either dialectical thought claims to conceptually grasp the absolute, and thereby poses as itself being absolute, or it declares the absolute to be something wholly other, beyond the grasp of dialectical thought, and thereby subscribes to a double truth theory reminiscent of outmoded medieval philosophy. Although Adorno's negative dialectics rejects any attempt to absolutize thought and its results,[50] it also regards positing two kinds of truth as "incompatible with the idea of the true" (ND 397/406). How can negative dialectics escape this dilemma without entirely giving up on metaphysics and thereby also surrendering the idea of truth which, as Adorno had said a few pages earlier, is the most important metaphysical idea (ND 394/401)?

Such talk of metaphysics, double-truth theory, and knowing the absolute might seem remote from both Adorno's social critique and feminist critical theory. Nevertheless, what motivates Adorno's concern here is not simply how to respond to the Western metaphysical tradition and Hegel's absolute idealism. Rather, it emerges from his own understanding of the dialectic of domination. For the "all-subjugating principle of identity" (ND 314/320) that governs all three modes of domination also governs the theoretical critique of domination. Yet resistance to blind domination requires the critical theorist to appeal to an emphatic idea of truth that points beyond identitarian domination. How is that possible?

Adorno's response involves several moves. First, he recognizes the double character of dialectical thought with respect to the universal history of domination. Dialectics is, he says, both the imprint (*Abdruck*) and the critique of this universal context of delusion or illusion (*Verblendungszusammenhang*). Second, he insists that, as such a critique, dialectical thought must challenge its own participation in domination. In "one last move," dialectics must "turn against itself" (ND 397/406). It must engage in self-critique. Third, in turning against itself, dialectical thought must also point beyond the dialectic of domination that until now has held sway, also within thought. Specifically, dialectical thought must point beyond the principle of identity and the economic exchange principle it mirrors and reinforces. For the capitalist economic principle that nothing has value except insofar as it can be exchanged for something else (and thereby generate private profit) is precisely what scientific and technological efforts to impose conceptual identity on things both echo and sustain. And pointing beyond the exchange and identity principles is precisely what Adorno does, throughout the entire book, to be sure, but especially in these concluding pages.

But what does pointing beyond the dialectic of domination come to? As Adorno immediately indicates, it involves logically grasping and resisting the coercive character (*Zwangscharakter*) of logic itself—the tendency in modern philosophy, science, and society, for example, to think that scientific truth is the only truth. In thereby relativizing the principle of identity, while still following it, negative dialectics can envision what truth would be like if the dialectic of domination were in fact superseded in both thought and society: truth would be to do justice to "the nonidentical that would emerge only after the identity-compulsion [*Identitätszwang*] dissolved" (ND 398/406). In the meantime, to pursue such truth requires, together with a self-critique of dialectical thought, "micrological" investigations of life and society. These would bring matters into a "legible constellation" from which we can begin to discern what things would be like if they were no longer ruled by the all-subjugating principle of identity—that is, what they would be like in their nonidentity. Because such micrological thinking is devoted to "the absolute"—because, in pursuing truth, it tries to do justice to the nonidentical that would emerge after the identity-compulsion has dissolved—it shows solidarity with metaphysics—which traditionally absolutized thought itself—"in the moment of its collapse" (ND 400/408).

This combination of dialectics and micrology—of Hegel and Walter Benjamin, if you will—yields a distinctive conception of truth in Adorno's philosophy. Truth, he often says, is a constellation, and it cannot be restricted to scientific truth. Thus, for example, as an alternative to Husserl's alleged "logical absolutism"—his idealizing the laws of logic and removing them from anything empirical—Adorno portrays truth as a "constellation" of both subjective and objective moments and as a "force field" that cannot be pinned down as "an entity" (ME 79/72). In other words, truth is relational and dynamic, and it is not a substance or nonrelational property, despite what most Western philosophers since Aristotle have thought.[51]

To that extent, then, Adorno's conception of truth resembles Foucault's: both of them regard truth as relational and dynamic. As a constellation, however, the idea of truth is more complex than the relation between epistemic subject and object that, with his concerns about scientific knowledge and disciplinary power, Foucault emphasizes. At various places Adorno calls attention to other intersecting polarities within the constellation of truth: along with the subject/object dialectic there are polarities between universal and particular, between concept and thing, and between identity and nonidentity. Truth consists in the ongoing mediation of such polarities. Unlike Foucault, however, Adorno thinks of these polarities as unfolding within a universal dialectic of domination, such that there is an important continuity across historical epochs.

For this reason, as I have argued in previous chapters, the dialectic between history and transcendence is the most decisive polarity in Adorno's conception of truth, and it has no parallel in Foucault's thought. Briefly, the dialectic between history and transcendence lies in a tension between the historical rootedness of the idea of truth and the possibility that the course of history could dramatically change. On the one hand, we would not have the idea of truth if it had not emerged from a dialectic of enlightenment in which, as Adorno says at one point, the subject "wrestles free from illusion [*Schein*]" (ND 368/375). On the other hand, even though until now such critique of untruth has repeatedly contributed to the domination of nature, self, and others, the idea of truth must also point to the possibility that untruth will not have the final word, that the history of domination from which this idea emerges could indeed give way to freedom and reconciliation. This possibility emerges both from the capacity thought retains to think otherwise and from the refusal of the dominated to submit entirely to an imposed identity (i.e., from the nonidentical).

Accordingly, as chapters 2 and 3 have indicated, Adorno says the "surplus beyond the subject" and "the truth-moment in what is thinglike . . . touch in the idea of truth" (ND 368/375). And what sustains such touching is the possibility that the course of history is not inevitable, that a fundamentally different society is possible, a society in which blind domination and needless suffering have ended. As we have seen, Adorno calls this possibility "the humanly promised other of history" (ND 396/404). The pursuit of truth, then, requires both an unsparing critique of domination and a persistent hope for complete social transformation.

Because such hope is required, the pursuit of truth cannot do without what Benhabib called utopian thinking. She was right to worry that Foucaultian social critique undermines this element in feminist theory. At the same time, however, Foucault's detailed exposés of how the pursuit of scientific truth both supports and receives support from disciplinary power makes one wonder whether and how a complete social transformation would in fact be possible. At what point does utopian thinking tip over into nothing more than socially necessary illusion?

Hence Foucault and Adorno leave feminist critical theorists with two interrelated challenges. One is to think through normative implications of the interrelation between truth and power. The other is to try to envision prospects for social transformation that neither ignore nor totalize the dialectic of domination. Let me offer preliminary responses to each challenge in turn.

Power, Truth, and Social Hope

SOCIAL DOMAINS OF TRUTH

Earlier I suggested that Foucault fails to consider whether certain forms of power and truth are better or worse, both intrinsically and in relationship to each other. Behind this suggestion lies the intuition, partially shared by Adorno, that in modern society there is more than one social domain of knowledge and hence more than one sort of truth. For example, one can regard artistic truth as a distinct sort of truth that cannot be either reduced to scientific truth or replaced by it. If that is so, then one can also ask how the sort of truth that art offers differs from scientific truth and provides something science lacks.

One can also consider both whether either art or science is more conducive to desirable forms of power and whether the more desirable forms of power are more likely to support either artistic or scientific truth. Even if it is so that disciplinary power is the predominant form of interactional power in contemporary society and that scientific truth is the primary way in which disciplinary power is produced and ratified, this would not preclude there being alternative forms of power and truth within the historically emergent architecture of society. Such alternative forms could allow resistance to take shape and help inspire a normative critique of dominant power relations. This could provide a more nuanced understanding of feminist struggles against subjugation. It could also provide a way out of the conceptual binds within Foucaultian feminist accounts of (de)subjection with respect to (individual) freedom and (societal) determinism.[52]

To recognize more than one social domain of truth need not commit one to a version of the double-truth theory, however. Adorno is right that the idea of truth rules out such dividing and conquering. But he also says truth is a constellation, and this suggests there can be more than one "star" (i.e., more than one social domain of truth) and yet all the stars make up one constellation. To posit one constellation and so avoid a double-truth theory, however, would require a holistic conception of truth that neither restricts it primarily to scientific truth, à la Foucault, nor renders it mostly counterfactual, à la Adorno ("*das Absolute wäre . . .*"). Moreover, to avoid simply counterfactualizing or subjunctivizing truth as a whole, one would need a more nuanced account of the interrelation between truth and power than Adorno and Foucault provide.

Normative Critique of Power

This is especially so with regard to the universal dialectic of domination in Adorno's philosophy of history. As we have seen, Adorno construes this dialectic as an emergent and antagonistic continuity among three modes of domination that both threatens complete destruction and makes possible a postdominative future. For that future to arrive, the principle of identity could no longer be imposed on nature, human relations, and individual lives. This understanding of domination as a universal-historical process raises two sorts of questions for which Adorno lacks adequate answers.

One question concerns normative alternatives to identitarian domination. If the imposition of identity governs destructive modes of domination, ones that in their violence create persistent suffering, human and otherwise, then what would be a better way to connect the pursuit of identity with the exercise of power? Although Adorno points to micrology as an alternative, it is hard to see how this theoretical model of nonidentitarian thought would either generate or support better ways to connect identity and power in either science or politics.

A second question concerns qualitative distinctions among the three modes of domination. Might Adorno's insistence on continuity in domination and a single all-subjugating principle occlude the sorts of nonidentities that not even the most pervasive dialectic can eliminate? Specifically, aren't there qualitative differences among the subjugation of nature, the exploitation of humans, and self-repression, such that, even within the continuity of domination, each points to its own sort of alternative and calls for its own sort of normative critique? For the exercise of human power with respect to so-called nature has different normative implications than it does with respect to either other humans or one's self. As I have argued elsewhere,[53] attempts to control nonhuman life and existence become problematic when they fail to promote interconnected flourishing among all creatures; they become destructive when they try to promote human well-being at the expense of other creatures. Patterns of thought that identify "nature" as no more than a realm of objects for human mastery are, as Adorno recognizes, inherently violent, and they feed into destructive control, into the subjugation of "nature."

Yet violence toward "nature" cannot be equated with violence toward other human beings. The exploitation of one class or gender or race by another, for example, involves a one-sided *social* distribution of power; it is not simply the exercise of human power with respect to nonhuman creatures. This one-sided distribution persistently promotes the apparent flourishing of one group at the ongoing expense of another, whose members suffer as a result. Such social violence is not only destructive—directly so for the exploited and indirectly for the exploiters—but also normatively problematic: it rejects fundamental expectations of solidarity and justice without which, as members of society, human beings cannot flourish.

So too, the domination of what Adorno calls inner nature—in the words of *Dialectic of Enlightenment,* the "denial of nature in the human being for the sake of mastery [*Herrschaft*] over extrahuman nature and over other human beings" (DA 78/42)—is qualitatively different from either the subjugation of "nature" or the exploitation of other humans. How an individual relates to one's own corporeal needs and sensuous happiness is different from how humanity relates to "nature" and how groups engage in social struggle. Moreover, not all self-denial is destructive or illegitimate, as Adorno himself recognizes; without some degree of self-denial individuals could hardly have agency or exercise power. So we need to distinguish between self-denial that is indeed problematic and that which is not. I mark this distinction with the words *repression* and *sublimation*. Whereas repressing one's own needs and desires is problematic, sublimating them into a larger life-project, into pathways of personal flourishing, is not.

Reformulated, then, Adorno's thesis of historical continuity in domination claims that subjugation of nature, social exploitation, and self-repression unavoidably feed into and off one another both historically and in late capitalist society. To break the grip of domination would require undoing all three modes of domination. Hence the urgency of challenging the "all-subjugating principle of identity." If, however, these are not the only ways in which power has been and currently is exercised—if, in fact, nonviolent control, nonexploitative social struggle, and nonrepressive self-relations have occurred in the past and are currently available—then the critique of domination can become more nuanced, and the hope for social transformation can become less desperate.

Collaboration and Social Hope

Here the shape of interactional and macrostructural forms of power and their interrelation, which both Adorno and Foucault thematize, become decisive. For if the only forms of interactional power historically available are power-over (influence) and power to (agency), as Foucault's diagnosis of disciplinary power suggests; if macrostructural forms of political and economic power hold sway in contemporary society, as Adorno claims; and if these forms of interactional and macrostructural power not only interlink but also reinforce each other, as both Foucault and Adorno seem to indicate, then critique and resistance would seem futile and social transformation impossible. Then the utopian hope that Benhabib rightly says feminists need would become merely utopian in a pejorative sense. I call this the dilemma of historically ill-founded utopian hope.

I can envision two ways to respond to this dilemma. One would be to acknowledge a third and intrinsically intersubjective form of power in human history and contemporary society, a form Amy Allen calls "power-with." Derived from Hannah Arendt's definition of power as the human ability to act in concert, power-with is a capacity people enact together to accomplish a shared end. We can call it *collaboration*. In describing it, however, I have modified Allen's definition. Allen defines power-with as "the ability of a collectivity to act together for the attainment of an agreed-upon end or series of ends."[54] I have modified her definition because not all power-with involves collectivity (e.g., in a friendship or intimate partnership), and I do not think prior agreement is always required in order to exercise power-with. Indeed, it is important to break completely with a contractualist notion of power if one wants to understand the distinctive qualities and potentials of collaborative power.

As Allen points out, feminism and other collective movements of resistance and critique depend heavily on collaboration. So do many of the interrelations and practices that make up the fabric of daily social life. Unless one regards all such collaboration as merely a conduit or target of disciplinary power and domination—a position I regard as both cynical and empirically inaccurate—one can look to such social movements and modes of interaction for ways to empower social transformation.

A second way to respond to the dilemma of ill-founded hope would be point to historically emergent and shared, albeit contested, expectations concerning social life. I call these expectations societal principles, and I argue that they hold for the entire array of interrelations, practices, institutions, and macrostructures that organize life in contemporary society. Together with the pursuit of interconnected flourishing, fidelity to such expectations is the hallmark of truth. For, as I have argued elsewhere, truth as a whole is a dynamic correlation between human fidelity to societal principles and a life-giving disclosure of society.[55] And truth is not an otherworldly idea.

Rather, the process from which these shared expectations and possibilities for flourishing emerge is the same history where disciplinary power and a dialectic of domination occur.

These expectations and possibilities are, if you will, the penumbra of problematic power. They emerge not in the absence of power but in the very exercise of power both interactional and macrostructural. For people cannot be faithful to societal principles such as solidarity and justice without collaborating, exerting influence, and exercising agency. Nor can they pursue interconnected flourishing in a power vacuum. Accordingly, every social domain of truth, whether science, art, or religion, for example, is simultaneously a domain of power, and a normative critique of power must ask which sorts of power are most conducive to truth in each domain.

Politics, I have argued elsewhere, is one such domain.[56] It is the domain where people struggle for power to achieve justice and where they struggle over justice from positions of relative power. Such empowered struggles for justice typically aim to liberate people and other creatures from oppression. Accordingly, the exercise of political power is subject to normative constraints: it must either promise or actually accomplish justice and freedom, and it must be suitable in this regard. Moreover, the justifiability and suitability of power is intrinsic to politics as a social domain of truth. Without them, in the long run, neither justice nor freedom would be achieved.

If justice and freedom have in fact been achieved in the past, and if justifiable and suitable forms of political power are available in the present, then there are genuinely political reasons to hope for social transformation. Such hope need not be merely utopian, even though there is more to the social transformation needed than politics alone can achieve. For contemporary society as a whole needs what I call a "differential transformation,"[57] and that will not occur in the absence of fundamental economic change.

Like Foucault and Adorno, feminist critical theorists have offered sophisticated critiques of power. But we have become stuck, it seems to me, because we have not developed a sufficiently nuanced account of the normative interrelation between truth and power. To do that, I have suggested, feminist critical theorists need to reexamine Foucault's genealogy and Adorno's negative dialectics and ask what forms of power these have ignored or overlooked. And, given the prominence of truth for both Foucault and Adorno, that will also require a new conception of truth, one that neither restricts truth to science nor treats it as a counterfactual idea, but locates it instead in the historically emergent and malleable social domains of truth. We turn next to artistic truth, the social domain where Adorno himself found a dialectical alternative to science-driven domination.

6

"Weh spricht vergeh"

Truth in Adorno's *Aesthetic Theory*

> It would be preferable that some fine day art would vanish altogether than that it forget suffering, which is art's expression and in which form has its substance. . . . What sort of history writing would art be, if it shook off the memory of accumulated suffering?
>
> —Theodor W. Adorno (ÄT 386–87/260–61)

Adorno's *Ästhetische Theorie*, published posthumously in 1970, appeared at a transitional moment in the history of Western aesthetics. Compared with other writings in philosophical aesthetics at the time, its comprehensiveness and social-critical edge made it both pathbreaking and highly relevant. After the book appeared, however, the themes of social critique and ecological aesthetics became so commonplace that it quickly came to seem out of date. There is a peculiar untimely timeliness to Adorno's aesthetics.

In this chapter I tie such (un)timeliness to the conception of artistic truth at the center of Adorno's aesthetics. First I situate *Ästhetische Theorie* within postwar Western philosophical aesthetics, summarize its dialectical autonomism concerning art in society, and review two responses to how this autonomism undergirds Adorno's conception of artistic truth. Then I show how the polarities discussed in previous chapters not only permeate this conception but also make it distinctive. I conclude by considering what Adorno's conception of artistic truth has to offer within the contemporary culture-political landscape.

Untimely Timeliness

Postwar Aesthetics

Few philosophers after World War Two attempted a comprehensive approach to the topics of philosophical aesthetics, and, unlike Adorno, those who did usually did not combine this with a critique of society as a whole, including the relation between art and nature. The most comprehensive approaches in postwar Anglo-American aesthetics prior to 1970 tend toward conceptual analysis, metacriticism, or nominalism with respect to art. One thinks here of Susanne K. Langer's *Feeling and Form* (1953), Monroe Beardsley's *Aesthetics* (1958), and Nelson Goodman's *Languages of Art* (1968). All three focus on theories of art, and none of them discuss either natural beauty or the critical role of art in contemporary society. In fact, the terms "nature" and "society" do not appear in the index to any of these three books. Although Langer and Beardsley do have concluding chapters titled "The Work and Its Public"[1] and "The Arts in the Life of Man,"[2] neither one comes close to the critique of society that runs throughout *Aesthetic Theory* and crystallizes in the chapter titled "Society" (ÄT 334–87/225–61).[3] Nor do they and Goodman provide anything like Adorno's discussion of "Natural Beauty" (ÄT 97–121/61–78).[4] Perhaps the most important exception to this pattern of omission is *The Structure of Aesthetics* (1963), a sadly neglected work by Francis Sparshott, which discusses the concept of beauty in detail and includes chapters on both "art and nature" and "art and society."[5]

In Western Europe, postwar approaches to philosophical aesthetics before 1970 have a similar focus on theories of art, and they show similar blind spots toward social critique. With their roots in phenomenology and hermeneutics, however, they do demonstrate interest in the social construction of art and in the relation between art and nature. One recalls, for example, Mikel Dufrenne's 1953 *Phénoménologie de l'expérience esthétique*, which begins by discussing artistic performance and art publics as well as the relation between aesthetic and natural objects.[6] So too, Hans-Georg Gadamer's 1960 *Wahrheit und Methode* wrests its play-based and performance-oriented ontology of art from a critique of Kant's subjectivized natural-beauty aesthetics.[7] Moreover, although Roman Ingarden's 1968 *Vom Erkennen des literarischen Kunstwerks* does not explicitly deal with such topics, the point of his project is to ask how our cognition of (literary) artworks lines up with other sorts of knowledge and other modes of existence.[8] Yet, among the comprehensive philosophical aesthetic theories on offer in postwar Western

Europe, there was no precedent for the scope of social critique built into Adorno's *Aesthetic Theory*.

To find anything like that, one would need to turn to works by Eastern Europeans such as the Hungarian Marxists Arnold Hauser and Georg Lukács. Nevertheless, Hauser's *Sozialgeschichte der Kunst und Literatur* is more historical than philosophical, and it restricts its one chapter about twentieth-century art mostly to the sociology of film, saying little about society as a whole.[9] So too, Lukács's *Die Eigenart des Ästhetischen* (The Specificity of the Aesthetic), the only published portion of his massive three-part aesthetics, does not really take up contemporary social issues.[10]

After 1970, with the spread of deconstruction and poststructuralism, the blossoming of feminist theory and ecological thought, and, especially in Anglo-American countries, the rise of neopragmatism and postanalytic philosophy—not to mention an increasing emphasis on postcolonial theory and non-Western thought—the landscape of Western philosophical aesthetics changed dramatically. Soon Adorno's attention to nature and his critique of society came to seem mainstream, even as his focus on modern art and his indebtedness to Kant, Hegel, and Marx came to seem dated or problematic. This peculiar untimely timeliness was obvious when the author published a book titled *Adorno's Aesthetic Theory* in 1991, one year after literary theorist Fredric Jameson had declared Adorno "one of the greatest of twentieth-century Marxist philosophers."[11] Although Jameson intended this as praise, it was unclear then who in the academic world would consider it a compliment. By the early 1990s, it seemed that *Aesthetic Theory* both grasped its own time in thought, to adapt Hegel's well-known description of philosophy,[12] and remained oddly out of sync with its philosophical contemporaries—simultaneously outrunning the main currents of Western philosophical aesthetics and lagging behind them.

Dialectical Autonomism

A key to the untimely timeliness of Adorno's unfinished magnum opus lies in its combination of academic askesis and modernist engagement. On the one hand, apart from frequent references to Heidegger and to Western Marxist thinkers such as Walter Benjamin, Bertolt Brecht, Max Horkheimer, Lukács, and Herbert Marcuse, with whom Adorno had long-standing debates, the book seldom addresses the work of Adorno's contemporaries in philosophical aesthetics. In passing, the "Draft Introduction" favorably refers to John Dewey twice (ÄT 498/335, 525/353), but, for example, the book never mentions the work of Gadamer, whom Adorno knew as a colleague. The book's philosophical discussion partners come mainly from Greek philosophy (primarily Plato and Aristotle) and the German intellectual tradition from Immanuel Kant through Sigmund Freud. Such academic askesis lines up with the draft introduction's questionable judgment that, when Benedetto Croce "introduced radical nominalism into aesthetic theory," "important thinking left behind the so-called fundamental problems of aesthetics" (ÄT 494/333). Adorno's restricting his philosophical discussion partners to fellow travelers and traditional figures generates intense and illuminating critical appropriations from his own primary sources. Yet it makes the book seem oddly out of step with contemporaneous developments in Anglo-American, French, and even German aesthetics.

On the other hand, in keeping with Adorno's philosophical commitment to the "priority of the object" (*Vorrang des Objekts*) (ND 184–87/183–86; cf. ÄT 166/109, 494–99/333–35), *Aesthetic Theory* focuses on the issues and achievements of modern art, broadly construed. This does not preclude Adorno's discussing "classics" of the Western fine art tradition—in music, for example, Bach, Mozart, Beethoven, Wagner, Brahms, and Mahler. Yet Adorno's modernist engagement leaves mostly to the side both premodern and emerging postmodern art, as well as other artforms that have received increasing philosophical attention since 1970—popular art, mass-mediated art, and what one could loosely label situated art (e.g., political art, landscape art, and liturgical art)[13]—and the many aesthetic phenomena and events in daily life that do not have the social status of art. Although some of these artforms and aesthetic phenomena achieved much greater prominence in Western society *after* Adorno died, such that he could not have addressed them well, what I have labeled Adorno's "paradoxical modernism"[14] makes his *Aesthetic Theory* less relevant for addressing them. At the same time, of course, the book is incomparable in its sophisticated engagement with modern art.

If the combination of academic askesis and modernist engagement contributes to the book's untimely timeliness, then so does the dialectical autonomism that pervades Adorno's modernism. Art—especially modern art—is "the social antithesis of society," Adorno claims (ÄT 19/8), and therein lies both art's truth and its falsity. Briefly put, whatever independence art has in late capitalist society is made possible by destructive tendencies and patterns in that very same society, especially in its polity and economy. Yet the particular manner in which art depends on society for its existence also places art in unavoidable opposition to society as it is currently constituted. This particular manner requires the production and reception of relatively independent works of art whose internal dynamics bring to expression the underlying contradictions of society as a whole.

Aesthetic Theory elaborates this dialectical conception of art's autonomy in many different directions. Perhaps the direction that most contributes to the book's untimely timeliness pertains to truth and politics. Adorno regards the truth content (*Wahrheitsgehalt*) of autonomous artworks as the key to any art-generated social critique and social transformation: through truth content, (modern) art can help people resist late capitalism and imagine a postcapitalist society. Yet such resistance and imagination are plainly not enough, as Adorno himself recognizes, even as any other path to world-changing politics appears to lie blocked. Hence the politically important truth of art, made possible by art's societally constituted autonomy, is also politically impotent.

By embracing such important impotence, the dialectical autonomism of Adorno's *Aesthetic Theory* has proved not only provocative but also deeply unsatisfying, both for those who hope for real social transformation—such as feminists, ecological activists, and the progressive left—and for those who prefer the societal status quo. Dismissing his unfinished book, however, or simply picking up bits and pieces would also be unsatisfying.[15] To go beyond both dismissal and eclecticism, one needs to take up the complex conception of artistic truth that lies at the center of Adorno's aesthetics, always keeping in view his understanding of art as the social antithesis of society.

Truth Content or Truth Potential?

One can see the importance of taking up Adorno's conception of artistic truth from conflicts between Albrecht Wellmer and J. M. Bernstein, two astute interpreters of Adorno's *Aesthetic Theory*. Their disagreements also show how one's understanding of his paradoxical modernism and dialectical autonomism will shape what one makes of this conception. Although both Wellmer and Bernstein understand Adorno's conception of artistic truth as a response to the aporias of modern art within a secularly differentiated society, they have dramatically opposed assessments of this conception. Whereas Wellmer thinks Adorno's conception of artistic truth needs significant revision in order to illuminate the cognitive roles of art under modern conditions of cultural differentiation, Bernstein applauds Adorno's conception precisely because it recognizes and reinforces how modern art challenges such differentiation. So too, whereas Wellmer denies that art can "literally" be true, Bernstein resists the restriction of truth to "truth-only cognition" that seems to support Wellmer's denial. Let me briefly review their positions.

In "Truth, Semblance, Reconciliation," an essay first presented at the 1983 Adorno conference in Frankfurt, Albrecht Wellmer develops a critical interpretation of what he describes as "Adorno's aesthetic redemption of modernity."[16] Although Wellmer's provocative and seminal essay resists a simple summary, two issues stand out.[17] One is that, by treating artistic truth as a model of reconciliation both among human beings and between them and nature, Adorno inscribes a gap between historically developed society and a utopian future. The gap is so huge that "bridging it can no longer constitute a meaningful goal of human praxis," and historical reality "becomes fixed transcendentally . . . in negative terms."[18] In other words, Adorno's conception of artistic truth underwrites a problematic form of abstractly utopian politics. The other issue Wellmer raises is that, by retaining an "emphatic concept of truth" and pitting this against instrumental rationality,[19] Adorno removes artistic truth from the "living praxis" in which art can have a transformative cognitive role.[20] For Wellmer, this issue is closely related to what he describes as the "artificial" traits of the "aporetic constructions" in *Aesthetic Theory* and the "latent traditionalism" of Adorno's aesthetic judgments concerning mass culture and popular art.[21]

Wellmer addresses the first issue by turning Adorno's supposedly otherworldly idea of reconciliation into the "inner worldly" idea of "non-violent communication" that, following Habermas, Wellmer considers intrinsic to ordinary communicative action and discourse.[22] He responds to the second issue by replacing Adorno's concept of the truth content (*Wahrheitsgehalt*) internal to works of art with the concept of art's truth potential (*Wahrheitspotential*) in experience. According to Wellmer, aesthetically valid artworks have the potential to mobilize ordinary experience in which the three dimensions of communicative validity are interwoven. These three dimensions—propositional truth, normative rightness, and personal truthfulness—differentiate the "everyday concept of truth," he says, but none of them applies straightforwardly to artworks as such. At most, the so-called truth of art can be defended as "a phenomenon of interference between the various dimensions of truth." Strictly speaking, however, art itself is neither true nor false.[23]

With these modifications to Adorno's conception of artistic truth, Wellmer surrenders precisely those insights that Jay Bernstein considers most important in Adorno's aesthetics. In *The Fate of Art*, a penetrating and wide-ranging study of the theme of aesthetic alienation in continental philosophy, Bernstein challenges the assumptions on which Wellmer's critical interpretation of Adorno rests.[24] Two assumptions are especially relevant here. One is Wellmer's "acceptance of the Weber-Habermas thesis that the categorial separation of truth into knowledge, moral rightness and aesthetic validity represents *the* cognitive achievement of modernity."[25] Perhaps we can label this assumption the thesis of progressive cultural differentiation. The other assumption, closely related to the first, is Wellmer's Habermasian subscription to "a continuist conception of historical change from capital to its successor social formation"—in contrast to what Bernstein describes as Adorno's "discontinuist conception of historical change."[26] Let's call this assumption the thesis of sociohistorical evolution.

Because of the first thesis, Wellmer fails to recognize that what Bernstein calls "modernist art" does not simply accept the aesthetic niche into which it has been slotted by modern cultural differentiation. Rather, by suspending aesthetic meaning in ever new ways, modernist art fundamentally and repeatedly questions its own nature and purpose in modern society. Whereas Adorno makes such "categorial self-reflection" in "modernist artistic production" central to his account of artistic truth, Wellmer simply refuses to engage with "modernism's self-reflective character," Bernstein says.[27] Contra Wellmer, modernist works of art do not so much mobilize ordinary experience, with its supposedly interwoven validity dimensions, as question the differentiated conditions of cultural modernity that govern such experience. That is what, according to Bernstein, Adorno's conception of artistic truth content recognizes and Wellmer's conception of artistic truth potential forgets.

As an interpretation and defense of Adorno, Bernstein's critique of Wellmer is surely right. Adorno's conception of artistic truth is indeed inextricable from the dialectical autonomism I have already described. Simply to assume the theses of sociohistorical evolution and progressive cultural differentiation is to give up the radical social critique and paradoxical modernism that pervade Adorno's negatively dialectical aesthetics. Yet the insightfulness of Bernstein's criticisms does not resolve the concerns that motivate Wellmer's revisionist "stereoscopic reading of Adorno,"[28] namely, whether and how Adorno's conception of artistic truth remains valid and viable.

Bernstein commends Adorno's conception for aiming to reunify, without subsumption, the "categorial spheres" of beauty, truth, and goodness that were "dirempted by Kantian modernity"; for showing that "art's truth content is . . . a categorial truth claim . . . about art and the nature of truth (reason) in modernity"; and for recognizing how both (modernist) art and philosophy are "political or ethical stand-ins for an absent politics," for "a politics that has never been."[29] One wonders, however, whether Adorno's conception of artistic truth has more to offer than such a categorial self-reflection of modernity. Once we recognize just how problematic the modern restriction of truth to propositional truth and the aestheticizing of art have been, how should we reconceive artistic truth and its political role?

Artistic Truth

Perhaps a systematic reconstruction of Adorno's conception of artistic truth, organized around the three polarities already highlighted, will help. I propose next to examine how the polarities in Adorno's negative dialectical constellation of truth show up in his philosophy of art. As discussed in this book, Adorno's central alethic polarities are the subject/object dialectic, the tension between concept and thing or subject matter (i.e., between the conceptual and the nonconceptual), and the conflict between history and transcendence. These show up within Adorno's conception of artistic truth in the dialectics of semblance and expression, of form and content, and of historical possibility, respectively. I take up the dialectic of semblance and expression first.

Semblance and Expression

Although *Aesthetic Theory* devotes a chapter to the dialectic of subject and object in art (ÄT 244–62/163–75), the importance of this dialectic in Adorno's conception of artistic truth especially comes to the fore in an earlier chapter on the dialectic of semblance and expression (*Schein und Ausdruck*, ÄT 154–79/100–118).[30] Midway through this earlier chapter, shortly before a paragraph titled "Subjekt-Objekt und Ausdruck" (a title shortened in the translation to simply "Subject-Object"), Adorno writes, "Expression and semblance are fundamentally antithetical" (ÄT 168/110). In the immediate context, this sentence crystallizes Adorno's claims about the unavoidable and historically variable tensions between dissonance and consonance in music and other arts. But it also encapsulates a subject/object dialectic that he considers central to artistic truth. This dialectic has to do with how a subject that has become object—that is, the artwork as semblance (*Schein*)—mediates and is mediated by an object that has become subject—that is, the artwork as expression (*Ausdruck*). Let me explain.

On the preceding pages (ÄT 154–68/100–110), Adorno lays out many ways in which artworks can be a semblance or illusion: they take distance from empirical reality; they strive for a unity and meaning they cannot fully achieve; they cover up the traces of their own production and pretend to be completely self-contained; they point to possibilities they cannot actualize. All of these ways are rendered problematic by modern art, which "wants to shake off its illusoriness [*Scheincharakter*] like an animal trying to shake off its antlers" (ÄT 157/102). Yet it cannot do so without eliminating art altogether. That is what Adorno calls the modern crisis of semblance.

What unites these various meanings of *semblance* in Adorno's account is the fact that artworks are human products aiming to disclose something humans cannot produce. As artifacts, they are semblance; yet they aim to disclose what is true. That, Adorno says, is the fundamental paradox of art and aesthetics: "How can making bring into appearance what is not the result of making; how can what according to its own concept is not true nevertheless be true? This is conceivable only if import [*Gehalt*] is distinct from semblance; yet no artwork has import other than through semblance. . . . The center of aesthetics therefore would be the redemption of semblance; and the emphatic right of art, the legitimation of its truth, depends on this redemption" (ÄT 164/107). The fact that a subject-become-object (a humanly produced artwork) can carry truth content (*Wahrheitsgehalt*) is both the conundrum of art and the focus of Adorno's aesthetics.

How, then, can a cultural process (*Geist*) aimed at making products *not* simply produce falsehood when it produces art? How can artistic truth content be so "unmetaphorically true" that art can "discard the semblance produced by its artifactuality" (ÄT 164/107)? Although part of Adorno's answer has to do with peculiarities in how art is made, as much has to do with how a different process—that of the object becoming subject—mediates the artifactuality of art. This other process is what he calls *expression* (*Ausdruck*).

For Adorno, artistic expression is not an utterance of the artist who makes or presents an artwork. Neither is it an eliciting of emotions from an artwork's audience. Rather, artistic expression is the voice that speaks from the artwork. What it bespeaks is the mimetic connection between subject and object beyond the polarity between them. In this sense the artwork as expression approaches a "transsubjective" form of knowledge, even as it relies on the objectification inherent to the artwork's artifactual character. Artistic expression is, Adorno writes, "the objectification of the non-objective," such that "it becomes a second-order nonobjectivity: It becomes what speaks out of the artifact [but] not as an imitation of the subject" (ÄT 170/111).

Although artistic expression does not convey artists' lives or feelings, it does rely on artists' mimetic conduct when they fashion artworks, listening for what the works would say. Because of this mimetic process, the expression of artworks recapitulates, as it were, the emergence of subjectivity from a prerational connection with nonobjects. Artistic expression is, Adorno says, "the nonsubjective in the subject" and an echo of the "protohistory of subjectivity" (ÄT 172/112–13). In that sense, artistic expression represents a process of the object (artwork) becoming a protosubject (a voiceless voice). And what, in general, artworks articulate is the language of suffering (ÄT 169/110), the repeatedly suppressed pain of an alienation between subject and object. That is why Adorno describes expression as "the lamenting face of artworks" [*das klagende Gesicht der Werke*]" (ÄT 170/111).

Artistic expression would not be possible, however, without the self-reflective labor that goes into the production of artworks. Hence the "subjective paradox of art," the paradox every serious artist faces, is how to produce something unintentional (expression) through formal reflection (semblance) (ÄT 174/114). This is a counterpart to the paradox already mentioned, namely, how a humanly produced artifact can be true. In both forms, the paradox turns on how the process of subject-becoming-object (making the artwork) and the process of object-becoming-subject (artwork becoming expressive) mediate each other. Or, to put this in the "objective" language Adorno prefers, the paradox turns on how the artwork as semblance and the artwork as expression are mutually mediated.

A key to understanding this paradox is to recognize that artistic production is a unique form of social labor and yields a unique sort of product.[31] Even though artistic production, like all other social labor, participates in the alienation between subject and object, it relies on a mimetic relation to objects that originally preceded this alienation and potentially points beyond it. So too, although, as a product, the artwork results from a form of domination, because of the mimetic impulses it encapsulates the artwork frees spirit "from the aims of domination." In principle, then, art's form of knowledge achieves what conceptual knowledge misses, and it corrects the domination of nature that conceptual knowledge too often serves: "Art corrects conceptual knowledge because, in isolation, it carries out what conceptual knowledge awaits in vain from the nonpictorial [*unbildlich*] subject-object relation: that through a subjective achievement what is objective would be unveiled. Art does not postpone this achievement ad infinitum but demands it of its own finitude at the price of its illusoriness

[*Scheinhaftigkeit*]. Through spiritualization—the radical domination of its own nature—art corrects the domination of nature as the domination of an other" (ÄT 173/113).

Accordingly, the mediation of subject and object accounts for two ways in which art can be true. First, as a social domain, (modern) art can interrupt the patterns of domination that pervade society as a whole and can point to the possibility of reconciliation between subject and object. Second, in each authentic artwork, voice can be given to the suffering that domination inflicts and to the happiness that society-wide reconciliation would promise. For Adorno, truth in this sense is not a propositional matter to be asserted and justified. Instead, it is a relation to be inhabited and carried out. Contra Wellmer, the truth of artworks is not simply the potential they have to disclose the experience of their audiences. Rather, it is the disclosive import (*Gehalt*) they carry within both despite and amid their semblance character. And, contra Bernstein, the truth of (modern) art as a social domain is not simply its refusal to accept the modern categorial differentiation that makes it possible. It is also an ability to voice potentials that surpass categorization. The significance of such import and ability stems from a second polarity in Adorno's conception of artistic truth, namely, that between concept and thing.

Form and Content

The polarity between concept and thing has at least two configurations in Adorno's conception of artistic truth. One has to do with the tension between philosophical concepts and artistic phenomena, which I take up later. The other pertains to the dialectic between form (*Form*) and content (*Inhalt*) within works of art. Although Adorno discusses this dialectic throughout *Aesthetic Theory*, the most sustained treatment occurs in the chapter titled "Coherence and Meaning" (*Stimmigkeit und Sinn*, ÄT 205–44/136–63), to which I turn next.[32]

First, however, a brief comment on terminology is needed. Like Hegel, Adorno uses two different terms—*Inhalt* and *Gehalt*—that English translations commonly render as "content." Yet these are not synonyms in Adorno's usage, and sometimes he explicitly distinguishes *Gehalt* from *Inhalt*. To mark this distinction, I render *Gehalt* as "import" and retain "content" as a translation of *Inhalt*. In many passages *Wahrheitsgehalt* might be better rendered as "truth-import." Nevertheless, I continue to use "truth content," the standard translation, for that.

The form of artworks, Adorno writes, is "the quintessence of all elements of logicality [*Logizität*]" and "coherence [*Stimmigkeit*]" in them (ÄT 211/140). Like Susanne K. Langer, who emphasizes the nondiscursive "logic" in music and other artforms,[33] Adorno insists that artworks are "logical," even though they are not conceptual and do not make or present conceptual judgments or propositional assertions. In their striving for consistency among their disparate elements and achieving an internal necessity, they are like syllogisms, he says: "The logic of art is . . . a syllogism [*Schlussverfahren*] without concept or judgment" (ÄT 205/136).

As a nonconceptual logicality, artistic form offers an alternative to the conceptual domination of nature, Adorno claims. Rather than impose conceptual identity on objects, artistic form can call for "a communication between objects," for an "affinity" among moments that are not conceptually identified (AT 208/138). And that makes the knowledge art provides an "implicit critique of the nature-dominating *ratio*," even as art also participates in such domination (ÄT 209/139).

The key to art's alternative rationality lies in the relation between form and content (*Inhalt*). On the one hand, form is what Adorno calls "sedimented and modified content" (ÄT 210/139). It can never completely cut its ties to the sociohistorical reality from which artistic content comes. On the other hand, content becomes artistic precisely through the distance artistic form establishes between artworks and reality. That is why Adorno says aesthetics must conceive of artistic form "not only . . . in opposition to content but through it" (ÄT 211/140). So too, content not only resists form but is constituted by it.

From this complex form/content relation two aspects to Adorno's conception of artistic truth emerge. One is his attention to the attunement of form to content. The other is his emphasizing the suspension of form on behalf of content. Both attunement and suspension surface in a passage where Adorno calls form "an unfolding of truth." Let me quote it and then comment.

> Aesthetic form is the objective organization into coherent eloquence [*zum stimmig Beredten*] of everything that appears within an artwork. It is the nonviolent synthesis of the diffuse that nevertheless preserves it [*bewahrt es*] as what it is, in its divergence and contradictions, and hence actually an unfolding of truth [*eine Entfaltung der Wahrheit*]. A posited unity [*gesetzte Einheit*],

and as posited, [form] constantly suspends itself; essential to it is interrupting itself by way of its other, essential to its coherence, not cohering.... [As] the law [*Gesetz*] of the transfiguration of what exists, form represents freedom toward what exists. (ÄT 215–16/143)

In this passage, Adorno identifies form as essential to art's expressive quality, to its speech-likeness (*Sprachcharakter*),[34] even as form is also decisive to art's status as semblance (*Scheincharakter*): form organizes an artwork's content into a coherent voice. Unlike so much of conceptual logic, such organization carries out a "nonviolent synthesis." That is because, in principle, artistic form can be attuned to content in its diversity. It can recognize discrete moments for what they are in relation to other moments without imposing conceptual identity and consistency on them. Although Adorno does not explicitly say so here, he clearly regards such nonviolent synthesis as a partial model for conceptual thought. The sort of relation between "concept" and "thing" exemplified by an artistic attunement between form and content is a prerequisite for attaining truth.

Yet there is more to Adorno's position. Form that is fully attuned to content does not cover up the tensions and conflicts within the content of an artwork. Instead, it allows these to come to expression. Part of doing that is to acknowledge form's semblance character, its being posited and not simply emerging from the content. In this acknowledgement, form suspends itself for the sake of that which needs to speak. Form thereby exercises self-critique, just as, in Adorno's negative dialectics, conceptual thought criticizes its own imposition of identity. In this way, too, the relation between artistic form and content exemplifies what is required for attaining truth. Moreover, in both respects, in both attunement and self-suspension, the relation of form to content in art sets forth a model of social freedom, Adorno suggests, an expressive semblance of how domination could give way to reconciliation, how a false society could be reconfigured. In that sense, too, artistic form is "an unfolding of truth."

That is why, as was suggested earlier, it is important not to equate the notion of content (*Inhalt*) with that of import (*Gehalt*). For the import of an artwork is not simply what form organizes into coherent nonconceptual expression. Nor is it that on behalf of which form exercises self-critique. Instead, import is the entire dialectic that plays out within an artwork between form and content and what this dialectic discloses not only about the artwork itself but also about the social dynamic that comes to expression in it. This form/content dialectic and its significance are the substance (*Gehalt*) or spirit (*Geist*) of an artwork. It can be either true or false.

The truth or untruth of an artwork's import is not itself conceptual. Yet it does call for the right sort of conceptual understanding and critique and the right sort of relation between conceptual interpretation and artistic import. This interpretation/import relation involves a second sort of concept/thing polarity within Adorno's conception of artistic truth. Because it is closely tied to the polarity of history and transcendence, let me take up the second concept/thing polarity in that context.

SEMBLANCE OF TRUTH

The polarity of history and transcendence has special prominence in the chapter "Enigmaticalness, Truth Content, Metaphysics" (*Rätselcharakter, Wahrheitsgehalt, Metaphysik*, ÄT 179–205/118–36),[35] which lies between the two chapters already discussed. In the chapter's second half (ÄT 193–205/127–36), Adorno presents the idea of artistic truth content as central to what he calls "the metaphysics of art" (ÄT 198/131).[36] These are the pages whose utopian and "theological" language especially elicited Wellmer's concerns. They are also mostly ignored by Bernstein, who at one point calls Adorno's "language of redemption" mystifying.[37] What I find mystifying, by contrast, is why two such perceptive interpreters of Adorno seem compelled to either neutralize or avoid such language. For, as already argued in previous chapters, Adorno's utopian and "otherworldly" language provides a decisive orientation to his conception of truth and to the other polarities he emphasizes. This is nowhere more evident than in his *Aesthetic Theory*.

To see this, one can ask why, as Adorno had suggested earlier, the "redemption of semblance [*Rettung des Scheins*]" would be the center of aesthetics (ÄT 164/107) and why he now says "the metaphysics of art revolves around the question of how something spiritual that is made"—that is, the import of an artwork—"can be true." Immediately he says this question concerns "the rescue of semblance as the semblance of the true [*seiner Errettung als des Scheins von Wahrem*]" (ÄT 198/131). Why is this question so crucial for Adorno's *Aesthetic Theory*, as it clearly is? Is it because, à la Wellmer, the book wants to explain how aesthetically valid artworks can mobilize ordinary communicative action and discourse? Is it because, à la Bernstein, Adorno's aesthetics aims to highlight and reinforce modern art's refusing the diremption of beauty, truth, and goodness? Or is it because Adorno thinks authentic (modern) art can hold open the possibility of historical transcendence, the societal possibility of what *Negative Dialectics* calls "the humanly promised other of history" (ND 396/404)? Adorno's discussion of truth content and the metaphysics of art strongly points in this latter direction.

Adorno's answer to the question how artistic semblance can be true advances three interrelated claims. First, that truth content emerges from artifactual artworks, yet it transcends their artifactuality, by way of their artifactuality. Second, that such transcendence of artifactuality depends to a significant degree on how artworks are philosophically interpreted. Third, that artistic truth content is a sedimentation of history in artworks that, by virtue of this sedimentation, points to possibilities not yet actualized in history. In all three respects—the transcendence of artifactuality, the dependence on philosophical interpretation, and the possibilizing sedimentation of history—the truth of an artwork's import can hold open the societal possibility of historical transcendence. Let me explain.

Mediated Transcendence

In the long paragraph titled "On the Truth Content of Artworks" (ÄT 193–97/127–30), which opens the second half of the chapter under consideration here, Adorno collects many thoughts around a simple paradox concerning artworks: "They have truth content and they do not have it" (ÄT 194/128). Artworks have truth content in the sense that it emerges from the complex mediation of subject and object and of form and content within them. But they do not have truth content in the sense that it cannot be pinned down to any single element or complex of elements within them: neither their facticity (*was an den Werken der Fall ist*) nor their logicality (*Logizität*) or form, neither their philosophical idea nor what the artist intends, neither their sensuous qualities nor how artworks configure these qualities (ÄT 194–95/128–29). Rather, truth content is mediated by everything within an artwork. And the more highly artworks are internally elaborated, the more likely that their import is true. Yet not even mediation is enough. For truth content is the sociohistorical import (*geistiger Gehalt*) in which artworks *transcend* their mediation *by way of* their mediation. Moreover, not even a high degree of artifactual achievement guarantees that an artwork is true: it could be highly accomplished ideology. As Adorno says, "Many works of the highest quality are true as the expression of a consciousness that is false in itself" (ÄT 196/129).[38]

Such self-transcendence on the part of artworks would be unintelligible, however, if they could not be properly experienced and interpreted. And for that, Adorno says, philosophical reflection is needed. Truth content may be "the objective solution of the enigma" posed by every artwork, but it can be attained "only by philosophical reflection," he writes (ÄT 193/127–28). Artworks might resist conceptual interpretation—that's one reason they are enigmatic—and yet they also depend on it, for otherwise their truth content would not unfold. They need what Adorno calls the "establishing [*Herstellung*] of their truth content" (ÄT 194/128), for which philosophical interpretation is required. Not just any philosophical interpretation will do, however. It must pay attention to the particularity of artworks and follow their internal mediation from within, all the while staying attuned to the wider social and historical dynamics in which art participates.

This introduces the second concept/thing dialectic, mentioned earlier, in Adorno's conception of artistic truth, namely, the dialectic between the philosophical concept and the work of art. These converge, Adorno says, in truth content: "Philosophy and art converge in their truth content: The progressive self-unfolding truth of the artwork is none other than the truth of the philosophical concept" (ÄT 197/130). This "none other than" is a *dialectical* identity, however. In principle, artistic truth is nonconceptual, and philosophical truth is not. The truth content of artworks can depend on philosophical interpretation for its unfolding without itself becoming conceptual, just as the truth content of philosophy can help unfold artistic truth without itself becoming nonconceptual.

Indeed, one reason for Adorno's insistence on conceptual constellations is to attune philosophy to the particularity of artworks and other objects *without* denying or avoiding philosophy's conceptual character. The task of a philosophical interpretation of artworks is to sort out whether these are true or false, that is, whether indeed they disclose a self-transcending truth content, whether their sociohistorical import is true. In principle (*der Idee nach*), such philosophically interpretable and artifactually mediated truth "coincides with philosophical truth," Adorno claims (ÄT 197/130–31). In true dialectical fashion, however, he regards this coinciding not as a fusion of similarities but as a *coincidentia oppositorum*, a unity of opposites. Accordingly, interpretations of Adorno that say he wishes to make philosophy artistic are just as mistaken as those that claim he wants to make art philosophical.[39]

Historical Possibility

The urgency of Adorno's insistence on both the artwork's self-transcendence and its philosophical unfolding stems from the third sense of transcendence in his conception of artistic truth, namely the transcendence of history toward its humanly promised other. This third sense is really the overriding one, the one that orients his conceptions of artistic truth content and philosophical interpretation. It shows up in each extended paragraph of the half chapter under consideration. In the paragraph on the concept of artistic truth content, Adorno talks about art as the "negative appearance of utopia" (ÄT 196/130). In the next paragraph, on the convergence of philosophy and art, he mentions the appearance of a social collectivity in artist truth content (ÄT 198/131). His paragraph on the metaphysics of art emphasizes how artworks testify to the possibility of what is historically possible (ÄT 199–200/132–33). And the final two paragraphs, on the negativity of artistic truth content (ÄT 200–205/133–36), explore how, even in their modernist negativity, artworks participate in reconciliation and anticipate the nonidentical.

Let me focus on the paragraph about the metaphysics of art before I more briefly consider the final two paragraphs. Immediately this paragraph's caption confronts us with a problem of interpretation. In German the caption reads "Wahrheit als Schein des Scheinlosen," which Hullot-Kentor translates as "Truth as Semblance of the Illusionless" (ÄT 199/vi). This caption is most puzzling. Does it suggest that truth is no more than a semblance? If so, then what would be the truth of which truth is a semblance? If Adorno really did believe that truth is a semblance—even if truth is a semblance of that which is without semblance—then all of his efforts to spell out what artistic truth content comes to would lose their point. For then artistic truth content would come down to little more than an illusion, and neither the dialectic between semblance and expression nor the polarity of form and content would matter. Although such an outcome might be acceptable to readers who regard Adorno as an alethic negativist or as little more than a latter-day Nietzsche, it clearly does not jibe with my own approach.

In the paragraph itself, however, Adorno does not say truth is an illusion. Rather, he writes, "Wahrheit hat Kunst als Schein des Scheinlosen," which Hullot-Kentor translates as "Art has truth as the semblance of the illusionless" (ÄT 199/132). Adorno's word order is important—"Wahrheit hat Kunst," he writes, not "Kunst hat Wahrheit"—and so is the context where this sentence occurs. Adorno's argument in this passage is that, as humanly fabricated products, artworks "stand in the most extreme tension to their truth content," which can appear only in such artifacts, yet negates them in their artifactuality. Every artwork promises that its truth content would realize itself and "leave the artwork behind simply as a husk" (ÄT 199/131–32). That is why, Adorno says, the notion of aesthetic semblance does not suffice to define art, for the semblance gives rise to truth. Accordingly, it is not *truth* that is the "semblance of the illusionless." Rather, it is *art*, in its artifactuality, that is a semblance of what lacks semblance—that is, art is a semblance of truth. Hence a more accurate, albeit less elegant, rendering of the sentence in question would be: "Truth is had by art as the semblance of the illusionless," where the "as" connects "art" and "semblance" and does not connect "truth" and "semblance." Art, not truth, is a semblance of truth.

What, then, is the truth that art, in its semblantic artifactuality, "has"? Although Adorno gives various descriptions in different passages, what stands out in the immediate context is the utopian possibility of sociohistorical transcendence, the possibility that society could be completely different from what it has historically come to be. And this possibility arises from the social history that until now has blocked it. Authentic artworks long, Adorno claims, for their truth content not to be null. They long for it to become actual. Yet they transcend this longing insofar as "neediness" not only is inscribed in what historically exists (*das geschichtlich Seiende*) but also summons "its fulfillment and change" and finds articulation in artworks. Authentic artworks express the longing of what is for something different, for the other whose elements already exist and would "require only a small displacement into a new constellation to find their right position" (ÄT 199/132).

This other, this no longer dominative and need-thwarting society, is historically possible. Artworks have no power over whether what is historically possible becomes actual. Yet the fact that they exist attests to its being possible: their reality "testifies to the possibility of the possible" (ÄT 200/132). And what makes such testimony possible, in turn, is the fact that artworks simultaneously participate in history and take a critical stance toward it. From such critical participation the truth content of artworks emerges and points beyond. Unlike the artifactual artwork, such truth content is not fabricated. Artistic truth content is not a semblance. It is the "unposited" and possibilizing sedimentation of social history (ÄT 200/133).

Accordingly, the urgency of Adorno's insisting on the artwork's self-transcendence and its philosophical unfolding derives from the dialectic between history and transcendence that, I have argued, sets the direction for polarities between subject and object and between concept and thing in Adorno's conception of truth. For Adorno, the overriding significance of dialectically autonomous art in contemporary society is to express the possibility of sociohistorical transcendence via critical participation in the social history that has blocked this possibility. Just as the history of society both makes possible and blocks its "humanly promised other," so too art's participation in this history both makes artistic truth content possible and blocks its actualization.

Broken Promise

That is why, according to the last two paragraphs in this half chapter, the historically sedimented truth content in artworks does not straightforwardly *affirm* the possibility of sociohistorical transcendence. Rather, truth content is "only something negative [*nur ein Negatives*]" (ÄT 200/133). Artworks can point to the other only by configuring how things historically are. In opposing society, art cannot step outside it. Instead, art "achieves opposition only through identification with that against which it remonstrates" (ÄT 201/133). Even in artworks that formally achieve distance from a dominative society, an "echo of social violence" remains (ÄT 202/134). Although artworks can and do undertake a reconciling comportment toward the nonidentical, they nevertheless do so through a distanced and negative stance toward contemporary society. They themselves cannot achieve the societal reconciliation toward which they point. Their truth content is negative.

Nevertheless, art both anticipates "what would finally be itself" and recollects "the possible in opposition to the actual that suppresses it." Hence, within their negativity, and by way of it, "artworks make a promise" (ÄT 203–4/135). They make a promise of what is historically blocked and yet historically possible. As Adorno says at the very end of this chapter, a truth-oriented experience of art—what in this context he calls *aesthetic experience (ästhetische Erfahrung)*—is the experience of "possibility, promised by its impossibility. Art is the promise of happiness that is broken" (ÄT 205/136). This does not mean, however, that the promised possibility is irrevocably impossible. Nor does it mean that the promise of happiness can never be kept. It simply means that what expresses the promise—that is, art or, more precisely, the truth content of authentic artworks—cannot actualize the possibility or keep the promise. For that to happen, society itself would have to change.

It is only in light of art's promise that it can express suffering. Artworks give voice to suffering in longing for its removal. Art, in this sense, is "the imaginary reparation of the catastrophe of world history," and it stands for a freedom from societally induced suffering that has not yet "come to pass" (ÄT 204/135). If art's promise of happiness were not broken, then either the humanly promised other of history would have been achieved or art itself would have become fundamentally untrue. Neither neutralizing nor ignoring Adorno's "metaphysical" language of redemption can do justice to the overriding hope in his aesthetics for the transformation of society as a whole. That hope is the secret to his conception of artistic truth, even as it makes his aesthetics seem untimely and problematic to those who have a less utopian approach to the politics of art.

Art and Politics

Encapsuled Praxis

Adorno's complex conception of artistic truth, together with the dialectical autonomism that undergirds it, leads to what one could label an oblique approach to the politics of art. Authentic artworks do make a political contribution, he writes. But this contribution does not occur in direct impact on people's political actions or attitudes, by inciting or supporting their social protests, for example. Instead, the political contribution lies in what their truth content implies: "Praxis is not the effect [*Wirkung*] of works; rather, it is encapsuled [*verkapselt*] in their truth content" (ÄT 367/247). Hence, the proper relation of authentic artworks to political praxis is indirect. It occurs via what Adorno calls "the scarcely apprehensible transformation of consciousness," a transformation that "could become a transformation of [social] reality" (ÄT 360–61/243). At bottom, the requisite transformation of consciousness is to break with the need for self-preservation that sustains the domination of nature both within and without and also unavoidably contaminates political action (ÄT 358–59/241–42). This transformation happens within the truth-oriented experience of art, in the moment of our being shaken up or shocked (*Erschütterung*) by the truth-laden artwork: "The experience of art as that of its truth or untruth is . . . the irruption of objectivity into subjective consciousness" (ÄT 363/244–45).

Contrary to Bernstein's otherwise insightful interpretation, this oblique approach to the politics of art does not reduce art to a political stand-in "for an absent politics."[40] Adorno clearly recognizes that artistic truth can contribute to existing politics, even though he thinks the proper contribution is oblique, and existing politics is, to say the least, problematic. Neither, however, does Adorno's truth-oriented politics of art reduce this contribution to what Wellmer describes as an "phenomenon of interference" among the three validity dimensions of ordinary communicative action.[41] The change of consciousness Adorno envisions is not a slight disturbance that leaves ordinary ways of acting and speaking intact. Rather it is a transformative upheaval in the very structure of consciousness, one that reorients us toward not only the object that has priority and the content that form articulates but also the humanly promised other of history. For Adorno, the political stakes of artistic truth are high.

Nevertheless, Adorno's oblique approach contributes to the seeming untimeliness of *Aesthetic Theory*. Given current cultural politics, his approach is at odds both with those who see and seek overt connections between art and politics (including many critical theorists in the broad sense) and those who prefer art to be apolitical. For convenience, let me label these the politically engaged and the apolitical approaches, respectively.

To those who endorse art's political engagement—and who often deny that art ever is not politically engaged—Adorno's oblique approach problematically defers the impact of art's political contributions to a utopian future. He thereby ignores or distorts the important roles that art actually fulfills in current political struggles. By contrast, to those who prefer art's political neutrality—and who often think overt political engagement necessarily distorts art's vocation or diminishes its quality—Adorno's oblique approach gives far too much credence to the socially transformative potential of art. In this way he places demands on artists and their audience that hardly anyone can fulfill. In other words, the engaged find Adorno's truth aesthetics to be insufficiently "political" for the purposes of, say, resisting racism, dismantling patriarchy, or challenging the hegemony of turbocapitalism and the administrative state. And the apolitical regard Adorno's truth aesthetics as wildly overwrought with respect to the falsity of society as a whole and art's transformative potential in that regard.

What bothers both ends of the current culture-political spectrum, it seems to me, is the dilemma of historically ill-founded utopian hope mentioned in the previous chapter. Both sides are troubled by Adorno's locating art's political role in a transformation of consciousness that, under his own description of the dialectic of domination, seems currently impossible. Or, if it is possible within a truth-oriented experience of authentic artworks, it is unclear how this art-induced transformation would in fact play out in actual political struggles. This disturbs the politically engaged because they expect art to make a more direct contribution to political struggles. And it bothers the apolitical because they think art should not be burdened with such an "unrealistic" expectation.

Artistic and Political Truth

I, too, find the dilemma of ill-founded hope troubling, and the previous chapter suggests ways to address it. Yet, in the context of current cultural politics, I also believe this point of disturbance is precisely what makes Adorno's apparently untimely truth aesthetics most timely. For he suggests a way to think about both the sort of political change needed and the scope of art's political contribution that neither politicizes nor depoliticizes art yet keeps alive the hope for radical social transformation. He thereby challenges both ends of the culture-political spectrum to reconsider the terms of their debates. Let me explain.

Implicit in Adorno's aesthetics is the intuition that art and politics are distinct social domains. Although Adorno does not share my view of politics as a social domain of truth, he recognizes that what art contributes to political struggles presupposes that the art making the contribution is true. Moreover, the truth of art is distinct from, and not reducible to, its effectiveness in the political arena. And this distinction applies not only to the sort of "autonomous" artworks, such as Samuel Beckett's *Endgame*, that Adorno prefers, but also the more overtly political art, such as social protest art, that he tends to value not for its political role but for its intrinsic truth content. Adorno's point, which I endorse, is that art cannot be politically true if it is not intrinsically true, even though, I would add, intrinsic artistic truth does not guarantee political truth. In his words, "No artwork . . . can be socially true that is not also true in-itself; conversely, social false consciousness is equally incapable of becoming aesthetically authentic" (ÄT 368/248).[42]

In my own terms, art is true when products or events of art cogently and imaginatively disclose the worlds of their creators and interpreters and, in the case of artworks, the world of the artwork. These products and events do not need to be autonomous artworks in Adorno's sense in order to provide such disclosure, even though artworks, by virtue of their having been institutionally constituted to be relatively independent, can achieve a truth content or import that other art products or events might lack. What is decisive for artistic truth is not whether *autonomous artworks* carry it but whether what the product or event discloses is imaginatively and cogently disclosed.[43] Social protest art, too, can be either true or false in this sense, even though its imaginative disclosure is overtly in the service of a political movement or cause. Whether or not it is artistically true is a different question, however, from whether it is politically effective, and the two questions have independent answers: what is artistically true can be politically ineffective, and what is politically successful can be artistically untrue.

This implies, in turn, that political *effectiveness* is not the same as political *truth*. Otherwise, I would need to give up the earlier claim, derived from Adorno, that art cannot be politically true if it is not intrinsically true—that is, if it does not accomplish a cogent imaginative disclosure. For I have just suggested that politically effective art can be artistically untrue. To explain this, I need to articulate a notion of political truth that, so far as I can tell, Adorno does not share.

In the previous chapter I described politics as the domain in society where people engage in struggles for justice from positions of relative power, typically to achieve liberation from oppression. This is a normative description; built into it is the expectation that the power exercised and achieved is justifiable and suitable vis à vis justice and freedom. Political truth occurs when the exercise of justifiable and suitable power serves interlinked justice and freedom. On this account, a decision, action, strategy, or policy can be politically effective without being politically true. For it could well be a clever way to exercise power without being either justifiable or suitable with respect to achieving justice and freedom.

So too, a piece of art, whether or not it is overt propaganda, can be effective as a way to exercise political power and yet fail to serve the ends of justice and liberation. In that case it would be politically effective but not politically true. Moreover, because the requirements of justice and the shape of liberation are themselves always sites of political struggle, there is no politically "neutral" way to determine whether or not, in any particular case, what is artistically true is also politically true. Yet it is highly unlikely—indeed, I want to say it is impossible—that art products or events that serve our seeking justice and freedom on the basis of justifiable power would not themselves cogently and imaginatively disclose the worlds of their creators and interpreters. The converse, however, does not appear to hold. Art products and events can cogently and imaginatively disclose and yet not serve the justifiably empowered pursuit of justice and freedom, either because they are cordoned off from political struggles or because they are politically abused.

In establishing such a two-way relation between artistic and political truth, I follow Adorno's lead to take issue with both the politically engaged and the apolitical approaches to art and politics. On the one hand, the stance of political engagement threatens either to make artistic truth completely subservient to political truth or to equate political truth with political effectiveness, to the detriment of artistic truth. If, in the end, the worth of art is reduced to whether or not it is politically effective, then, I would argue, both art and politics will suffer. For then the cogency and imaginativeness of artistic disclosure will not matter, nor will the concern whether the exercise of political power does indeed further justice and freedom. Such replacing of truth by effectiveness is a hallmark of what I call the politicizing of art.

On the other hand, the stance of political neutrality threatens to isolate artistic truth from political truth, to the detriment of both. If we reduce the truth of art to whether or not it is intrinsically true, without regard for art's role in politics, then we will lose sight of why artistic truth matters in the first place. It matters because art can disclose the worlds we inhabit, and without such disclosure, social transformation is hard to imagine. Included in such transformation is the pursuit of political truth that, I have suggested, artistic truth supports. The demotion of art to political irrelevance is what distinguishes what I call the depoliticizing of art.

How, then, can art properly contribute to politics? More specifically, how does what I have described as cogent imaginative disclosure contribute to the justifiably empowered and liberating pursuit of justice in society? Let me suggest three ways: first, by giving voice to social needs; second, by challenging current arrangements of power; and third, by inspiring commitments to pursuing social justice. In all three ways artistic truth serves both social critique and social imagination, not only exposing injustice, oppression, and unjustifiable power but also helping us envision new conditions of justice and freedom.

The social needs to which artistic truth gives voice are both widely shared and shaped by the current societal formation—for example, adequate food and shelter. In giving voice to unmet social needs, true art is, as Adorno suggests, a language of human suffering. Yet, when voicing their satisfaction, it is also a language of celebration and, contra Adorno, not simply a "broken promise" of happiness. In this sense, artistic truth can both help us reject what destroys life and embrace what liberates from injustice and oppression. It thereby supports political truth.

So too, cogently imaginative and disclosive art can help challenge current arrangements of power. Under conditions of oppression and injustice, some people wield power at the expense of others. Power that oppresses others and denies them their rights is unjustifiable, and it needs to be resisted and overturned. Through cogent imaginative disclosure, true art can call attention to the destructive effects of oppressive power and point toward conditions under which justice is no longer denied, whether through social protest, collective lament, or utopian vision. By itself, such cogently disclosive art does not bring about political change. But without it, oppressive power would more easily remain in effect, and paths to justice and freedom would more likely remain blocked.

Expressing social needs and challenging oppressive power, true art can also inspire commitments to the cause of justice. Often oppressive power can seem so deeply entrenched, and failures to achieve justice so pervasive, that political cynicism or despair takes hold. To remain committed to the cause of justice in such circumstances, people need reminders of historical possibilities. And, as Adorno emphasizes, that is what true art can provide: the nuances of meaning it discloses include the historical possibilities of the present day, both how our personal and social worlds might have evolved differently than they did and how they might change in the future. When art cogently and imaginatively discloses either personal and social worlds or the world of the artwork, it brings to the fore historical possibilities—ways things could be or could have been—that inspire both critique and hope: critique of how things have been, and hope for a better future. It thereby encourages faithfulness to the societal principle of justice, despite both the historical record and the current odds.

In these three ways, then, artistic truth supports political truth. Art does not need to be directly involved with actual politics in order for its truth to support political truth. But when art *is* politically involved, its direct contribution to the pursuit of justice and freedom will depend on its being artistically true. What Adorno said concerning the import of the autonomous artwork also holds for politically engaged art: its political contribution depends on its artistic truth.

Timely Truth Content

To arrive at this conclusion, however, one needs to take distance from the dialectical autonomism of Adorno's aesthetics. As I have argued elsewhere, the autonomy of the work of art is not a necessary condition for achieving artistic truth. Art products and events that are *not* institutionally constituted as autonomous artworks are also capable of cogent imaginative disclosure.[44] I have also modified the utopian dimension to Adorno's conception of truth. Although I agree with him that hope for social transformation is intrinsic not simply to artistic truth but truth as a whole, I do not agree that until now the path toward such transformation has been blocked. Rather, the possibilities for genuine justice, solidarity, and interconnected flourishing are just as much woven into the fabric of sociohistorical reality as are the institutions, systems, and structures that currently work against their coming to fruition. In this sense, my conception of artistic truth is less "pessimistic" than Adorno's.

Here, however, one needs to tread carefully. For the dialectic between history and transcendence in Adorno's conception of artistic truth, when not either ignored or dismissed altogether, has often been misunderstood. From many examples one could cite, let me mention in conclusion the interpretation of Paul Guyer, a leading figure in Anglo-American aesthetics and a well-known Kant scholar. The third volume of Guyer's extensive *History of Modern Aesthetics* discusses Adorno's aesthetics in a chapter on postwar German scholarship. Having traced three main themes in the history of modern aesthetics in the two previous volumes—truth, emotion, and play—Guyer locates Adorno's work, like Heidegger's, exclusively in the cognitivist strand. Then he argues that Adorno's specific version of cognitivism leads to a highly "pessimistic" view of art: "The truth that art delivers is that of the impossibility of the happiness that it says is possible. Adorno's aesthetic theory expresses a pessimism that makes that of Schopenhauer seem halfhearted: For Schopenhauer, art offered only momentary respite from pessimism, but asceticism could offer enduring relief from it, while for Adorno art promises a better world with one hand but proves the impossibility of such a world with the other."[45]

Perhaps Guyer's assessment of extreme pessimism—the main theme in his discussion of Adorno's aesthetics—would make sense if Adorno thought art and society cannot change, such that the better world toward which authentic artworks point can never be achieved and the current society that authentic artworks critique can never be transformed. If Adorno thought this, then he would indeed be a radical disciple of Schopenhauer's resignation. Yet the entire point of Adorno's conception of artistic truth is to hold open the possibility of real sociohistorical transformation in society as a whole, in a society that encourages everyone to think nothing fundamental can change. Adorno might have had too restricted a view of which art can help offer the requisite critique. He might also have overlooked social tendencies and agencies beyond art that can contribute to genuine sociohistorical transformation. Yet he never said, nor as Benjamin-inspired Hegelian Marxist could he have said, that fundamental change is impossible.

At least some art is able to meet what *Negative Dialectics* describes as a necessary condition for all truth (ND 29/17–18): it can satisfy the need to let suffering speak. And by giving voice to suffering, art expresses a longing for its removal. While that does not make Adorno an aesthetic optimist, it does indicate why any assumed contrast between optimism and pessimism is singularly unsuited for understanding the conception of artistic truth that pervades his modernist and autonomist aesthetic theory.

For Adorno, modern art is the language of societally induced suffering. Such suffering is to be neither accepted nor forgotten (ÄT 386–87/260–61). It is because (modern) art gives voice to societally induced suffering that its promise of happiness is "broken" (ÄT 205/136).[46] Yet it is in the expression of suffering that art's promise is made. As *Negative Dialectics* (ND 203/203) says, quoting Friedrich Nietzsche (without citation) from Zarathustra's roundelay and the fourth movement of Gustav Mahler's Third Symphony: *Weh spricht: Vergeh*—Woe implores: Go.[47] Were society to change in fundamental ways and no longer induce human suffering, then art's promise of happiness would be kept. Such a transformation is not impossible. Amid apparent untimeliness, that is the still timely truth content of Adorno's *Aesthetic Theory*.

7

Promises of Truth

In semblance, nonsemblance is promised.

—Theodor W. Adorno (ND 397/405)

Truth, Adorno claims, is a dynamic constellation. So too, I have argued, is Adorno's conception of truth, a constellation in which the crisscrossing polarities of subject and object, of concept and thing, and of history and transcendence stand out. In describing truth as a dynamic historical process, Adorno takes issue with all those philosophers, from Parmenides and Plato onward, who think truth is eternal and unchanging. And by calling truth a constellation, he takes distance from those, like Hegel, who regard truth as a holistic system.

In both respects, the emphasis on historical process and that on constellation, Adorno's conception of truth conflicts with dominant tendencies within recent philosophy in the West. On the one hand, recent truth theory in analytic philosophy, with its tangled roots in logical positivism, tends to focus on questions about the relation, if any, between propositional truth bearers (such as sentences, statements, assertions, and propositions) and appropriate truth makers, if any (such as objects, facts, and states of affairs).[1] Although Adorno does not ignore such questions, he clearly thinks there is much more to truth than propositional truth. Moreover, propositional truth itself needs to be conceived not as a static correspondence between propositions and facts but as a historically emergent—and often historically blocked—mediation between concepts and objects. That is one of the essential points in Adorno's critique of logical positivism and its analytic aftermath. Not even the idea of scientific truth can be split off from the idea of "a true society," he says.[2]

On the other hand, much of recent continental philosophy, with its troubled indebtedness to Heidegger's existentialism, takes a skeptical stance toward propositional truth,[3] even as it casts doubt on anything like an "emphatic concept of truth," which for Adorno includes the thought of society having "the right organization."[4] By failing to provide a robust conception of propositional truth, continental philosophy inadvertently reinforces the narrowness it rejects in analytic philosophy.

Placed in this context, Adorno's conception of truth as a dynamic constellation provides a significant alternative to dominant trends in both analytic and continental philosophy, even as it invites dismissal from both sides. At the same time, as I have already suggested, Adorno's conception poses its own problems. It is in articulating and addressing these problems that one can critically retrieve the alethic insights his philosophy offers. Returning to issues raised in previous chapters, let me first discuss propositional truth and its relation to truth as a whole. Then I shall conclude with reflections on the tasks of a truth-oriented social critique.

Propositional Truth

In chapters 2 and 3 I argued that Adorno rightly distinguishes propositional truth from truth as a whole but fails to provide an adequate account of propositional truth and how it relates to truth as a whole. There are two sides to this failure. First, although Adorno rightly critiques patterns of domination in society as a whole, he problematically tends to equate predication with dominative identification, such that even ordinary claims about what things are cannot do justice to their objects. This tendency is the reason why some Adorno scholars regard him as an alethic negativist—incorrectly, in my view.

Second, although he rightly insists on the priority of the object, Adorno tends to restrict the object's availability to how it addresses mimetic dimensions of thought and experience. These dimensions are inherently prepredicative. Hence, to do justice to the object, the cognitive subject must continually find prepredicative ways to counter its predicatively imposing identity on the object. This tendency is the reason why other Adorno scholars regard him as what could be called an alethic aestheticist, as someone who thinks only art and aesthetic experience can do justice to cognitive objects—another incorrect interpretation of Adorno, it seems to me.

As a result of both tendencies, Adorno cannot provide an adequate account of propositional truth. He cannot explain how, when we make correct assertions, we can in fact do justice to the identity of objects, and objects can reliably disclose their identity to us—that is, how we can achieve propositional truth. This achievement is due, in general, to interrelations between life practices and the objects of those practices and, in particular, to what I call *predicative interrelations* between disclosive predicative practices and the predicative self-disclosure of practical objects.

The underlying idea here is that, as predicative practices, the referring and predicating that occur in ordinary speech acts, such as my asserting "This house is green," do indeed identify objects. These practices also either implicitly or explicitly distinguish objects from one another and point out relations among them. Asserted in a particular context, "This house is green" not only singles out a particular house and specifies its color but also thereby distinguishes it from other houses nearby and relates it to them in terms of color. In these ways, the ordinary practices of referring and predicating serve to disclose the identity of specific objects in specific respects. Yet no presumption is built into such ordinary predicative practices that what they single out is all there is to the object's identity, nor that the identity of the object is simply whatever the speech act specifies. In other words, predicative identification is not necessarily a dominative imposition of identity. Rather, when carried out in proper interrelation with practical objects, predicative practices help disclose objects in their own identity.

Predicatively disclosing the identity of practical objects presupposes that these do in fact have an identity that goes beyond that singled out by any particular assertion or combination of assertions. Obviously, for example, there is more to a house than its color, and there are many more aspects to what it is than what the use of "house" as a referring term identifies. This "surplus beyond the subject," if you will, is precisely what, in the context of explaining propositional truth, Adorno's insistence on the nonidentical paradoxically identifies but wants to shield from conceptual imposition. At the same time, however, intrinsic to the full identity of practical objects is their offering themselves for human practices, and among these practices are those of referring and predicating. Moreover, practical objects can be available for predicative practices in ways that align with their being available for relevant nonpredicative practices. A house's availability for predications about its color can align with its availability for color perception.

Indeed, these two sorts of practical availability—predicative and nonpredicative—*must* align in order for assertions about a practical object to be correct and for the propositions asserted to be accurate. I call such alignment between predicative and nonpredicative availability within the object on the occasion of a predication the *predicative self-disclosure* of the object. The object offers itself in a certain way; it self-discloses in interrelation with predicative practices. It is by virtue of the object's predicative self-disclosure in interrelation with the practices of reference and predication that we can achieve propositional truth.

Yet propositional truth requires more than the correctness of assertions and the accuracy of propositions. It also requires that the propositions we assert align properly with each other in patterns of inference. In other words, they must be logically valid.[5] The truth of propositions involves an interlinkage between accurate insight into predicatively self-disclosing practical objects, on the one hand, and inferential validity with respect to the other propositions stated or implied when we make an assertion, on the other.

This account of propositional truth, which I have articulated at greater length elsewhere,[6] might appear to turn contemporary society into a fantasy land of sweetness and light. For if ordinary predicative practices do not necessarily dominate their objects, and if ordinary practical objects do not resist predicative identification, then Adorno's entire critique of domination and his repeated calls for the epistemic subject's critical self-negation seem to go missing. Whereas chapter 2 argues that Adorno rightly says social hope and social critique interlink in the idea of truth and correctly calls attention to a negative relation between epistemic subject and epistemic object, now I seem to have abandoned his social critique and his insistence on a negative epistemic relation. In response, I need to say a little more about the idea of truth as a whole and how propositional truth relates to that.

Truth as a Whole

To begin, let me suggest that the interlinkage between accurate insight and inferential validity offers an important clue into what truth as a whole is like. It offers a clue because a dynamic correlation *within propositional truth* both echoes and participates in the dynamic correlation *within truth as a whole*. Let me explain.

In order for inferential validity and accurate insight to interlink, those who make assertions must not only try to think logically but also do justice to what they make assertions about. In fact, their fidelity to the societal principle of logical validity must correlate with their doing justice to the object's predicative self-disclosure. Moreover, this correlation is dynamic, for each side inflects the other: our fidelity serves to promote the object's disclosure, and our doing justice to the object's predicative self-disclosure partly depends on how faithful we are to the principle of logical validity.

Now I submit that this dynamic correlation *within* propositional truth both echoes and participates in the fidelity/disclosure correlation that characterizes truth *as a whole*. Just as propositional truth requires a dynamic correlation between fidelity to logical validity and a propositional disclosure of the object, so in general truth consists in a dynamic correlation between human fidelity to societal principles and a life-giving disclosure of society. Moreover, a version of this general correlation also shows up in every *nonpropositional* sort of truth, such as artistic truth. And that is why, as Adorno recognized in his own way, among the various sorts of truth, propositional truth is not the primary sort. Indeed, there is no primary *sort* of truth. What is primary, when it comes to truth, is *truth as a whole*, not one of its types or kinds.

Yet propositional truth is important. Deliberate lying, bullshit, and misinformation undermine logical fidelity and accurate insight. They thereby damage not only the path of propositional truth but also the pursuit of truth as a whole. For infidelity to one societal principle—logical validity, in this case—both encourages and reinforces infidelity to other societal principles—such as solidarity and justice—even as the refusal to pursue accurate insight both fosters and strengthens other refusals to pursue what is societally good. So, propositional truth is important, important both in its own right—human beings need accurate and inferentially valid insight—and for its role within truth as a whole—it helps foster a dynamic correlation between fidelity to societal principles and a life-giving disclosure of society. Yet propositional truth is not alone in having such double importance, and it is limited in ways that nonpropositional sorts of truth are not. Although important, then, propositional truth is not all-important. The same goes for scientific truth, which takes propositional truth to a new level.

In portraying truth as a whole to be a dynamic correlation between fidelity to societal principles and a life-giving disclosure of society, however, I need to state explicitly what has been suggested at various points along the way: Adorno's conjectural or subjunctive conception of truth as a whole is as problematic as it is significant. By a "subjunctive conception" I mean what Adorno articulates when he talks about "the utopia of the whole truth, which is still to be realized" (H 325/88) and when he identifies the absolute as "the nonidentical that would emerge only after the identity compulsion dissolved" (ND 398/406).

There are two problems with this conception of truth as a whole. First, it inadvertently dehistoricizes the idea of truth, contrary to Adorno's own Hegelian insistence on the historical character of truth. If, as a whole, truth is still to be realized, and if the nonidentical would not emerge until after the identity-compulsion dissolved, then truth as a whole can be historical only in a proleptic sense: it could become historical in the future, but only if the present course of history were to shift radically. Until that *Umschlag* (reversal) occurs, truth as a whole is not, strictly speaking, historical. It does not unfold *within* the practices, institutions, and macrostructures that make up the historical fabric of society and human life.

The second problem with Adorno's conception of truth as a whole is socioepistemological. The entire weight of his critique of domination rests on the possibility that one can conceive of the whole truth that "reveals the whole to be untrue in all its moments," as Adorno puts it (H 325/88). Yet the only conception Adorno can offer of the whole truth is conjectural and negative, namely, what life and society would be like if blind domination ended. Moreover, what life and society would then be like is extremely difficult for Adorno to say: if he were to spell it out, he would violate his own understanding of and commitment to determinate negation. Hence Adorno's critique of domination appears to be caught in the socioepistemological bind of a necessary but cognitively inaccessible idea of truth as a whole.

Despite these two problems, I think Adorno is right to insist on the idea of truth as a whole and to assign it a futural dimension. This allows him not only to interlink social hope and social critique in the idea of truth but also to insist on a negative relation between epistemic subject and object—two of his most important contributions to contemporary truth theory. The challenge is to retain and rearticulate these insights without dehistoricizing truth as a whole and rendering it cognitively inaccessible.

As already indicated, and as elaborated elsewhere, I propose to do this by understanding truth as a whole as a dynamic correlation between human fidelity to societal principles such as justice and solidarity, on the one hand, and a life-giving disclosure of society, on the other. Without going into the details here, let me suggest such an understanding retains the futural orientation of Adorno's conception without dehistoricizing the idea of truth as a whole. For the societal principles to which we can be faithful are themselves historically still evolving within the practices, institutions, and macrostructures of contemporary society. And the life-giving disclosure of this society is an open-ended process. The dynamic correlation between fidelity and disclosure is not cognitively inaccessible either. We can know

now what fidelity to societal principles requires, and that allows us to put content into the notion of life-giving disclosure. Hence, for example, we can say that a true society would be one in which justice and solidarity prevail and all inhabitants flourish in an interconnected way. Moreover, we can spell out in some detail how contemporary society both blocks such a "utopian" condition and opens possibilities for its arrival.

As a result, one can not only retain the link between social critique and social hope in Adorno's conception of truth but make it even stronger. For the identification of historically blocked possibilities can come paired with substantial proposals about removing the blockage. One can also retain Adorno's insistence on a negative relation between epistemic subject and object. For being faithful to societal principles necessarily requires resistance toward whatever stands in the way of our practicing justice and solidarity. Moreover, in the specific domain of propositional truth, where predicative interrelations support our pursuing a dynamic correlation between accurate insight and inferential validity, it is the critique of failures to achieve accuracy or validity or both that tells us whether and how to renew this pursuit. It is in such propositional self-critique that disparities between the subject's conceptual identifications and the object's identity show up. Such self-critique is intrinsic to the discursive confirmation of truth claims whereby the truth of propositions unfolds. And the unfolding of propositional truth both belongs to and contributes to the unfolding of truth as a whole, which, as Adorno rightly insists, is much more than propositional.

Nevertheless—and here Adorno and I part ways—propositional self-critique presupposes the prior interrelation between subjective predicative practices and the objective predicative self-disclosure that makes propositional truth possible in the first place. So too, resistance to injustice and exclusion presupposes a prior attachment to historically embedded societal principles. Truth is indeed a dynamic constellation. As a whole, however, it is always already historically unfolding, also via social resistance and propositional self-critique.

Social Critique

To this point the proposed critical retrieval of Adorno's conception of truth has assumed that the possibility of the humanly promised other of history is not as thoroughly blocked in contemporary society as Adorno often suggests. Previous chapters have indicated various reasons for making this assumption. In chapter 4 I suggested that, unlike Heidegger, who locates the blocked possibility in a nearly irretrievable "other beginning," Adorno locates it in contemporary society as it has historically developed, with a view toward a transformed society where needless suffering would end. If this possibility does lie blocked *in* contemporary society, however, then it seems it must also have historically unfolded in this society. And that raises questions about how, specifically, the humanly promised other of history has unfolded in the past and how its prior unfolding prepares for a potentially different future.

So too, in distinguishing Adorno's social critique from Foucault's, chapter 5 suggested that three refinements are needed in order to retain the utopian dimension in Adorno's conception of truth that Foucault's conception lacks. One is to recognize multiple social domains of truth and thereby neither privilege nor dismiss the social domain of scientific truth. A second refinement is to distinguish more clearly than Adorno did between subjugation, exploitation, and repression and thereby develop both a more nuanced critique of domination and a more textured hope for social transformation. A third is to point to collaboration (power-with) as a third existing form of power, alongside influence (power-over) and agency (power-to), and thereby secure additional support for pursuing truth in its various social domains.

The upshot of such refinements, when combined with questions about the history of utopian possibility, would be both a less monolithic social critique and a more differentiated social vision. Hence, for example, to understand how subjugation, exploitation, and repression play out in mutually reinforcing ways, one would need to see specifically how they take shape in different macrostructures and social institutions. So too, to understand how a basis to hope for a different future has unfolded in the past, one would need to see how, amid such mutually reinforcing patterns of domination, truth-conducive patterns of ecocare, power-sharing, and flexible sublimation have also taken shape. As a result, we could view the hoped-for transition to a postdominative society not only as not historically impossible but also as indeed historically possible. The transition might currently be blocked by the normative deficiencies and structural hegemony of a turbocapitalist economy and administrative state. Yet contemporary society harbors historical possibilities for a different future. One task of a truth-oriented social critique would be to say what those possibilities are.

As critically retrieved via Adorno's conception of truth, a truth-oriented social critique would try to articulate, within society as a whole, what truth consists in, how its unfolding is blocked, and how the barriers to truth's unfolding could be removed. Unlike Adorno, I do not believe there are only traces of truth in contemporary society. Ever-emerging societal principles such as solidarity and justice are deeply interwoven into the historical fabric of society, and struggles to honor them have helped shape contemporary institutions and societal structures. So too, the desire for interconnected flourishing is not a philosopher's pipe dream. Many people and communities long for this, even when they come into conflict over what it means and requires. To ignore these existing guidelines and openings while pointing out society's pervasive falsehood would all-too-easily reinforce the truth-nihilism of current post-truth politics.

Accordingly, the first task of a truth-oriented social critique is to ask what fidelity to societal principles, life-giving disclosure of society, and a dynamic correlation between fidelity and disclosure come to within and across diverse social domains. As Adorno and the Frankfurt School recognized in their own way, this is an inherently interdisciplinary and collaborative effort, one that philosophers cannot carry out on their own. Nevertheless, philosophy can certainly help establish what the leading societal principles are, what they mean and require, how they link up with specific practices and institutions, and how to be faithful to them. In collaboration with other academic disciplines and social domains, philosophy can also help establish what life-giving disclosure would be like under current social conditions and suggest how fidelity to specific societal principles can contribute to this.

There's a danger, of course, that by emphasizing this task of finding guidelines and openings to truth, social critique will ignore blatant signs of untruth. Ignoring these signs, which are all around us, would defeat the entire socially transformative point of trying to establish what is true. One cannot help people overcome falsehood if one covers up the many ways in which contemporary society is untrue and, in its falsehood, induces widespread suffering. Indeed, the second task of social critique is to identify the roadblocks contemporary society erects to pursuing fidelity to societal principles and achieving life-giving disclosure.

These barriers to the unfolding of truth take three forms, which I label normative deficiencies, structural distortions, and directional dead ends. By *normative deficiencies* I mean the ways in which society in its current organization subverts the meaning of specific societal principles. For example, as Adorno clearly saw, the global capitalist system, measured by both its potential and its failure to remove human and nonhuman suffering, is a deficient economy. But I would want to add that, in light of the societal principle it should uphold, namely, the expectation of resourcefulness, global capitalism is *normatively* deficient. Instead of carefully stewarding human and nonhuman potentials for interconnected flourishing, global capitalism exploits and appropriates them for private profit, usually at the expense of disadvantaged people and vulnerable habitats. Although the capitalist system does not completely ignore the expectation of resourcefulness, its response to this expectation subverts what resourcefulness comes to and thereby burdens other social institutions, whether governmental or civil societal, to compensate for the economic system's normative deficiencies.

Such normative deficiencies both induce and reinforce structural distortions. By *structural distortions* I mean how, within an institutionally differentiated society, some social domains thrive at the expense of others. This especially occurs when wealth and power consolidate in specific sorts of social institutions. In *Art in Public*, for example, I examined how, due to wealth and power becoming concentrated in the capitalist economy and administrative state, the arts continually undergo systemic pressures of hyper-commercialization and performance fetishism.[7] The same systemic pressures impinge on universities and undermine the pursuit of scientific truth. In response to the hegemony of the capitalist economy and administrative state, universities all too frequently not only give in to such pressures but also readily internalize them in their own structures of scholarship, education, governance, and administration.[8] In this manner structural distortions among social domains engender and reinforce structural distortions within them.

Together with normative deficiencies and structural distortions, directional dead ends also block the unfolding of truth. By *directional dead ends* I mean the blockages that arise when society as a whole or a leading sector within it heads in a life-destroying direction, usually with heartfelt allegiances to this direction from those who pursue it. Exposing directional dead ends used to be called ideology critique. It is both necessary for a truth-oriented social critique and controversial. One can see just how controversial it is from the so-called positivist dispute in German sociology mentioned earlier. Adorno questioned what he perceived as Popper's blind endorsement of the late-capitalist status quo, and Popper rejected what he characterized as Adorno's irrational promotion of an illiberal revolution.[9] At bottom, like Adorno's critique of Heidegger, this dispute was a struggle over the direction of society.

Although controversial, such attempts to expose dead ends are necessary. Any philosopher who cares about truth as a whole, as Adorno plainly did, will need to address the direction in which society is headed and challenge tendencies that point it away from what makes for goodness in social life. When these become deeply entrenched in society—as Adorno thought exchange-anchored domination had—then one should not hesitate to call them *societal evil*: deeply entrenched and life-destroying tendencies that are difficult to recognize, to take responsibility for, and to resist. In the end, a truth-oriented social critique must also be a critique of societal evil.

Yet the exposure of normative, structural, and directional barriers to the unfolding of truth is not enough. A truth-oriented social critique also needs to envision how these can be removed. That is its third task, in addition to asking what truth comes to and what blocks its unfolding. Contra Adorno, it does not suffice to say the whole is the false. Contra Hegel, it is not enough to say the true is the whole. The critique must also say how the whole is not wholly false and what a wholly true society would be like. It needs to envision how, if the truth already in society were no longer blocked, truth as a whole would unfold.

As a continually unfolding process, truth as a whole points to a future none of us fully comprehends. Yet, how truth currently unfolds, and how it has unfolded in the past, create possibilities for how it can unfold in the future, and these *can* be understood. They are historical possibilities, tied to the practices and institutions that have come to organize social life as well as the ever-emerging societal principles that current practices and institutions help articulate. Given the current societal formation, with both its openings and its barriers, what historical possibilities does society hold for the future unfolding of truth—that is, for fuller fidelity to societal principles, in dynamic correlation with a more completely life-giving disclosure of society? And, in light of that question, how does society as a whole need to change?

Clearly such questions have a speculative element. Yet the future-oriented envisaging of historical possibilities need not be abstractly utopian. Rather, it can help people imagine a historically achievable society where all Earth's inhabitants more fully flourish—as well as our own part in achieving it.

The threefold task of a truth-oriented social critique, then, is to spell out, with a view to society as a whole, what societal fidelity and life-giving disclosure come to, which barriers block them, and how, in light of genuine historical possibilities, these barriers could be removed. In the pursuit of this task, social critique both aligns itself with artistic truth and makes a political contribution. Like art that is true, a truth-oriented social critique will not only expose injustice, oppression, and unjustifiable power. It will also help us envision new conditions of justice and freedom. Both art and social critique can contribute to a hopeful politics of truth.

Unlike many radical social critics who have become completely disillusioned, Adorno never gave up hope for the humanly promised other of history. Despite stunning atrocities and systemic failures, he never gave up hope, even though he considered the possibilities for such a society to be thoroughly, albeit temporarily, blocked: the thickest context of illusion (*Verblendungszusammenhang*) still carries the promise of truth. I have tried, in a preliminary fashion, to suggest a different way to think about such possibilities. By saying where the unfolding of truth currently occurs, exposing barriers to it, and envisioning their removal, a truth-oriented social critique can help rearticulate the central insights in Adorno's conception of truth.

Hegel once wrote that "it is the nature of truth to prevail when its time has come."[10] Adorno did not share Hegel's confidence. Yet he also did not think that falsehood would triumph. Even in a society that, as a whole, he regarded as false, Adorno embraced the "folly" of not giving up on truth. In the end, the hope of a truth-oriented social critique is to find and foster truth. For "in semblance, nonsemblance is promised" (ND 397/405).

Appendix

Reflections from Damaged Life: Theodor W. Adorno (1903–69)

The subtitle to *Minima Moralia* (1951), Adorno's eloquent book of wartime aphorisms, describes all of his mature writings. They are "reflections from damaged life." Their author was born on September 11, 1903, in Frankfurt am Main, the only child of Oscar Wiesengrund, an assimilated Jewish merchant, and Maria Calvelli-Adorno, a devout Catholic of Corsican descent. Baptized Catholic as Theodor Ludwig Wiesengrund and later confirmed as a Protestant, he grew up in a sheltered and cultured middle-class home. Maria's sister Agathe Calvelli-Adorno lived with his parents and was like a second mother to him. The two sisters were accomplished musicians, Maria a singer and Agathe a singer and pianist. Teddie, as his family and friends called him, learned his passion for music from them. His attachment to Maria and Agathe shows up in the hyphenated name he used as a young adult: Theodor Wiesengrund-Adorno. Later, during the Nazi era, he shortened his Jewish patronym to the initial "W."

Music, Philosophy, and Social Critique

Still in his midteens when the First World War ended, Adorno avoided direct experience of the conflict. Even as a schoolboy, however, he rejected the rampant nationalism and war propaganda that flooded German culture. Soon he would be caught up in the revolutionary fervor spreading across postwar Europe and articulated in the early 1920s by the Western Marxist philosophers Ernst Bloch, Karl Korsch, and Georg Lukács. From these years stem the conviction, which Adorno never lost, that society as a whole needed to be transformed. Or, as *Minima Moralia* puts this, parodying Hegel's *Phenomenology of Spirit,* "The whole is the false."

Having been admitted in 1921 to the recently founded Goethe University Frankfurt, the precocious twenty-one-year-old obtained his philosophy doctorate in 1924. By then he had met the older men who would mentor and collaborate with him in later years, including the writer and film theorist Siegfried Kracauer, the essayist and cultural critic Walter Benjamin, and the philosopher and sociologist Max Horkheimer. A year later Adorno moved to Vienna, his "second home," to pursue his musical passions in the Second Viennese School surrounding Arnold Schoenberg. There he studied composition with Alban Berg and piano with Eduard Steuermann. He also befriended Hanns Eisler, one of Schoenberg's most accomplished students and a musical collaborator of Bertolt Brecht. In later years, after most of these Jewish intellectuals had fled Nazi Germany to the United States, Adorno cowrote a book with Eisler on movie music titled *Composing for the Films* (1947). It was through a circle of radically left-wing artists in Berlin, including Benjamin, Brecht, and Eisler, that Adorno met Gretel Karplus. They married in 1937, shortly before they emigrated to the United States, and remained partners for life.

Adorno was not yet thirty when he completed his second dissertation (*Habilitationsschrift*) and became an instructor (*Privatdozent*) at Frankfurt University. He wrote it on Søren Kierkegaard, under the supervision of the philosophical theologian Paul Tillich. Two years later, the dissertation appeared in book form as *Kierkegaard: Construction of the Aesthetic* on the day that Adolf Hitler came to power. Soon afterward the Nazi regime forced all Jewish faculty members and many left-wing intellectuals out of their university positions across Germany.

Their ranks included the members of Frankfurt Institute for Social Research, collectively known as the Frankfurt School. Founded in 1923 as an independent center for interdisciplinary Marxist scholarship and led after 1930 by its director Max Horkheimer, the Institute included the philosopher Herbert Marcuse, literary sociologist Leo Löwenthal, social psychologist Erich Fromm, and other scholars in economics and political theory. In the 1930s they developed an interdisciplinary research program called Critical Theory. Adorno gave his controversial Benjamin-inspired inaugural lecture, "The Actuality of Philosophy," at the Institute in 1931. It argued that only a radical change in philosophical approach, one neither imitating the social sciences nor aiming at systematic completeness, would suffice for a critical understanding of contemporary society.

Adorno and Benjamin did not become members of the Institute until it had moved to New York City in 1935. Their famous field-shaping debate on the political potential of mass-mediated culture took place in the *Zeitschrift für Sozialforschung* (Journal for Social Research), the Institute's journal of record. Benjamin's essay "The Work of Art in the Age of Mechanical Reproduction" (1935) and Adorno's rejoinder "On the Fetish-Character in Music and the Regression of Listening" (1938) have become classics in cultural studies and related fields. Whereas Benjamin suggested that film as a mass medium has democratic and emancipatory potential, Adorno argued that, for the most part, the entertainment industry simply secures the capitalist status quo.

Wartime Writings

Adorno expanded and deepened this argument in *Dialectic of Enlightenment*, a groundbreaking book he cowrote with Horkheimer in southern California during the Second World War. In it, they set out to explain why a world with so much potential for good had become so unrelentingly bad, why the dawn of enlightenment had become the nightmare of fascism, why the social promise of happiness had been broken. Interweaving philosophy, literary commentary, and social critique, they tried to show that reason, the purported agency of enlightenment, had become irrational. Whereas the purpose of reason was to liberate people, it had instead served to trap them in patterns of blind domination. By not serving its own purpose, and instead serving as a tool for domination, reason had become irrational.

According to Horkheimer and Adorno, blind domination occurs in three tightly interlinked forms: human subjugation of nature, psychological repression, and social exploitation. What drives all three forms in contemporary society is an ever-expanding capitalist economy, wedded to massive state power, and fed by the latest science and technology. Moreover, the contemporary tendency toward such domination has ancient roots.

This diagnosis became definitive for first-generation Critical Theory. It also turned into a target of criticisms from second-generation Critical Theorists, led by Adorno's former assistant Jürgen Habermas. Contrary to some interpretations, the diagnosis in *Dialectic of Enlightenment* does not mean the authors give up on rationality and have no hope for social transformation. Their attempt at a comprehensive critical diagnosis is an exercise of dialectical reason. It aims to recall and project the origin and goal of thought itself, namely, freedom—not blind domination but thoughtful reconciliation, not the subjugation of nature and repression of needs and desires and exploitation of disadvantaged people but rather their liberation. And, within *Dialectic of Enlightenment* itself, their diagnosis yields powerful insights into both the culture industry as "mass deception" and the psycho-social roots of antisemitism in "false projection."

Adorno incorporated such insights into his *Philosophy of New Music* (1949). He also expressed them in *Minima Moralia*, originally presented to Horkheimer as a fiftieth birthday gift in 1945 and then published after they had returned to Frankfurt. Meanwhile Adorno also coauthored *The Authoritarian Personality* (1950), a landmark American study in qualitative social psychology. It identifies antidemocratic tendencies and personality traits among those who incline toward fascism, a project that regains relevance today with the rise of authoritarian populism in supposedly democratic countries.

Postwar Interventions

With the exception of *Minima Moralia*, most of Adorno's wartime works were little-known in postwar Germany. *Dialectic of Enlightenment*, originally published by a Dutch press in 1947, did not receive wide circulation until it was reissued in 1969, the year Adorno died. Yet Adorno himself quickly gained prominence in the 1950s and 1960s as a university professor and public intellectual who continued the trajectory of radical social critique that his wartime works had set. He became the director of the Institute for Social Research when Horkheimer retired; contributed frequently to newspapers, radio, and other public media; and produced one book after another on philosophy, music, literature, sociology, and cultural criticism. He also played a key role in German academic debates.

Perhaps his most famous scholarly interventions were in the positivism dispute in German sociology, which erupted in 1961 when Adorno squared off with Sir Karl Popper over value neutrality in the social sciences, and Adorno's scathing critique of Heideggerian rhetoric, which he published as *The Jargon of Authenticity* in 1964. Whereas Adorno argued against Popper that we cannot separate the idea of scientific truth from the idea of a true society freed from the grip of blind domination, he argued against Heidegger's followers that the source of truth, whether scientific or societal, cannot lie in the purported authenticity of either individual experience or communal life. The stances he took in these debates still speak today, in an allegedly post-truth society riven by various forms of identity politics.

While participating in these debates, Adorno became caught up in intense struggles over university reform. Although a progressive, he found himself on the receiving end of harsh criticisms and dismissive "actions" by his own students. After he called the police in January 1969 to remove student protestors at the Institute for Social Research, they retaliated by disrupting his lectures and trying to humiliate him in public. Eventually he had to cancel his lecture course on dialectical thought, attended by up to one thousand people. It was to be his last lecture course. On vacation with Gretel in Switzerland, Adorno suffered a heart attack and died on August 6, 1969, a month before his sixty-sixth birthday.

Given the wide range of Adorno's interests and the interdisciplinary character of his writings, it is hard to distill what his contributions come to. Perhaps his greatest legacy for philosophers lies in the two books that most absorbed his scholarly attention in the 1960s and overlapped with the courses he was teaching: *Negative Dialectics* (1966) and *Aesthetic Theory*, published posthumously in 1970. Together with a volume he had planned on moral philosophy but did not live to write, these are the books Adorno himself wanted to have "weighed in the balance." Both are complex and uncompromising summations of Adorno's philosophy; the first focused on questions about experience, knowledge, history, and metaphysics, and the second addressing aesthetics, beauty, art, and society.

The two books also work out the implications of Horkheimer and Adorno's wartime social critique for the radical change in philosophical approach already envisioned in Adorno's inaugural lecture of 1931. If, according to *Dialectic of Enlightenment*, the key to contemporary societal regression lies in late capitalism's threefold nexus of blind domination, then the challenge for Adorno's philosophy is to expose such domination and point to an alternative. In *Negative Dialectics* he does this by insisting on nonidentity, dialectics, and the priority of the object. In *Aesthetic Theory* he emphasizes aesthetic modernity, social antithesis, and artistic truth. In each case, what Adorno emphasizes serves not only to uncover the subjugation, repression, and exploitation that pervade late capitalist society but also to gesture toward the possibility of a world free from this domination.

To understand Adorno's philosophy, it helps to know how it stems from his readings of Kant, Hegel, and Marx. Briefly, Adorno agrees with Kant that human knowers constitute the objects of their knowledge. We can know things, according to Kant, only insofar as our fundamental concepts and perceptions make this possible. But according to Adorno, how we know them is governed by deep-seated patterns and trends in society as a whole, such that our knowledge simultaneously does violence to its objects. Adorno's emphasis on society as a whole comes, in turn, from Hegel, with a twist, as we have seen: the totality Hegel claimed to comprehend in truth has become the whole that is untrue. Adorno's understanding of such global falsity comes from Marx's critique of capital, with the proviso that the patterns of exploitation Marx found deep within the economy have, according to Adorno, become the dominant principle in society as a whole. Adorno calls this the exchange principle (*Tauschprinzip*); a society dominated by it is an "exchange society" (*Tauschgesellschaft*).

According to Adorno, the principle of exchange is both highly abstract and all-pervasive in late capitalist society. The principle comes down to the imperative that nothing has value except insofar as it can be exchanged for something else and, in this exchange, generates a profit for those who control the conditions under which exchange occurs. Moreover, exchange is how the threefold nexus of blind domination works. In a late capitalist society, people subjugate nature, repress their needs and desires, and exploit one another by following the principle of exchange. This explains why a society with the potential to mitigate so much suffering continually destroys nature, perpetuates repression, and generates vast disparities and disadvantages in wealth and power.

Negative Dialectics and Aesthetic Theory

That is how Adorno turns a Hegelian Marxist theory of reification, proposed by Georg Lukács in the early 1920s, into the radically social-critical philosophy he calls "negative dialectics." Lukács had argued that capitalist commodification has spread to all of life. Although Adorno agrees, he claims that commodification expresses an even deeper tendency toward domination that works through exchange. To help expose and resist an all-pervasive domination in exchange, Adorno's *Negative Dialectics* sets out to break the grip of identity thinking in modern philosophy, to challenge the project of pinning down the identity of things in concepts. It is through conceptually pinning down identity that philosophy reflects and fosters the societal tendency to treat everything and everyone as exchangeable. According to Adorno, identity thinking fails to honor the ways in which things are not identical with their concepts. Instead, in trying to impose identity, one ignores the diversity and particularity of things. Such identity thinking goes hand in hand with a society whose exchange principle demands the equivalence of all nonequivalents, a society where, for example, even one's most unique qualities can be digitized, stored in databases, and exploited for commercial or political purposes. Adorno persistently criticizes false conceptual identifications in other philosophies. And he tries, using expressive language, to lend a voice to that which is not identical, to what he calls the nonidentical (*das Nichtidentische*).

The alternative to identity thinking lies in negative dialectical thought. Dialectics, as Adorno understands it, is the continual effort to think through the contradictions in thought in order to uncover the tensions and antagonisms in culture and society: class conflicts, economic anomalies, and ecological disasters, to name a few. The point of this, however, is not simply negative. The point is also to gesture toward the possibility of a transformed society, one not fundamentally antagonistic, not pervaded by domination, and not driven by the principle of exchange, a society where thought would shed the compulsion to dominate through conceptual identification. In other words, negative dialectics gestures, however obliquely, toward the possibility of reconciliation.

That is why, in opposition to a philosophical commitment from Kant onward to constitutive subjectivity, Adorno insists on what he calls the "priority of the object" (*Vorrang des Objekts*). A protean phrase, this refers to the dimensions of experience and existence that resist subjugation, repression, and exploitation, the ways in which things are not identical with their concepts, and the worth of matters beyond their exchange value. By insisting on the priority of the object, Adorno wishes to remind us that thought itself is societally constituted, that identity thinking cannot fully grasp what it tries to know, and that, despite the societal pressure to impose conceptual identity on objects, the true goal of thought is to honor objects in their nonidentity. To do this, thought must open itself to the preconceptual layers of experience to which expressive language lends a voice, a mandate Adorno tries to meet in his own writing.

Working on *Aesthetic Theory* in the late 1960s, Adorno became convinced that nonidentity, dialectics, and the priority of the object required a dramatically new mode of textual presentation. Given his subject matter, he could not proceed in a linear fashion, arguing step by step to a final conclusion. Rather, he would need to adopt a paratactical mode of presentation. The resulting text, as edited by Rolf Tiedemann and Gretel Adorno, largely dispenses with explicit coordination among sentences, paragraphs, and passages. Each main section (not really a chapter in the traditional sense) has its own ever-shifting constellation of concepts. This constellation intersects with those in other sections, such that they all shed light on one another and on the book as a whole. Of Adorno's many books, *Aesthetic Theory* comes closest to the ideal of atonal music that he inherited from Schoenberg and the early Second Viennese School: every tone should lie equally close to the center. Together with the fact that Adorno did not live to complete this project, the book's paratactical organization complicates any attempt to interpret it. Let me simply summarize its emphasis on aesthetic modernity, social antithesis, and artistic truth.

Adorno aimed to write a book in which neither philosophy nor art are missing. More specifically, he set out to reconstruct the modern art movement in light of philosophical aesthetics and to reconstruct the tradition of philosophical aesthetics—especially that of Kant and Hegel—from the perspective of modern art. He focuses on modern art for both historical and social-critical reasons. Historically, he thinks the issues and achievements of modern art illuminate all art heretofore, and they raise unavoidable questions about how philosophers in the past have interpreted art. Social-critically, he regards modern art as a unique arena within late capitalist society that challenges the dominance of exchange, giving expression to the nonidentical.

Art, especially modern art, is, he claims, the "social antithesis of society." It holds a mirror up to society even as it points toward a different possibility. In fact, the opposition between art and society is so severe that *Aesthetic Theory* begins and ends with updated Hegelian concerns about the possible death of art: can art even survive in a late capitalist society? Yet Adorno also emphasizes that, within its opposition, art owes its existence and character to the larger society to which it antithetically belongs. Even art's autonomy—the relative independence that allows it to resist—is made possible by the economic and political tendencies art challenges. And that raises updated Marxian questions about whether and how art can help transform society as a whole.

The key to any contribution art can make to social transformation lies in what Adorno calls artistic truth content (*Wahrheitsgehalt*). Autonomous modern works of art are like monads of society as a whole, he claims. The unavoidable tensions within them between content and form give articulation to underlying antagonisms in society as a whole, antagonisms that the culture industry covers up. At the same time, however, because authentic artworks deploy form to accommodate rather than dominate their content, they also suggest ways in which societal antagonisms can be resolved and how blind domination can end. This, however, they can only suggest: actual reconciliation would require economic and political transformations that art as such is powerless to bring about.

Adorno's aesthetics is, of course, richer in detail and insight than a brief summary can indicate. Together with *Negative Dialectics*, which it supplements and assumes, *Aesthetic Theory* marks the culmination of a singular body of work: Adorno's radically critical reflections from damaged life.

Notes

Chapter 1

1. In "Goldmann and Adorno: To Describe, Understand and Explain," appendix 3 to Lucien Goldmann, *Cultural Creation in Modern Society*, trans. Bart Grahl (Oxford: Basil Blackwell, 1976), 142.

2. Adorno's debate with Goldmann, quoted in this chapter's epigraph, took place in 1968 at the second international colloquium on the sociology of literature at Royaumont, France.

3. See the introduction to *Truth in Husserl, Heidegger, and the Frankfurt School: Critical Retrieval* (Cambridge, MA: MIT Press, 2017), 1–16, and the section titled "Metacritique" in *Social Domains of Truth: Science, Politics, Art, and Religion* (New York: Routledge, 2023), 283–86.

4. See especially *Adorno's Aesthetic Theory: The Redemption of Illusion* (Cambridge, MA: MIT Press, 1991) and *Social Philosophy after Adorno* (Cambridge: Cambridge University Press, 2007).

5. Theodor W. Adorno, "Anmerkungen zum philosophischen Denken," in *Stichworte: Kritische Modelle 2*, GS 10.2 (Frankfurt am Main: Suhrkamp, 1977), 598–607, quotation from 604; "Notes on Philosophical Thinking," in *Critical Models: Interventions and Catchwords*, trans. Henry W. Pickford (New York: Columbia University Press, 1998), 127–34, quotation from 131.

6. Walter Benjamin, *Origin of the German Trauerspiel* (1928), trans. Howard Eiland (Cambridge, MA: Harvard University Press, 2019), 10–11. In German the sentence reads, "Die Ideen sind ewige Konstellationen und indem die Elemente als Punkte in derartigen Konstellationen effasst werden, sind die Phänomene aufgeteilt und gerettet zugleich." Walter Benjamin, *Ursprung des deutschen Trauerspiels* (Frankfurt am Main: Suhrkamp Taschenbuch, 1978), 17.

7. On this point, see Simon Jarvis, *Adorno: A Critical Introduction* (New York: Routledge, 1998), 175–76. For more extensive accounts of Adorno's indebtedness to and departures from Benjamin's account of truth and other ideas as constellations, see Susan Buck-Morss, *The Origin of Negative Dialectics: Theodor W. Adorno, Walter*

Benjamin, and the Frankfurt Institute (Hassocks, Sussex, UK: Harvester Press, 1977), 77–81, 90–95; Richard Wolin, *Walter Benjamin: An Aesthetic of Redemption* (New York: Columbia University Press, 1982); and especially David Kaufmann, "Correlations, Constellations and the Truth: Adorno's Ontology of Redemption," *Philosophy and Social Criticism* 26, no. 5 (2000): 62–80.

    8. Alison Stone, "Adorno and Logic," in *Theodor Adorno: Key Concepts*, ed. Deborah Cook (Stocksfield, UK: Acumen, 2008), 59. Stone shows how Adorno's approach not only takes issue with Hegel but also involves tensions between the notions of *conceptual* and *objectual* constellations.

    9. Kaufmann, "Correlations, Constellations and the Truth," 73. Kaufmann argues that "the reflection of transcendence that reveals the truth of the object is a constant [Benjamin-inspired] motif in Adorno's thought" (74).

    10. Adorno, "Anmerkungen," 601; "Notes," 129.

    11. Adorno, "Anmerkungen," 604; "Notes," 131.

    12. Owen Hulatt, *Adorno's Theory of Philosophical and Aesthetic Truth* (New York: Columbia University Press, 2016), 86–88.

    13. Hulatt, *Adorno's Theory*, 92.

    14. Hulatt, *Adorno's Theory*, 98–104.

    15. Kaufmann, "Correlations, Constellations and the Truth," 72, 75.

    16. Fabian Freyenhagen, *Adorno's Practical Philosophy: Living Less Wrongly* (Cambridge: Cambridge University Press, 2013), 52–53, 65, and passim.

    17. Freyenhagen, *Adorno's Practical Philosophy*, 4–5.

    18. Freyenhagen, *Adorno's Practical Philosophy*, 7, 209.

    19. Freyenhagen, *Adorno's Practical Philosophy*, 210–14.

    20. Freyenhagen, *Adorno's Practical Philosophy*, 226–28. Although Freyenhagen says utopian elements such as "the experiences involved in art, theology, and metaphysics" also "provide us with the strength" to see that things ought to be different (228), I do not think he explains how.

    21. Kaufmann, "Correlations, Constellations and the Truth," 75–76.

    22. Kaufmann, "Correlations, Constellations and the Truth," 77.

    23. In this connection, see Roger S. Foster's discussion of Adorno's approach to philosophical interpretation in chapter 3 ("The Internal History of Truth") of *Adorno and Philosophical Modernism: The Inside of Things* (Lanham, MD: Lexington Books, 2016), 133–65.

    24. Iain Macdonald, *What Would Be Different: Figures of Possibility in Adorno* (Stanford, CA: Stanford University Press, 2019), 103–56.

Chapter 2

A first draft of this chapter was presented at "Adorno's *Negative Dialectics* at Fifty," a conference organized by Peter Gordon and Max Pensky and held at Harvard

University on November 18–19, 2016. I thank the conference organizers for their invitation and the conference participants for their inspiring conversation. Later versions were presented in March 2017 at the annual meeting of the Association for Adorno Studies at Duke University organized by Henry Pickford and on November 3, 2017, to the Philosophy Colloquium led by Andrew Spear at Grand Valley State University. Again, my thanks go to the event organizers for their invitations and to the participants for their instructive comments and questions.

1. I take the cue for this reading from Albrecht Wellmer, "Metaphysics at the Moment of Its Fall," in *Endgame: The Irreconcilable Nature of Modernity; Essays and Lectures*, trans. David Midgley (Cambridge, MA: MIT Press, 1998), 183–201, even though I have significant reservations about Wellmer's interpretation and critique of Adorno. See Lambert Zuidervaart, *Social Philosophy after Adorno* (Cambridge: Cambridge University Press, 2007), 48–76.

2. Quoted in Peter E. Gordon, *Adorno and Existence* (Cambridge, MA: Harvard University Press, 2016), 159.

3. Gordon, *Adorno and Existence,* 160.

4. Deborah Cook, "Through a Glass Darkly: Adorno's Inverse Theology," *Adorno Studies* 1, no. 1 (January 2017): 66–78.

5. For a recent collection of essays on this topic, see Maxi Berger and Philip Hogh, eds., *Der Vorrang des Objekts: Negative Dialektik heute* (Berlin: J. B. Metzler, 2022).

6. Brian O'Connor, *Adorno's Negative Dialectics: Philosophy and the Possibility of Critical Rationality* (Cambridge, MA: MIT Press, 2004), 45–98.

7. Andrew Bowie, *Adorno and the Ends of Philosophy* (Cambridge: Polity, 2013), 38–74.

8. See Axel Honneth, *Reification: A New Look at an Old Idea*, ed. Martin Jay (Oxford: Oxford University Press, 2008).

9. See "Performing Justice: Adorno's Introduction to *Negative Dialectics*," in Axel Honneth, *Pathologies of Reason*, trans. James Ingram et al. (New York: Columbia University Press, 2009), 71–87.

10. "Truth and Authentication: Heidegger and Adorno in Reverse," chapter 4 in Lambert Zuidervaart, *Truth in Husserl, Heidegger, and the Frankfurt School: Critical Retrieval* (Cambridge, MA: MIT Press, 2017), 77–101.

11. Theodor W. Adorno, *Metaphysics: Concept and Problems* (1965), ed. Rolf Tiedemann, trans. Edmund Jephcott (Stanford, CA: Stanford University Press, 2000), 132–33.

12. Iain Macdonald, "Adorno's Modal Utopianism: Possibility and Actuality in Adorno and Hegel," *Adorno Studies* 1, no. 1 (January 2017): 1–12.

13. Adorno, *Metaphysics*, 142.

14. Zuidervaart, *Social Philosophy after Adorno*, 66–69, 98–101.

15. Martin Shuster, *Autonomy after Auschwitz: Adorno, German Idealism, and Modernity* (Chicago, IL: University of Chicago Press, 2014).

16. Immanuel Kant, *Critique of Practical Reason*, in Immanuel Kant, *Practical Philosophy*, trans. and ed. Mary J. Gregor (Cambridge: Cambridge University Press, 1996), 228–58; AK 5:110–48.

17. Part of the difficulty here is that Adorno and Horkheimer might have different views of reason in history. Espen Hammer has given good reasons to regard Habermas's presupposition as incorrect with respect to Adorno—see the discussion of "reason and domination" in *Adorno's Modernism: Art, Experience, and Catastrophe* (Cambridge: Cambridge University Press, 2015), 32–44. Martin Jay has given equally good reasons to consider Habermas's presupposition more or less correct with respect to Horkheimer, especially in Horkheimer's *Eclipse of Reason*—see the chapter titled "The Critique of Instrumental Reason: Horkheimer, Marcuse, and Adorno" in *Reason after Its Eclipse: On Late Critical Theory* (Madison: University of Wisconsin Press, 2016), 97–113. And I have taken issue with Habermas's *The Theory of Communicative Action* and *The Philosophical Discourse of Modernity* for giving reductionist readings of both Horkheimer and Adorno's critique of reason—see the chapter titled "Globalizing Dialectic of Enlightenment" in Zuidervaart, *Social Philosophy after Adorno*, 107–31.

18. That is my loose translation of the following passage in Max Horkheimer, *Die Sehnsucht nach dem ganz Anderen: Ein Interview mit Kommentar von Helmut Gumnior* (Hamburg: Furche-Verlag, 1970), 61–62: "Theologie ist . . . die Hoffnung, dass es bei diesem Unrecht, durch das die Welt gekennzeichnet ist, nicht bleibe, dass das Unrecht nicht das letzte Wort sein möge. . . . [Theologie ist] Ausdruck einer Sehnsucht, einer Sehnsucht danach, dass der Mörder nicht über das unschuldige Opfer triumphieren möge."

19. Zuidervaart, *Social Philosophy after Adorno*, 70–76.

20. See Ernst Tugendhat, "Heidegger's Idea of Truth," in *The Heidegger Controversy: A Critical Reader*, ed. Richard Wolin, 2nd ed. (Cambridge, MA: MIT Press, 1991), 245–63.

21. For an eloquent and comprehensive account, see Oshrat C. Silberbusch, *Adorno's Philosophy of the Nonidentical: Thinking as Resistance* (Cham, Switzerland: Springer, Palgrave Macmillan, 2018).

22. Hammer, *Adorno's Modernism*, 106.

23. Hammer, *Adorno's Modernism*, 112.

24. Hammer, *Adorno's Modernism*, 115, 117.

25. Owen Hulatt, *Adorno's Theory of Philosophical and Aesthetic Truth* (New York: Columbia University Press), 27–104.

26. Philip Hogh, *Communication and Expression: Adorno's Philosophy of Language*, trans. Antonia Hofstätter (London: Rowman & Littlefield International), 98–101.

27. Hogh, *Communication and Expression*, 101–3.

28. Hogh, *Communication and Expression*, 109.

29. Hogh, *Communication and Expression*, 113.

30. Gordon, *Adorno and Existence*, 11.

Chapter 3

A first draft of this chapter was presented at the Fifth Annual Meeting of the Association for Adorno Studies at the Université de Montréal in 2016. I thank Iain Macdonald for the invitation to present it and the conference participants for their engaged and constructive conversations. I also acknowledge with gratitude the instructive comments I subsequently received from two anonymous referees for *Symposium: Canadian Journal of Continental Philosophy*.

1. See, for example, the use of Adorno's essay "Subject-Object" to explicate his "atonal philosophy" in Martin Jay, *Adorno* (London: Fontana Paperbacks, 1984), 56–81.

2. See especially Jürgen Habermas, *The Theory of Communicative Action*, trans. Thomas McCarthy (Boston, MA: Beacon Press, 1984), 1:366–99. For a brief and helpful discussion of Habermas's critique of Adorno, see Brian O'Connor, *Adorno's Negative Dialectic: Philosophy and the Possibility of Critical Rationality* (Cambridge, MA: MIT Press, 2004), 165–70.

3. O'Connor, *Adorno's Negative Dialectic*, 15–43.

4. For an illuminating overview of Adorno's decades-long engagement with Husserlian phenomenology and Heideggerian ontology prior to *Negative Dialectics*, see chapter 2 ("Ontology and Phenomenology") in Peter E. Gordon, *Adorno and Existence* (Cambridge, MA: Harvard University Press, 2016), 37–83.

5. Because Adorno's criticism tends to conflate Husserl's early conception of categorial intuition and later conception of eidetic intuition, arguably he fails to do justice to Husserl's extensive and painstaking work on the latter.

6. Cf. *Logische Untersuchungen*, vol. 2, found in Edmund Husserl, *Husserliana*, vol. 19 (The Hague: Martinus Nijhoff, 1984), 669–70; trans. J. N. Findlay as *Logical Investigations*, ed. Dermot Moran (London: Routledge, 1970, 2001), 2:279–80.

7. For purposes of focus, my summary ignores the fact that Adorno seems to restrict Husserl's notion of intentionality to signitive acts, even though Husserl also plainly regards intuitive and meaning-fulfilling acts as intentional.

8. The lectures in *Ontologie and Dialektik* bear out the strong connection Adorno sees between Husserl's "categorial intuition" and "eidetic intuition," on the one hand, and Heidegger's conception of Being, on the other. The first lecture ends with a paragraph (omitted in the English translation) that calls Husserl's notion of a direct, intuitive "consciousness of essence" the presupposition for all of Heidegger's philosophy (OD 21). Lectures 6 and 18 return to this point, elaborate it, and refer to Adorno's own discussion of Husserl's categorial intuition in *Zur Metakritik der Erkenntnistheorie*—see OD 89–93/58–61 and 262–75/186–95. See also the portion of lecture 19 (OD 281–85/200–203) that parallels the section titled "On Categorial Intuition" in *Negative Dialectics* (ND 87–90/80–83).

9. I discuss this account at greater length in *Truth in Husserl, Heidegger, and the Frankfurt School: Critical Retrieval* (Cambridge, MA: MIT Press, 2017), 19–45, 125–46.

10. Husserl, *Husserliana* 19: 667–70; *Logical Investigations* 2:278–80.

11. Indeed, the phrase "medium of exemplary thought" points to Adorno's emphasis on constructing constellations of concepts and fashioning dialectical models of thought, as alternatives to both deductive systems and inductive histories. See the insightful discussion of Adorno's constellations and models in Martin Shuster, *Autonomy after Auschwitz: Adorno, German Idealism, and Modernity* (Chicago, IL: University of Chicago Press, 2014), 172–74.

12. Here Adorno's term "existential judgment" (*Existentialurteil*) designates a judgment in which something is claimed to exist or to exist in a certain way. It does not refer to Heidegger's notion of the ontological "existentials" (*Existenzialien*) that constitute Dasein's Being-in-the-world.

13. Parallel passages in Adorno's lectures on *Ontology and Dialectics* label this ontic meaning of the copula "synsemantic," as distinct from "autosemantic." For this terminology, Adorno cites Oskar Kraus's introduction to the first volume of Franz Brentano's *Psychologie vom empirischen Standpunkt* (Leipzig: Felix Meiner, 1924). The lectures contrast the "synsemantic" meaning of the copula with the copula's "syntactic" function as a universal form of judgment. See OD 298–309/213–22.

14. See Immanuel Kant, *Critique of Pure Reason*, trans. and ed. Paul Guyer and Allen W. Wood (Cambridge: Cambridge University Press, 1998), 366–83; A 260–92/B316–49. In his 1959 lectures on Kant's First Critique, Adorno had already claimed that the amphiboly chapter provides Kant's solution "to what nowadays has become the fashionable problem of *Being*" (K 60/36).

15. Kant, *Critique of Pure Reason*, 371; A270/B326.

16. Kant points instead to the following relations between concepts, always with reference to how the objects of the concepts are presented to us: identity and difference, agreement and opposition, the inner and the outer, and the determinable and the determination (matter and form). Kant, *Critique of Pure Reason*, 367–70; A261–68/B317–24.

17. Kant, *Critique of Pure Reason*, 563–69; A592–602/B620–39. See also Adorno's brief comments on this passage, which he says is "of such outstanding importance" in Kant's First Critique (K 68–69/41–42).

18. Kant, *Critique of Pure Reason*, 567; A598–99/B626–27.

19. Adorno alludes to this work in his lectures on Kant's First Critique but does not really discuss it. See K 58/35, 324/214.

20. Originally a lecture in 1961 and published in 1962 and 1963, "Kants These über das Sein" is the last chapter in Martin Heidegger, *Wegmarken* (Frankfurt am Main: Vittorio Klostermann, 1967), 445–80. References are to the third edition of 1996, itself based on the second edition in Heidegger's Gesamtausgabe, vol. 9 (1978), and to "Kant's Thesis about Being" in *Pathmarks*, ed. William McNeill (Cambridge: Cambridge University Press, 1998), 337–63. So far as I can tell, Adorno never refers to this essay.

21. Heidegger, *Wegmarken*, 480; *Pathmarks*, 363.

22. Heidegger, *Wegmarken*, 455; *Pathmarks*, 344–45.

23. Kant, *Critique of Pure Reason*, 251; B141–42. Heidegger quotes this passage in *Wegmarken*, 459; *Pathmarks*, 347 (but in the Kemp Smith translation).

24. Heidegger, *Wegmarken*, 460; *Pathmarks*, 348.

25. Heidegger, *Wegmarken*, 462; *Pathmarks*, 350.

26. See Kant, *Critique of Pure Reason*, 321–26; A218–26/B265–74.

27. Heidegger, *Wegmarken*, 467; *Pathmarks*, 353.

28. Heidegger, *Wegmarken*, 473; *Pathmarks*, 358.

29. Heidegger, *Wegmarken*, 479; *Pathmarks*, 362–63.

30. This distinction in types of synthesis is not explicated in the passages under consideration, however.

31. See chapter 3 in *Truth in Husserl, Heidegger, and the Frankfurt School*, 47–73.

Chapter 4

Excerpts from a first draft of this chapter were presented in an online book session on Iain Macdonald's *What Would Be Different: Figures of Possibility in Adorno* at the annual conference of the Society for Phenomenology and Existential Philosophy on September 24, 2021. I thank Iain and my fellow commentator, Krzysztof Ziarek, for a productive and instructive discussion.

1. Letter to Gershom Scholem dated April 25, 1930, in *The Correspondence of Walter Benjamin, 1910–1940*, ed. Gershom Scholem and Theodor W. Adorno, trans. Manfred R. Jacobson and Evelyn M. Jacobson (Chicago, IL: University of Chicago Press, 1994), 365. Referring to his fellow Berliner Bertolt Brecht, Benjamin writes, "We were planning to annihilate Heidegger here in the summer in the context of a very close-knit critical circle of readers led by Brecht and me."

2. "I have never read anything of his. Hermann Mörchen once tried to convince me to read Adorno. I didn't." Martin Heidegger, as quoted by Richard Wisser, "Afterthoughts and Gratitude," in Günther Neske and Emil Kettering, eds., *Martin Heidegger and National Socialism: Questions and Answers* (New York: Paragon House, 1990), 89–124, quotation from 117. In this piece Wisser tells about his television interview with Heidegger on September 17, 1969 (broadcast a week later on September 24), as well as the conversations he had with Heidegger before and after the interview was filmed. The translated transcript of the television interview appears in the same volume under the title "Martin Heidegger in Conversation with Richard Wisser" (81–87). The interview's audio track, with English subtitles, is available on YouTube at https://www.youtube.com/watch?v=vcm05b8m6tQ.

3. See Herman Mörchen, *Adorno und Heidegger: Untersuchung einer philosophischen Kommunikationsverweigerung* (Stuttgart: Klett-Cotta, 1981), 13. Kurt Riezler represented the "ontological position" in the "Frankfurt discussion" mentioned several times in Adorno's 1932 lecture "The Idea of Natural History," which also directly

cites Riezler. Besides Adorno and Riezler, other discussion partners included Paul Tillich, Max Horkheimer, Friedrich Pollock, and Karl Mannheim, according to Dieter Thomä, "Verhältnis zur Ontologie: Adornos Denken des Unbegrifflichen," in *Theodor W. Adorno: Negative Dialektik*, ed. Axel Honneth and Christoph Menke (Berlin: Akademie, 2006), 29–48. Mikko Immanen, *Toward a Concrete Philosophy: Heidegger and the Emergence of the Frankfurt School* (Ithaca, NY: Cornell University Press and Cornell University Library, 2020) shows in convincing detail how Adorno's debates in the early 1930s with the "Frankfurt Heideggerians" (i.e., Riezler, Tillich, and the psychologist Max Wertheimer) helped set the trajectory of Adorno's philosophy.

4. Mörchen, *Adorno und Heidegger*. See also the preliminary study by Hermann Mörchen, *Macht und Herrschaft im Denken von Heidegger und Adorno* (Stuttgart: Klett-Cotta, 1980). Fred Dallmayr summarizes and comments on the former volume in "Adorno and Heidegger," *Diacritics* 19, no. 3–4 (1989): 82–100. The same essay appears as chapter 2 in Fred Dallmayr, *Between Freiburg and Frankfurt: Toward a Critical Ontology* (Amherst: University of Massachusetts Press, 1991), 44–71. Dallmayr had already signaled the importance of sorting out Adorno's critique of Heidegger in Fred Dallmayr, "Phenomenology and Critical Theory: Adorno," *Cultural Hermeneutics* 3 (1976): 367–405.

5. Jürgen Habermas, *The Philosophical Discourse of Modernity: Twelve Lectures* (1985), trans. Frederick G. Lawrence (Cambridge, MA: MIT Press, 1987).

6. In chronological order, see, for example, Hauke Brunkhorst, "Adorno, Heidegger and Postmodernity," *Philosophy and Social Criticism* 14, no. 3–4 (1989): 411–24; J. M. Bernstein, *The Fate of Art: Aesthetic Alienation from Kant to Derrida and Adorno* (University Park: Pennsylvania State University Press, 1992); Tom Huhn, "The Movement of Mimesis: Heidegger's 'Origin of the Work of Art' in Relation to Adorno and Lyotard," *Philosophy and Social Criticism* 22, no. 4 (July 1996): 45–69; Michael Bauer, "Adorno and Heidegger on Art in the Modern World," *Philosophy Today* 40, no. 3 (Fall 1996): 357–66; Andrew Bowie, "Adorno, Heidegger, and the Meaning of Music," *Thesis Eleven* 56 (1999): 1–24; and Oliver Garbrecht, *Rationalitätskritik der Moderne: Adorno und Heidegger* (Munich: Herbert Utz, 1999).

7. Again in chronological order, see Ute Guzzoni, *Identität oder nicht: Zur Kritischen Theorie der Ontologie* (Freiburg/Munich: Verlag Karl Alber, 1981); Herbert Schnädelbach, "Dialektik als Vernunftkritik: Zur Konstruktion des Rationalen bei Adorno," in *Adorno-Konferenz 1983*, ed. Ludwig von Friedeburg and Jürgen Habermas (Frankfurt am Main: Suhrkamp, 1983), 66–93; Jürgen Naeher, "Das ontologische 'Bedürfnis im Denken'; Der Erste Teil der *Negativen Dialektik* (67–136): Zum Verfahren der 'immanenten Kritik,' " in *Die Negative Dialektik Adornos: Einführung—Dialog*, ed. Jürgen Naeher (Opladen: Leske Verlag + Budrich, 1984), 204–34; Sabine Wilke, *Zur Dialektik von Exposition und Darstellung: Ansätze zu einer Kritik der Arbeiten Martin Heideggers, Theodor W. Adornos, und Jacques Derridas* (New York and Frankfurt am Main: Peter Lang, 1988); the essays by Josef Früchtl and Adolf Polti in Forum für Philosophie Bad Homburg, ed., *Martin Heidegger:*

Innen- und Aussenansichten (Frankfurt am Main: Suhrkamp, 1989); Alexander Garcia Düttmann, *Das Gedächtnis des Denkens: Versuch über Heidegger und Adorno* (Frankfurt am Main: Suhrkamp, 1991), trans. Nicholas Walker as *The Memory of Thought: An Essay on Heidegger and Adorno* (London: Continuum, 2002); and Brian O'Connor, "Adorno, Heidegger and the Critique of Epistemology," *Philosophy and Social Criticism* 24, no. 4 (1998): 43–62.

8. These include the German publication of two massive biographies in 2003, subsequently published in English as Stefan Müller-Doohm, *Adorno: A Biography*, trans. Rodney Livingstone (Cambridge: Polity, 2005); and Detlev Claussen, *Theodor W. Adorno: One Last Genius*, trans. Rodney Livingstone (Cambridge, MA: Belknap Press of Harvard University Press, 2008). Especially important in the English-speaking world was a three-day conference held at the Université de Montréal in 2004, which led to the publication of *Adorno and Heidegger: Philosophical Questions*, ed. Iain Macdonald and Krzysztof Ziarek (Stanford, CA: Stanford University Press, 2008). For additional information on publications listed in previous notes as well as other secondary literature about the Adorno-Heidegger debate, see the bibliography in Macdonald and Ziarek, eds., *Adorno and Heidegger*, 209–13.

9. Published posthumously as volumes in Adorno's *Nachgelassene Schriften*, these lecture courses, in their original chronological sequence, are Theodor W. Adorno, *Ontologie und Dialektik (1960/61)*, NS IV.7, ed. Rolf Tiedemann (Frankfurt am Main: Suhrkamp, 2002), trans. Nicholas Walker as *Ontology and Dialectics 1960/61* (Cambridge: Polity, 2019); *Zur Lehre von der Geschichte und von der Freiheit* (1964/65), NS IV.13, ed. Rolf Tiedemann (Frankfurt am Main: Suhrkamp, 2001), trans. Rodney Livingstone as *History and Freedom: Lectures 1964–1965* (Cambridge: Polity, 2006); Metaphysik: *Begriff und Probleme* (1965), NS IV.14, ed. Rolf Tiedemann (Frankfurt am Main: Suhrkamp, 1998), trans. Edmund Jephcott as *Metaphysics: Concept and Problems* (Stanford, CA: Stanford University Press, 2000); and *Vorlesung über Negative Dialektik: Fragmente zur Vorlesung 1965/66*, NS IV.16, ed. Rolf Tiedemann (Frankfurt am Main: Suhrkamp, 2003), trans. Rodney Livingstone as *Lectures on Negative Dialectics: Fragments of a Lecture Course 1965/1966* (Cambridge: Polity, 2008).

10. Of special note was "Adorno's *Negative Dialectics* at Fifty," a conference organized by Peter Gordon and Max Pensky and held at Harvard University on November 18–19, 2016. Although it did not result in a conference publication, many leading Adorno scholars from the German- and English-speaking worlds gave papers there.

11. In chronological order, see, for example, Udo Tietz, *Ontologie und Dialektik: Heidegger und Adorno über das Sein, das Nichtidentische, die Synthesis und die Kopula* (Vienna: Passagen, 2003); Samir Gandesha, "Leaving Home: On Adorno and Heidegger," in *The Cambridge Companion to Adorno*, ed. Tom Huhn (Cambridge: Cambridge University Press, 2004), 101–28; Thomä, "Verhältnis zur Ontologie"; Iain Macdonald, " 'What Is, Is More Than It Is': Adorno and Heidegger

on the Priority of Possibility," *International Journal of Philosophical Studies* 19, no. 1 (2011): 31–57; Peter E. Gordon, *Adorno and Existence* (Cambridge, MA: Harvard University Press, 2016), especially 37–157; Iain Macdonald, *What Would Be Different: Figures of Possibility in Adorno* (Stanford, CA: Stanford University Press, 2019), especially 103–56; Espen Hammer, "Adorno's Critique of Heidegger," in *A Companion to Adorno*, ed. Peter E. Gordon, Espen Hammer, and Max Pensky (Hoboken, NJ: Wiley Blackwell, 2020), 473–86; and Immanen, *Toward a Concrete Philosophy*, especially 113–201.

12. Here I would include the following monographs, again in chronological order: Simon Jarvis, *Adorno: A Critical Introduction* (New York: Routledge, 1998), 199–207; J. M. Bernstein, *Adorno: Disenchantment and Ethics* (Cambridge: Cambridge University Press, 2001), 420–29; Brian O'Connor, *Adorno's Negative Dialectic: Philosophy and the Possibility of Critical Rationality* (Cambridge, MA: MIT Press, 2004), 127–64; Lambert Zuidervaart, *Social Philosophy after Adorno* (Cambridge: Cambridge University Press, 2007), 77–106; Roger S. Foster, *Adorno and Philosophical Modernism: The Inside of Things* (Lanham, MD: Lexington Books, 2016), 51–132. Also of interest is Nikolas Kompridis, *Critique and Disclosure: Critical Theory between Past and Future* (Cambridge, MA: MIT Press, 2007). Although he focuses on Habermas rather than Adorno, Kompridis appeals to Heidegger's conception of world disclosure in order to move Critical Theory away from Habermas and in the direction of Adorno.

13. Emmanuel Faye, *Heidegger: The Introduction of Nazism into Philosophy in Light of the Unpublished Seminars of 1933–1935* (2005), trans. Michael B. Smith (New Haven, CT: Yale University Press, 2009). See also the debates over Faye's book in Gregory Fried, ed., *Confronting Heidegger: A Critical Dialogue on Politics and Philosophy* (London: Rowman & Littlefield International, 2020).

14. For an attempt to contextualize these notebooks with respect to Heidegger's published work by the scholar who edited them for Heidegger's *Gesamtausgabe*, see Peter Trawny, *Heidegger: A Critical Introduction* (2016), trans. Rodrigo Therezo (Cambridge: Polity, 2019). For an extensive critique of Trawny for his either covering up or excusing Heidegger's Nazism and antisemitism, see Richard Wolin, "On Heidegger's Antisemitism: The Peter Trawny Affair," *Antisemitism Studies* 1, no. 2 (2017): 245–79.

15. Victor Farias, *Heidegger and Nazism* (1987), ed. Joseph Margolis and Tom Rockmore (Philadelphia: Temple University Press, 1989). Pierre Bourdieu, *The Political Ontology of Martin Heidegger* (1988), trans. Peter Collier (Stanford, CA: Stanford University Press, 1991)—a reissued book that Bourdieu first published in 1975. For a thorough study of the debates before they reignited in the 2000s, see Tom Rockmore, *On Heidegger's Nazism and Philosophy* (Berkeley: University of California Press, 1992). For key documents in this controversy, see Richard Wolin, ed., *The Heidegger Controversy: A Critical Reader*, 2nd ed. (Cambridge, MA: MIT Press, 1991).

16. Adam Knowles, *Heidegger's Fascist Affinities: A Politics of Silence* (Stanford, CA: Stanford University Press, 2019). The neglect of Adorno in these debates is all the more peculiar given his role in producing *The Authoritarian Personality* (1950), a major social-psychological study published long before Heidegger became a source of inspiration for contemporary authoritarian populist movements and regimes, according to Beiner. See Ronald Beiner, *Dangerous Minds: Nietzsche, Heidegger, and the Return of the Far Right* (Philadelphia: University of Pennsylvania Press, 2018).

17. "Die Aktualität der Philosophie" (1931), "Die Idee der Naturgeschichte" (1932), and "Thesen über die Sprache des Philosophen" (1932?), all in Adorno, GS 1 (Frankfurt am Main: Suhrkamp, 1973), 325–44, 345–65, and 366–71, respectively. In English as "The Actuality of Philosophy," trans. Benjamin Snow, *Telos* 31 (Spring 1977): 120–33; "The Idea of Natural History," trans. Robert Hullot-Kentor, *Telos*, no. 60 (Summer 1984): 111–24; and "Theses on the Language of the Philosopher," trans. Samir Gandesha and Michael K. Palamarek, in *Adorno and the Need in Thinking: New Critical Essays*, ed. Donald A. Burke et al. (Toronto: University of Toronto Press, 2007), 35–40. See also the discussions of these early works by Palamarek, Gandesha, and Kathy Kiloh in this same volume, 41–77, 78–102, and 103–29, respectively.

18. Theodor W. Adorno, *Kierkegaard: Konstruktion des Ästhetischen* (1933), GS 2 (Frankfurt am Main: Suhrkamp, 1979); trans. Robert Hullot-Kentor as *Kierkegaard: Construction of the Aesthetic* (Minneapolis: University of Minnesota Press, 1989).

19. Eventually assembled into Theodor W. Adorno, *Zur Metakritik der Erkenntnistheorie: Studien über Husserl und die phänomenologischen Antinomien* (1956), in GS 5 (Frankfurt am Main: Suhrkamp, 1970), 7–245; trans. Willis Domingo as *Against Epistemology: A Metacritique; Studies in Husserl and the Phenomenological Antinomies* (Cambridge, MA: MIT Press, 1982).

20. In addition to the four lecture courses cited earlier, the following are also relevant for Adorno's Heidegger critique: *Einführung in die Dialektik (1958)*, NS IV.2, ed. Christoph Ziermann (Berlin: Suhrkamp, 2010), trans. Nicholas Walker as *An Introduction to Dialectics (1958)* (Cambridge: Polity, 2017); *Kants "Kritik der reinen Vernunft" (1959)*, NS IV.4, ed. Rolf Tiedemann (Frankfurt am Main: Suhrkamp, 1995), trans. Rodney Livingstone as *Kant's "Critique of Pure Reason"* (1959) (Stanford, CA: Stanford University Press, 2001); and *Philosophische Terminologie I und II* (1962/63), NS IV.9, ed. Henri Lonitz (Frankfurt am Main: Suhrkamp, 2016).

21. Theodor W. Adorno, *Jargon der Eigentlichkeit: Zur deutschen Ideologie* (1964), in GS 6 (Frankfurt am Main: Suhrkamp, 1973), 413–526; trans. Knut Tarnowski and Frederic Will as *The Jargon of Authenticity* (London: Routledge & Kegan Paul, 1973).

22. The first two Paris lectures, like the corresponding chapters in *Negative Dialectics* part 1, are titled "The Ontological Need" and "Being and Existence." Lectures 22B–23 in *Ontology and Dialectics* (OD 325–41/235–49) mostly replicate the third Paris lecture, titled "Negative Dialectics," and they are the source material

for several long sections in *Negative Dialectics* part 2 ("Negative Dialectics: Concept and Categories"), specifically, ND 140–46/137–43 and 178–87/176–86. For details, see the editor's foreword in OD 419–31/xi–xxi.

23. For an exhaustive review of the Heidegger citations in all of Adorno's writings (excluding his posthumous works), see Mörchen, *Adorno und Heidegger*, 31–136. Mörchen concludes that Adorno's selection of passages and works is "one-sided and arbitrary," ignoring not only much within the writings cited but also some of Heidegger's most important works (133).

24. After revising and expanding this letter, Heidegger published it along with "Platons Lehre von der Wahrheit" ("Plato's Doctrine of Truth") in 1947. Later he incorporated both the letter and the essay into his 1967 volume *Wegmarken* (*Pathmarks*). Adorno mostly cites from the second edition: Martin Heidegger, *Platons Lehre von der Wahrheit: Mit einem Brief über den "Humanismus,"* 2nd ed. (Bern: A. Francke AG, 1954).

25. "In his references to Heidegger's *Letter on 'Humanism'* (1946) Adorno mistakenly refers to *Plato's Doctrine of Truth*. According to Heidegger, the latter text was delivered as a lecture in 1930/31 and was first published in 1942, whereas the *Letter on 'Humanism'* first appeared as an 'appendix' in a 1947 Swiss edition of *Plato's Doctrine of Truth*. Adorno appears to have regarded these two texts as a single work, which is neither philologically nor philosophically justifiable" (OD 378n165/277n11).

26. In the German edition, see endnotes 3, 12, 14, and 21–23 to part 1, chapter 1, and endnotes 9–12 and 18 to part 1, chapter 2; the equivalent endnotes in the English edition are 3, 11, 13, and 20–22 for chapter 1, and 10–13 and 19 for chapter 2 (ND 403–5/410–12).

27. See "Skoteinos oder Wie zu lesen sei" ("Skoteinos, or How to Read Hegel"), chapter 3 in H 326–75/89–148.

28. See also the long endnote in which Rolf Tiedemann explains "immanent critique" as the "methodological centre" of Adorno's philosophy: OD 348–49n6/252–53n6.

29. For a contrary view, specifically concerning part 1 of *Negative Dialectics*, see Naeher, "Das ontologische 'Bedürfnis im Denken.' "

30. Gordon, *Adorno and Existence*, 121.

31. Gordon Finlayson, "A Critical Notice of *Adorno and Existence*," *International Journal of Philosophical Studies* 25, no. 5 (2017): 723–30, quotations from 728.

32. See, for example, Espen Hammer, *Philosophy and Temporality from Kant to Critical Theory* (Cambridge: Cambridge University Press, 2011); and John McCumber, *Time and Philosophy: A History of Continental Thought* (Montreal: McGill-Queen's University Press, 2011).

33. Thomä, "Verhältnis zur Ontologie," 46.

34. On the history of Western truth theories, see Richard Campbell, *Truth and Historicity* (Oxford: Clarendon Press, 1992).

35. See especially the chapter titled "Propositions, Time, and Eternity" in Wolfgang Künne, *Conceptions of Truth* (Oxford: Clarendon Press, 2003), 249–316.

36. This section, titled "False Need" (*Bedürfnis falsch*), has no equivalent in the *Ontology and Dialectics* lectures, where it would have occurred right after Adorno stopped reading from his first Paris lecture at OD 298/213. It appears to be a later formulation intended specifically to help conclude the first chapter in part 1 of *Negative Dialectics*. That gives the section added significance, as is indicated by its prominence among German commentators. Citing this section, Jürgen Naeher describes Adorno's critique of Heidegger as a *Bedürfnis-Kritik* (literally: need-critique) informed by Nietzsche's critique of religion and Marx's critique of ideology ("Das ontologische 'Bedürfnis im Denken,'" 211). By contrast, Dieter Thomä points out several problems with Adorno's using the concept of need both to historicize Heidegger's turn toward ontology and to interpret Heidegger's concept of Being as a quasipsychological projection. Thomä concludes that the "ideology-critical point" of Adorno's focus on the ontological need "remains blunt," and Naeher's thesis that Adorno's critique of Heidegger is a *Bedürfnis-Kritik* "comes up short" ("Verhältnis zur Ontologie," 41).

37. Adorno's formulation of this point relies on a problematic notion of "the most advanced consciousness" that calls for closer scrutiny than I can give here. It also employs indirection and double negatives, which tend to hide his apparent assumption that sometime, perhaps in the mid-nineteenth century (1848?), a genuine social revolution might have been historically possible in the capitalist societies of Europe and North America. Here is an attempt to translate the murky sentence in question: "Only because of a failure to arrange the world, such that it would no longer obey form-categories contrary to the most advanced consciousness, must the prevailing consciousness frantically champion those categories" (ND 102/95).

38. Macdonald, *What Would Be Different*, 103–56.

39. Tiedemann points out the mistake in an endnote (OD 350n15/254n14) but suggests that Adorno does not repeat it in *Negative Dialectics*.

40. Adorno ties this supposed hierarchy to a correlative distinction, which does have a basis in Heidegger's text, among (1) fundamental ontology, (2) regional ontologies, and (3) "ontic inquiry" (roughly, the empirical sciences). See OD 25–30/12–16.

41. See especially lectures 6 ("Separating Being and Beings"), 7 ("Mind in Relation to Beings [*Geist und Seiendes*]), and 8–9 (both titled "Ontologizing the Ontic"), OD 80–138/52–94.

42. I am aware that capitalizing "Being" has the disadvantage of incorrectly suggesting that it is some kind of super being, but I have not found a more effective way to designate the difference between *Sein* (Being) and *das Seiende* (being or beings), short of always using the German terms instead. I silently incorporate this English orthography when I cite Heidegger and other authors, including Adorno's *Ontology and Dialectics* and *Negative Dialectics*.

43. For an incisive criticism of Adorno's misreading Heidegger as reviving an essentially Platonic metaphysics of the highest or most general being, see Hammer, "Adorno's Critique of Heidegger," 474–77. Hammer argues that, in this regard, not only does Adorno not engage in immanent criticism but he also "simply misunderstands the nature of [Heidegger's] project" (477).

44. There's no mistaking the political burden of Adorno's critique. The section "Immanent Critique of Ontology" concludes by comparing the "claim to pure essentiality" in Heidegger's conception of Being to how "highly sensitive dictators" avoid "visits to concentration camps whose functionaries dutifully follow their orders" (ND 106–7/99–100).

45. "Heidegger repeats the Hegelian sleight-of-hand [*Eulenspiegel–Manöver*]. Except Hegel practiced it openly, while Heidegger, who does not want to be an Idealist, shrouds and beclouds the ontologization of the ontic" (ND 127/121). For a more extensive account of Adorno's argument in the "Copula" section, see the previous chapter. For an even more extensive discussion of these issues in Heidegger and Adorno, see Tietz, *Ontologie und Dialektik*.

46. See also Günther Anders, "On the Pseudo-Concreteness of Heidegger's Philosophy," *Philosophy and Phenomenological Research* 8, no. 3 (1948), 337–71, and the discussion of this essay in Gordon, *Adorno and Existence*, 129–36.

47. Although Adorno usually cites Hegel's tripartite *Science of Logic*, published in 1812, 1813, and 1816, Hegel's 1830 *Encyclopedia* Logic makes the same moves in a more succinct and transparent way. See "The Doctrine of Being" in G. W. F. Hegel, *Hegel's Logic: Being Part One of the* Encyclopaedia of the Philosophical Sciences (1830), trans. William Wallace (Oxford: Clarendon Press, 1975), 123–61.

48. See also OD 124–27/84–86, where Adorno makes the same unfavorable comparison between Hegel and Heidegger, but without reference to the concept of Being in Hegel's logic. Macdonald, *What Would Be Different*, 25–55, shows that this line of criticizing Hegel is central to Adorno's negative dialectics.

49. Adorno might have in mind the work of Max Scheler, who was briefly a colleague of Max Horkheimer in Frankfurt and whose philosophical anthropology was both the topic of Heidegger's 1929 lecture in Frankfurt titled "Philosophical Anthropology and Metaphysics of Dasein," which Adorno attended, and a target of Horkheimer's sustained criticisms. For details, see Immanen, *Toward a Concrete Philosophy*, 129–71, 201, 209–22, 238–48.

50. The parallel passage in Adorno's lectures explicitly links this person-oriented ideology of "the earthy and authentic" with antisemitic "instincts" (OD 321/232)—a linkage more fully developed in Adorno's *Jargon of Authenticity*.

51. Adorno uses the same adjective—*existentiell*—in his lectures (see OD 323/233). By rendering it as "existential" rather than "existentiell," the English translations of *Negative Dialectics* and *Ontology and Dialectics* obscure the real focus of Adorno's critique in these passages, namely, the reduction of truth to what the individual subject is and does. Heidegger's *existentialer Wahrheitsbegriff*—truth as disclosedness or unconcealedness—is not directly under discussion here.

52. Lecture 9, the second lecture titled "Ontologizing the Ontic," indicates that Adorno is especially concerned with how, because of the ontologizing tendency, Heidegger's concept of historicity lets "concrete history" and its "wholly concrete distress" fall through the cracks "as something unworthy of philosophy" (OD 127/87).

53. I say "if" because, as is well known, *Sein und Zeit* as it stands is incomplete, lacking both a third division on "Time and Being" and a second half that would have mapped a "phenomenological destructuring of the history of ontology" focused on Kant, Descartes, and Aristotle (see SZ 39–40).

54. Adorno, GS 1:330, 337–38; "The Actuality of Philosophy" (1931), 124, 128–29.

55. Adorno, GS 1:348–50, 354; "The Idea of Natural History" (1932), 113–14, 117.

56. Adorno, GS 1:353–54; "The Idea of Natural History," 116. Here the framework of Adorno's critique is fundamentally neo-Kantian: "historicity" is a "categorial subjective structure" of possibility (mis)applied to the "empirical multiplicity" of actual history. His later critique in *Negative Dialectics* is more Hegelian.

57. Adorno, GS 1:354; "The Idea of Natural History," 116.

58. Adorno, GS 1:357–58, 365; "The Idea of Natural History," 119, 124.

59. Adorno, *Zur Lehre von der Geschichte*, 420n177; *History and Freedom*, 300n7.

60. Although the translation renders this lecture title as "The History of Nature," Adorno clearly has in mind the same idea of "natural history" that he had explored in 1932. In fact, he directly quotes from the 1932 lecture and recapitulates some of its content. See Adorno, *Zur Lehre von der Geschichte*, 179–84; *History and Freedom*, 124–26.

61. Adorno, *Zur Lehre von der Geschichte*, 177–78; *History and Freedom*, 123.

62. Tiedemann recalls that, during the two lectures titled "Naturgeschichte," Adorno read from the typescript of "World Spirit and Natural History"—see *Zur Lehre von der Geschichte*, 418n171; *History and Freedom*, 299n1.

63. Macdonald, *What Would Be Different*, 155.

64. Macdonald, *What Would Be Different*, 4.

65. Macdonald, *What Would Be Different*, 6–7.

66. Although this specifically describes the futural temporality of understanding (in contrast to the orientations of attunement and falling prey toward past and present, respectively), an orientation toward future possibilities has priority in Heidegger's conception in Dasein's temporality: "Temporality temporalizes itself as a future that makes present, in the process of having been" (SZ 350).

67. Martin Heidegger, *Contributions to Philosophy (Of the Event)*, trans. Richard Rojcewicz and Daniela Vallega-Neu (Bloomington: Indiana University Press, 2012), § 267, p. 374.

68. Heidegger, *Contributions to Philosophy*, § 266, p. 369.

69. Macdonald, *What Would Be Different*, 111.

70. Macdonald, *What Would Be Different*, 114–15.

71. Macdonald, *What Would Be Different*, 125.

72. Initial formulations pointing in this direction occur in Heidegger's 1930 essay "Vom Wesen der Wahrheit" ("On the Essence of Truth"). See my discussion in *Truth in Husserl, Heidegger, and the Frankfurt School: Critical Retrieval* (Cambridge, MA: MIT Press, 2017), 147–74.

73. Hegel, *Hegel's Logic*, 132.

74. On the contrast between eternalist and temporalist positions concerning propositional truth, see Künne, *Conceptions of Truth*, 249–316.

75. I articulate the beginnings of such a conception in *Truth in Husserl, Heidegger, and the Frankfurt School* and in chapters 14 and 15 of *Religion, Truth, and Social Transformation: Essays in Reformational Philosophy* (Montreal: McGill-Queen's University Press, 2016), 277–313. The details are worked out in *Shattering Silos: Reimagining Knowledge, Politics, and Social Critique* (Montreal: McGill-Queen's University Press, 2022) and *Social Domains of Truth: Science, Politics, Art, and Religion* (New York: Routledge, 2023).

Chapter 5

An early draft of the Foucault materials in this chapter received illuminating comments from Joshua Harris, Dean Dettloff, and the late Deborah Cook. I wish to thank them here. I also thank Joshua Harris for his perceptive reading of the nearly final version of this chapter.

1. See, for example, Michel Foucault, *The Politics of Truth*, ed. Sylvère Lotringer, trans. Lysa Hochroth and Catherine Porter (Los Angeles: Semiotext(e), 1997, 2007).

2. See especially chapters 5 and 10 in Jürgen Habermas, *The Philosophical Discourse of Modernity: Twelve Lectures*, trans. Frederick G. Lawrence (Cambridge, MA: MIT Press, 1987), 106–30, 266–93. See also Richard J. Bernstein, "Foucault: Critique as a Philosophic *Ēthos*," in *The New Constellation: The Ethical-Political Horizons of Modernity/Postmodernity* (Cambridge, MA: MIT Press, 1991), 142–71.

3. Axel Honneth, *The Critique of Power: Reflective Stages in a Critical Social Theory*, trans. Kenneth Baynes (Cambridge, MA: MIT Press, 1991).

4. Amy Allen, *The End of Progress: Decolonizing the Normative Foundations of Critical Theory* (New York: Columbia University Press, 2016), 165. I should note that, whereas here Allen focuses on Foucault's early writings, especially his 1961 *History of Madness*, the criticisms I have cited from Habermas and Honneth pertain primarily to Foucault's middle writings, especially his 1975 *Discipline and Punish*.

5. Deborah Cook, *Adorno, Foucault and the Critique of the West* (London: Verso, 2018), 142–51. Cook briefly mentions Honneth's criticisms of Adorno and Foucault but does not address them.

6. In addition to the works already cited, see, for example, Thomas McCarthy, "The Critique of Impure Reason: Foucault and the Frankfurt School," in *Ideals and Illusions: On Reconstruction and Deconstruction in Contemporary Critical Theory* (Cambridge, MA: MIT Press, 1991), 43–75; Michael Kelly, ed., *Critique and Power: Recasting the Foucault/Habermas Debate* (Cambridge, MA: MIT Press, 1994); David Couzens Hoy and Thomas McCarthy, *Critical Theory* (Oxford: Blackwell, 1994); David Ingram, "Foucault and Habermas," in *The Cambridge Companion to Foucault*, 2nd ed., ed. Gary Gutting (Cambridge: Cambridge University Press, 2005), 240–83; and Danielle Petherbridge, *The Critical Theory of Axel Honneth* (Lanham, MD: Lexington Books, 2013).

7. This is not to deny the crucial work done in feminist epistemology and feminist science and technology studies on the topics of knowledge and truth, however. For a survey of such contributions, see Elisabeth Anderson, "Feminist Epistemology and Philosophy of Science," in *The Stanford Encyclopedia of Philosophy* (Spring 2020 ed.), ed. Edward N. Zalta, <https://plato.stanford.edu/archives/spr2020/entries/feminism-epistemology/>.

8. Amy Allen, "Feminist Perspectives on Power," in *The Stanford Encyclopedia of Philosophy* (Fall 2016 ed.), Edward N. Zalta (ed.), <https://plato.stanford.edu/archives/fall2016/entries/feminist-power/>.

9. In an earlier and more extensive discussion, Allen also distinguishes solidarity ("power-with") from influence and agency, arguing that a feminist conception of power must include all three senses of power in order to understand "masculine domination, feminine empowerment and resistance, and feminist solidarity and coalition-building." Amy Allen, *The Power of Feminist Theory: Domination, Resistance, Solidarity* (Boulder, CO: Westview Press, 1999), 123.

10. Under *critical theory* in the broad sense, I include what Allen distinguishes as radical, socialist, intersectional, and poststructuralist feminists. When referring specifically to the Frankfurt School tradition, I capitalize *Critical Theory*. Feminists in the tradition of Critical Theory usually align with critical theory in the broad sense rather than with, say, liberal feminism or care theory.

11. See Sally Haslanger, *Resisting Reality: Social Construction and Social Critique* (New York: Oxford University Press, 2012), 312–17.

12. Nancy Fraser, *Justice Interruptus: Critical Reflections on the "Postsocialist Condition"* (New York: Routledge, 1997), 19. Fraser argues that the best political and theoretical responses to the injustices women and people of color suffer would combine socialism and deconstruction (32).

13. Published in English as Michel Foucault, *Discipline and Punish: The Birth of the Prison* (1975), trans. Alan Sheridan (New York: Pantheon Books, 1977).

14. Published in English as Michel Foucault, *The History of Sexuality*, vol. 1, *An Introduction* (1976), trans. Robert Hurley (New York: Random House, 1978; Vintage Books, 1990).

15. Cook, *Adorno, Foucault*, 31–60; Amy Allen, *The Politics of Our Selves: Power, Autonomy, and Gender in Contemporary Critical Theory* (New York: Columbia University Press, 2008), 48–60.

16. Foucault, *History of Sexuality*, 1:49.

17. Allen, *Politics of Our Selves*, 49–50.

18. Michel Foucault, *"Society Must Be Defended": Lectures at the Collège de France, 1975–76*, trans. David Macey (New York: Picador, 2003), 29–30. For an earlier translation of the first two lectures (i.e., January 7 and 14, 1976), see Michel Foucault, "Two Lectures" (1976), in *Power/Knowledge: Selected Interviews and Other Writings 1972–1977*, ed. Colin Gordon (New York: Pantheon Books, 1980), 78–108.

19. Allen, *Politics of Our Selves*, 68. Foucault's account of subjection raises difficult questions about whether and how individual subjects can have the autonomy seemingly required to undertake both critical reflection upon, and deliberate transformation of, contemporary technologies of the self. Amy Allen argues in detail that Foucault does indeed give an account of such autonomy, although she thinks it needs to be supplemented by a more Habermasian approach, one that provides an "intersubjective account of subjectivity and autonomy" grounded in "communicative interaction" (69). Although I think such questions about autonomy are crucial, I do not address them here.

20. Foucault, *"Society Must Be Defended,"* 14–15.

21. Foucault, *"Society Must Be Defended,"* 24.

22. Foucault, *"Society Must Be Defended,"* 29–30. In a short 1977 interview, Foucault hypothesizes that power, which is "co-extensive with the social body," occurs in relations of power that take multiple forms (not simply prohibition or punishment) and are "interwoven with other kinds of relations (production, kinship, family, sexuality) for which they play at once a conditioning and a conditioned role." Moreover, the interconnections among diverse relations of power "delineate general conditions of domination," and domination is organized into "global strategies" that make use of these power relations—albeit not without resistance, since "there are no relations of power without resistances" that can also be "integrated in global strategies." Michel Foucault, "Powers and Strategies," in Gordon, ed., *Power/Knowledge*, 134–45; quotations from 142.

23. Foucault, *"Society Must Be Defended,"* 33.

24. Foucault, *"Society Must Be Defended,"* 35–36.

25. Foucault, *"Society Must Be Defended,"* 38–39.

26. Foucault, *"Society Must Be Defended,"* 39–40. Although he does not deny that, along with disciplinary mechanisms, sovereignty remains one of the two essential components within modern society's general mechanism of power, Foucault refuses to give sovereignty either explanatory or normative preference. It persists, he suggests, primarily as a way to conceal how disciplinary power operates even in the democratic procurement of individual rights (37).

27. Allen, *Politics of Our Selves*, 56.

28. Foucault, *History of Sexuality*, 1:139. Despite what the title to Foucault's 1978–79 lectures on biopolitics might suggest, they do not trace the development of state supervision over the health, birthrates, etc. of a population. Instead, these lectures examine the development of liberalism and neoliberalism as "the framework of political rationality for biopolitics." See Michel Foucault, *The Birth of Biopolitics: Lectures at the Collège De France, 1978–79*, ed. Michel Senellart, trans. Graham Burchell (New York: Palgrave Macmillan, 2008), 317.

29. Foucault, *History of Sexuality*, 1:141.

30. Allen, *The End of Progress*, 164, 250n1. In a more general way, David Couzens Hoy had already argued in 1994 that French poststructuralism—especially Foucault—is "an alternative way of continuing the tradition of [Frankfurt School] critical theory"—that is, an alternative to Habermas. See "Conflicting Conceptions of Critique: Foucault versus Habermas," in Hoy and McCarthy, *Critical Theory*, 144–71, quotation from 144.

31. In 1978, asked about how his thought related to the early Frankfurt School, Foucault said Adorno and his colleagues "had tried, earlier than I, to say things I had also been trying to say for years," especially with regard to "the effects of power in their relation to [modern] rationality. . . . Couldn't it be concluded that the Enlightenment's promise of attaining freedom through the exercise of reason has been turned upside down, resulting in a domination by reason itself, which increasingly usurps the place of freedom?" "Interview with Michel Foucault," in *Power: Essential Works of Foucault, 1954–1984*, vol. 3, ed. James D. Faubion, trans. Robert Hurley et al. (New York: The New Press, 2000), 239–97; quotations from 273.

32. See especially the chapter titled "The Critique of Instrumental Reason" in Jürgen Habermas, *The Theory of Communicative Action*, trans. Thomas McCarthy (Boston, MA: Beacon Press, 1984), 1:339–99.

33. Peter Dews, *Logics of Disintegration: Post-Structuralist Thought and the Claims of Critical Theory* (London: Verso, 1987), 210.

34. Cook, *Adorno, Foucault*, 39–55.

35. At the same time, however, unlike Martin Shuster, I also do not regard Adorno's philosophy of history, with its inherent critique of domination, as primarily motivated by a quasi-Benjaminian concern for the sacredness of "every unique human life" and "the irreducible singularity of every moment and every life." See Martin Shuster, "The Philosophy of History," in *The Routledge Companion to the Frankfurt School*, ed. Peter Gordon, Espen Hammer, and Axel Honneth (New York: Routledge, 2018), 48–64, quotations from 59.

36. Max Horkheimer, *Die Sehnsucht nach dem ganz Anderen: Ein Interview mit Kommentar von Helmut Gumnior* (Hamburg: Furche-Verlag, 1970).

37. Seyla Benhabib, "Feminism and Postmodernism: An Uneasy Alliance," in Seyla Benhabib, Judith Butler, Drucilla Cornell, and Nancy Fraser, *Feminist Contentions: A Philosophical Exchange* (New York: Routledge, 1995), 30. A longer version

of this essay appears as chapter 7 ("Feminism and the Question of Postmodernism") in Seyla Benhabib, *Situating the Self: Gender, Community and Postmodernism in Contemporary Ethics* (New York: Routledge, 1992), 203–41. The original exchange among Benhabib, Butler, and Fraser occurred at a symposium on feminism and postmodernism sponsored by the Greater Philadelphia Philosophy Consortium. It was published first in the journal *Praxis International* (July 1991) and then, expanded by a contribution from Drucilla Cornell, in a German volume titled *Der Streit um Differenz* (Frankfurt am Main: Fischer, 1993).

38. Judith Butler, "Contingent Foundations: Feminism and the Question of 'Postmodernism,'" in Benhabib et al., *Feminist Contentions*, 39.

39. For succinct summaries of the debate along these lines, with an emphasis on "the problem of the subject" and its relation to power, see Allen, *Politics of Our Selves*, 4–10, and Amy Allen, "Critical Theory and Feminism," in *The Routledge Companion to the Frankfurt School*, 528–41, especially 529–32.

40. Seyla Benhabib, "Subjectivity, Historiography, and Politics," in Benhabib et al., *Feminist Contentions*, 108.

41. Benhabib, "Subjectivity, Historiography, and Politics," 116. But see "Feminism and Postmodernism," where Benhabib acknowledges Cornell as a feminist who "seeks to retain this utopian element even while affirming postmodernist philosophy" (34n29).

42. Judith Butler, "For a Careful Reading," in *Feminist Contentions*, 142.

43. Nancy Fraser, "Pragmatism, Feminism, and the Linguistic Turn," in Benhabib et al., *Feminist Contentions*, 159, 164.

44. See Drucilla Cornell, "Rethinking the Time of Feminism," in Benhabib et al., *Feminist Contentions*, especially 148–49.

45. On the political importance of cultivating utopian hope, see the Ernst Bloch–inspired reflections in Kathi Weeks, *The Problem with Work: Feminism, Marxism, Antiwork Politics, and Postwork Imaginaries* (Durham, NC: Duke University Press, 2011), 175–225.

46. Michel Foucault, "Questions of Method: An Interview with Michel Foucault," in *After Philosophy: End or Transformation?*, ed. Kenneth Baynes, James Bohman, and Thomas McCarthy (Cambridge, MA: MIT Press, 1987), 100–117, quotation from 111. The interview stems from 1978. It first appeared in 1980, followed by an English translation in 1981.

47. See especially Michel Foucault, *The Archaeology of Knowledge and the Discourse on Language* (1969 and 1971), trans. A. M. Sheridan Smith (New York: Vintage Books, 1972). Although written before the genealogical studies of truth and power that I have cited, this book establishes key claims about objects of discourse and levels of knowledge that Foucault neither abandoned nor revoked. See also Maurice Florence, "Foucault," in Michel Foucault, *Aesthetics, Method, and Epistemology: Essential Works of Foucault, 1954–1984*, vol. 2, ed. James D. Faubion, trans. Robert Hurley et al. (New York: The New Press, 1998), 459–63, which describes

Foucault's project as a "critical history of thought" that analyzes "the conditions under which certain relations of subject to object are formed and modified, insofar as those relations constitute a possible knowledge [*savoir*]" (459). The editor explains that this entry from the early 1980s for the *Dictionnaire des philosophes* was written mostly by Foucault and signed pseudonymously "Maurice Florence."

48. Michel Foucault, "The Subject and Power" (1982), in *Power: Essential Works of Foucault*, 326–48, quotation from 340.

49. Although this is not the same issue as the alleged "cryptonormativism" in Foucault's genealogical critique of power, it is closely related. "Cryptonormativism" refers to Foucault's supposedly invoking norms that he cannot justify because to justify them would require an appeal to universals like "justice" whose validity transcends the current regime of truth. See Jürgen Habermas, *The Philosophical Discourse of Modernity*, 282–86, which favorably cites the 1981 version of the essay by Nancy Fraser, "Foucault on Modern Power: Empirical Insights and Normative Confusions," in *Unruly Practices: Power, Discourse, and Gender in Contemporary Social Theory* (Minneapolis: University of Minnesota Press, 1989), 17–34.

50. See in this connection Adorno's lectures on metaphysics, where he says the idea that "thought and its constitutive forms are *in fact* the absolute" is "really the thesis of the whole metaphysical tradition" (and not, for example, simply of Hegel's absolute idealism). Adorno refers in this connection to his own critique (in *Zur Metakritik der Erkenntnistheorie*) of Husserl's "logical absolutism" for treating the pure forms of thought as absolute rather than historically contingent. Theodor W. Adorno, *Metaphysics: Concept and Problems* (1965), ed. Rolf Tiedemann, trans. Edmund Jephcott (Stanford, CA: Stanford University Press, 2000), 99.

51. A few pages earlier, Adorno says Husserl's attempt to bracket out empirical existence is based on "that residual concept of truth which is common to all bourgeois philosophy, with the exception of Hegel and Nietzsche," a concept that treats truth as the residue left after the labor of actual thinking has been erased (ME 76–77/70). See also ME 23/15, H 256/7, and Adorno's lectures on Kant, K 43–45/25–26.

52. See in this connection the illuminating discussion of Judith Butler's work in chapter 4 ("Dependency, Subordination, and Recognition: Butler on Subjection") of Allen, *Politics of Our Selves*, 72–95.

53. See chapter 4 ("Globalizing Dialectic of Enlightenment") in Zuidervaart, *Social Philosophy after Adorno* (Cambridge: Cambridge University Press, 2007), 107–31.

54. Allen, *Power of Feminist Theory*, 127.

55. See chapter 6 in Zuidervaart, *Social Domains of Truth*, 122–56.

56. See chapter 8 in Zuidervaart, *Social Domains of Truth*, 205–30.

57. See chapter 13 in Lambert Zuidervaart, *Religion, Truth, and Social Transformation: Essays in Reformational Philosophy* (Montreal: McGill-Queen's University Press, 2016), 252–76.

Chapter 6

Excerpts from this chapter were presented to the Critical Theory Roundtable meeting held at McMaster University in October 2019. I thank the conference organizers and meeting participants for a stimulating conversation.

1. Susanne K. Langer, *Feeling and Form: A Theory of Art Developed from Philosophy in a New Key* (New York: Charles Scribner's Sons, 1953), 392–410.

2. Monroe C. Beardsley, *Aesthetics: Problems in the Philosophy of Criticism* (New York: Harcourt, Brace & World, 1958), 557–91.

3. The "chapters" in Adorno's *Aesthetic Theory* are not really chapters (the translator Robert Hullot-Kentor calls them "parts"), and the pages-long paragraphs within them are not really paragraphs. Nevertheless, I will refer to them as chapters and paragraphs, since other terms such as parts, sections, and subsections would be even more misleading.

4. In a subsequent three-volume work titled *Mind*, however, Langer does discuss the relation between art and nature at some length. See especially volume 1 in Susanne K. Langer, *Mind: An Essay on Human Feeling*, 3 vols. (Baltimore, MD: Johns Hopkins University Press, 1967–82).

5. Francis E. Sparshott, *The Structure of Aesthetics* (Toronto: University of Toronto Press, 1963), 91–101, 267–311.

6. Mikel Dufrenne, *The Phenomenology of Aesthetic Experience*, trans. Edward S. Casey et al. (Evanston, IL: Northwestern University Press, 1973), 3–146. Two decades after the publication of *Phénoménologie de l'expérience esthétique*, and in the same year as Marc Jimenez published a French translation of Adorno's *Ästhetische Theorie*, Dufrenne wrote a book on art and politics and discussed Adorno's work in that context—see especially the second half of chapter 4 in Mikel Dufrenne, *Art et politique* (Paris: Union générale d'éditions, 1974), 149–71.

7. Hans-Georg Gadamer, *Truth and Method*, 2nd, rev. ed., trans. and ed. Joel Weinsheimer and Donald G. Marshall (New York: Crossroad, 1989), 1–169.

8. See Roman Ingarden, *The Cognition of the Literary Work of Art*, trans. Ruth Ann Crowley and Kenneth R. Olson (Evanston, IL: Northwestern University Press, 1973).

9. Arnold Hauser, *The Social History of Art*, 4 vols., trans. Stanley Goodman (New York: Vintage Books, 1951), 4:226–59. But see Hauser's philosophical reflections on his own social-historical methodology in Arnold Hauser, *The Philosophy of Art History* (London: Routledge & Kegan Paul, 1958), and his comprehensive 1974 work translated as *The Sociology of Art*, trans. Kenneth J. Northcott (Chicago, IL: University of Chicago Press, 1982). Adorno briefly discusses Hauser's *Sozialgeschichte der Kunst und Literatur* in the excursus "Theories on the Origin of Art" (ÄT 480–91/325–31).

10. Georg Lukács, *Die Eigenart des Ästhetischen*, 2 vols. (Neuwied: Luchterhand, 1963). Undoubtedly the projected third part of this project, titled *Die Kunst als*

gesellschaftlich-geschichtliche Erscheinung, would have engaged in social critique, perhaps along the lines of Lukács's 1958 *Wider den missverstandenen Realismus*, translated as *Realism in Our Time: Literature and the Class Struggle*, trans. Johan and Necke Mander (New York: Harper & Row, 1964). This book famously drew Adorno's ire in the 1958 essay "Erpresste Versöhnung," translated as "Extorted Reconciliation." See Theodor W. Adorno, *Noten zur Literatur II*, in GS 11 (Frankfurt am Main: Suhrkamp, 1974), 251–80; *Notes to Literature*, trans. Shierry Weber Nicholsen (New York: Columbia University Press, 1991), 1:216–40. Adorno's dispute with Lukács about literary realism and modern art continues in *Aesthetic Theory*—see ÄT 70/43, 147/95, 213/141–42, 280/188, 477/322. I summarize the dispute in *Adorno's Aesthetic Theory: The Redemption of Illusion* (Cambridge, MA: MIT Press, 1991), 38–43 and 250–54, and explore it at greater length in "Methodological Shadowboxing in Marxist Aesthetics: Lukács and Adorno," *Journal of Comparative Literature and Aesthetics* 11 (1988): 85–113.

11. Fredric Jameson, *Late Marxism: Adorno, or, the Persistence of the Dialectic* (London: Verso, 1990), 4.

12. G. W. F. Hegel, *Elements of the Philosophy of Right*, ed. Allen W. Wood, trans. H. B. Nisbet (Cambridge: Cambridge University Press, 1991), 21.

13. This is not to ignore Adorno's important critique of the culture industry in other writings, but simply to point out that *Aesthetic Theory* has little to say about mass-mediated art. Nor, as Nicholas Wolterstorff notes, does Adorno show much interest in theorizing memorial art or the other sorts of situated art that Gadamer describes as either occasional or decorative. See Nicholas Wolterstorff, *Art Rethought: The Social Practices of Art* (Oxford: Oxford University Press, 2015), 2–3; and Gadamer, *Truth and Method*, 144–59.

14. Zuidervaart, *Adorno's Aesthetic Theory*, 151–77.

15. There is growing recognition, especially in the German-speaking world, of the need for serious study of the book as a whole. Examples include the text-critical edition of the heavily reworked third chapter in the "Kapitel-Ästhetik" draft of *Ästhetische Theorie* (i.e., the draft from 1966–68 that was organized in long chapters): Theodor W. Adorno, *Schein—Form—Subjekt—Prozesscharakter—Kunstwerk: Textkritische Edition der letzten bekanten Überarbeitung des III. Kapitels der "Kapitel-Ästhetik,"* ed. Martin Endres, Axel Pichler, and Claus Zittel, 2 vols. (Berlin: Walter de Gruyter, 2021). The editors of this work also published a collection of essays to help mark the fiftieth anniversary of the posthumous publication of *Ästhetische Theorie* in 1970: *Eros und Erkenntnis: 50 Jahre "Ästhetische Theorie"* (Berlin: Walter DeGruyter, 2019). For a collection of essays devoted to each "chapter" in the 1970 version, see Anne Eusterschulte and Sebastian Tränkle, eds., *Theodor W. Adorno: Ästhetische Theorie* (Berlin: Walter de Gruyter, 2021).

16. Albrecht Wellmer, "Wahrheit, Schein, Versöhnung: Adornos Ästhetische Rettung der Modernität," in *Zur Dialektik von Moderne und Postmoderne: Vernunftkritik nach Adorno* (Frankfurt am Main: Suhrkamp, 1985), 9–47; Albrecht Wellmer,

"Truth, Semblance, Reconciliation: Adorno's Aesthetic Redemption of Modernity," in *The Persistence of Modernity: Essays on Aesthetics, Ethics, and Postmodernism*, trans. David Midgley (Cambridge, MA: MIT Press, 1991), 1–35.

17. For a more extensive discussion and critique of Wellmer's essay, see chapter 11 ("History, Art, and Truth") in Zuidervaart, *Adorno's Aesthetic Theory*, 275–307.

18. Wellmer, "Wahrheit, Schein, Versöhnung," 19–20; "Truth, Semblance, Reconciliation," 12.

19. See Albrecht Wellmer, "Adorno, Anwalt des Nicht-Identischen: Eine Einführung," in *Zur Dialektik von Moderne und Postmoderne*, 149.

20. Wellmer, "Wahrheit, Schein, Versöhnung," 38–43; "Truth, Semblance, Reconciliation," 29–34.

21. Wellmer, "Wahrheit, Schein, Versöhnung," 9; "Truth, Semblance, Reconciliation," 2.

22. Wellmer, "Wahrheit, Schein, Versöhnung," 19–23, 43–44; "Truth, Semblance, Reconciliation," 11–15, 34–35.

23. Wellmer, "Wahrheit, Schein, Versöhnung," 30–38; "Truth, Semblance, Reconciliation," 22–29.

24. J. M. Bernstein, *The Fate of Art: Aesthetic Alienation from Kant to Derrida and Adorno* (University Park: Pennsylvania State University Press, 1992). By "aesthetic alienation" Bernstein means art's becoming autonomous from "truth-only cognition" (e.g., science) and "principled morality" and, more specifically, "art's alienation from truth . . . caused by art's *becoming* aesthetical, a becoming that has been fully consummated only in modern societies" (4).

25. Bernstein, *Fate of Art*, 246–47.

26. Bernstein, *Fate of Art*, 247, 256.

27. Bernstein, *Fate of Art*, 245–46.

28. Wellmer, "Wahrheit, Schein, Versöhnung," 44; "Truth, Semblance, Reconciliation," 35.

29. Bernstein, *Fate of Art*, 241, 244, 272, 240, italics removed. For elaborations of the mostly implicit conceptions of politics and ethics in *The Fate of Art*, see J. M. Bernstein, *Recovering Ethical Life: Jürgen Habermas and the Future of Critical Theory* (New York: Routledge, 1995), and *Adorno: Disenchantment and Ethics* (New York: Cambridge University Press, 2001).

30. For a summary and assessment of this chapter, see Sebastian Tränkle, "Schein und Ausdruck," in *Theodor W. Adorno: Ästhetische Theorie*, 105–21.

31. For a more extensive account of how Adorno sees artistic production as a form of social labor, see chapter 4 in Zuidervaart, *Adorno's Aesthetic Theory*, 93–121.

32. In this connection, see the commentary on this chapter by Lydia Goehr, "Stimmigkeit und Sinn," in *Theodor W. Adorno: Ästhetische Theorie*, 139–54.

33. See Susanne K. Langer, *Philosophy in a New Key: A Study in the Symbolism of Reason, Rite, and Art*, 3rd ed. (Cambridge, MA: Harvard University Press, 1957), 79–102; and *Feeling and Form*, 24–41.

34. On the challenges of rendering this concept in English, see the translator's note in Adorno, *Aesthetic Theory*, 371n5.

35. For a commentary on this chapter, see Antonia Hofstätter, "Rätselcharakter, Wahrheitsgehalt, Metaphysik," in *Theodor W. Adorno: Ästhetische Theorie*, 123–38.

36. In the German edition, extra white space separates the second half of this chapter from the first. This separation disappears in the Hullot-Kentor translation—compare ÄT 193/127.

37. Bernstein, *Fate of Art*, 260. Bernstein more frequently cites the first half of this chapter, about the enigmatic character of art. When he does reference pages in the second half, it is to emphasize Adorno's conception of what Bernstein calls "the intelligible structure of recognition of non-identical others" (250). See Bernstein, *Fate of Art*, 239, 242, 250, 254, 259. In a subsequent essay, however, he argues convincingly that the rescue or redemption of semblance thematized in *Aesthetic Theory* supports the development of a materialist ethics. See J. M. Bernstein, "Why Rescue Semblance? Metaphysical Experience and the Possibility of Ethics," in Tom Huhn and Lambert Zuidervaart, eds., *The Semblance of Subjectivity: Essays in Adorno's Aesthetic Theory* (Cambridge, MA: MIT Press, 1997), 177–212.

38. In elaborating this point, Adorno employs two different and perhaps incompatible notions of artistic truth content: (1) truth content as the successful artistic expression of consciousness, even if the latter is false (some of Richard Wagner's operas or Leni Riefenstahl's films might fit this description), and (2) truth content as the genuine insight or disclosure toward which an artwork points (e.g., the import of Samuel Beckett's *Endgame*). In *Adorno's Aesthetic Theory*, 197–200, I try to unpack the unacknowledged contradiction that arises from Adorno's using both notions.

39. Here I take issue with Rüdiger Bubner, an influential German critic of Adorno, who in effect faults him for both aestheticizing theory and theoreticizing art. See Rüdiger Bubner, "Concerning the Central Idea of Adorno's Philosophy," in Huhn and Zuidervaart, *Semblance of Subjectivity*, 147–75.

40. Bernstein, *Fate of Art*, 272.

41. Wellmer, "Wahrheit, Schein, Versöhnung," 31; "Truth, Semblance, Reconciliation, 23.

42. As hinted earlier, Adorno's claim that social false consciousness cannot yield authentic artworks seems incompatible with his claim that many of the best artworks are true as expressions of false consciousness (ÄT 196/129).

43. For a more elaborate account, see Lambert Zuidervaart, *Artistic Truth: Aesthetics, Discourse, and Imaginative Disclosure* (Cambridge: Cambridge University Press, 2004).

44. See *Adorno's Aesthetic Theory*, 217–47; *Artistic Truth*, 118–39; and chapter 7 ("Relational Autonomy") in Lambert Zuidervaart, *Art in Public: Politics, Economics, and a Democratic Culture* (Cambridge: Cambridge University Press, 2011), 207–40.

45. Paul Guyer, *A History of Modern Aesthetics, Volume 3: The Twentieth Century* (Cambridge: Cambridge University Press, 2014), 72.

46. Guyer, *History of Modern Aesthetics*, 72, puts great weight on this passage, quoting it from Hullot-Kentor's translation: "Art is the ever broken promise of happiness" (ÄT 205/136). By emphasizing the word "ever," Guyer can interpret Adorno as an extreme pessimist. This word, however, is a translator's interpolation; its equivalent does not occur in Adorno's German text: "Kunst ist das Versprechen des Glücks, das gebrochen wird." Adorno's claim that the promise is broken (*gebrochen wird*) does not imply that the promise must always and forever be broken or that what art brokenly promises—yet still does promise it!—must always and forever be impossible. One small word—"ever"—inserted into the English translation can make a huge difference between reading Adorno as an extreme pessimist, as Guyer does, or taking him, as I do, to be a radical social critic for whom societally induced suffering cannot have the final word.

47. Cf. Friedrich Nietzsche, *Also Sprach Zarathustra* (1883–1885), in *Nietzsche Werke: Kritische Gesamtausgabe*, part 6, vol. 1, ed. Giorgio Colli and Mazzino Montinari (Berlin: Walter de Gruyter, 1968), 282; *Thus Spoke Zarathustra*, trans. Walter Kaufmann (New York: Penguin Books, 1966), 227.

Chapter 7

1. See, for example, Richard L. Kirkham, *Theories of Truth: A Critical Introduction* (Cambridge, MA: MIT Press, 1992); Michael Lynch, ed., *The Nature of Truth: Classic and Contemporary Perspectives* (Cambridge, MA: MIT Press, 2001); and Wolfgang Künne, *Conceptions of Truth* (Oxford: Clarendon Press, 2003).

2. Theodor W. Adorno, "Einleitung zum *Positivismusstreit in der deutschen Soziologie*," GS 8: 309; "Introduction," in Theodor W. Adorno et al., *The Positivist Dispute in German Sociology*, trans. Glyn Adey and David Frisby (London: Heinemann, 1976), 27. In this lengthy introduction Adorno discusses both the early Ludwig Wittgenstein and Rudolph Carnap as background to the critical rationalism of Sir Karl Popper and Hans Albert.

3. See, for example, Barry Allen, *Truth in Philosophy* (Cambridge, MA: Harvard University Press, 1993); and José Medina and David Wood, eds., *Truth: Engagements across Philosophical Traditions* (Malden, MA: Blackwell, 2005).

4. Theodor W. Adorno, "Zur Logik der Sozialwissenschaften," GS 8: 565; "On the Logic of the Social Sciences," in Adorno et al., *Positivist Dispute in German Sociology*, 122.

5. Here I do not restrict the term *logical validity* to that which is deductively valid. It refers to whatever makes for goodness in logical reasoning, including, for example, inductive and abductive forms of thought.

6. See chapter 8 in *Truth in Husserl, Heidegger, and the Frankfurt School: Critical Retrieval* (Cambridge, MA: MIT Press, 2017), 175–85; and chapters 2–3

in *Social Domains of Truth: Science, Politics, Art, and Religion* (New York: Routledge, 2023), 26–73.

7. *Art in Public: Politics, Economics, and a Democratic Culture* (Cambridge: Cambridge University Press, 2011), 176–90.

8. See the discussion of science's "societal autonomy" in *Social Domains of Truth*, 190–95.

9. See Popper's rejoinder, added to the English translation and titled "Reason or Revolution?," in Adorno et al., *Positivist Dispute in German Sociology*, 288–300.

10. G. W. F. Hegel, *Phenomenology of Spirit*, trans. A. V. Miller (Oxford: Oxford University Press, 1977), §71, p. 44. The longer sentence from Hegel's preface reads, "We must hold to the conviction that it is the nature of truth to prevail when its time has come, and that it appears only when this time has come, and therefore never appears prematurely, nor finds a public not ripe to receive it; also we must accept that the individual needs that this should be so in order to verify what is as yet a matter for himself alone, and to experience the conviction, which in the first place belongs only to a particular individual, as something universally held."

Bibliography

Adorno, Theodor W. "The Actuality of Philosophy" (1931). Translated by Benjamin Snow. *Telos* 31 (Spring 1977): 120–33.
Adorno, Theodor W. *Aesthetic Theory* (1970). Translated by Robert Hullot-Kentor. Minneapolis: University of Minnesota Press, 1997.
Adorno, Theodor W. *Against Epistemology: A Metacritique; Studies in Husserl and the Phenomenological Antinomies* (1956). Translated by Willis Domingo. Cambridge, MA: MIT Press, 1982.
Adorno, Theodor W. "Anmerkungen zum philosophischen Denken." In *Stichworte: Kritische Modelle 2*, GS 10.2, 598–607. Frankfurt am Main: Suhrkamp, 1977.
Adorno, Theodor W. *Ästhetische Theorie*. GS 7. 2nd ed. Frankfurt am Main: Suhrkamp, 1972.
Adorno, Theodor W. *Drei Studien zu Hegel*. In GS 5, 247–381. Frankfurt am Main: Suhrkamp, 1970.
Adorno, Theodor W. "Einleitung zum *Positivismusstreit in der deutschen Soziologie*." GS 8, 280–353.
Adorno, Theodor W. "Erpresste Versöhnung." In *Noten zur Literatur II*, GS 11, 251–80. Frankfurt am Main: Suhrkamp, 1974.
Adorno, Theodor W. "Extorted Reconciliation: On Georg Lukács' *Realism in Our Time*" (1958). In *Notes to Literature*, vol. 1, edited by Rolf Tiedemann, translated by Shierry Weber Nicholsen, 216–40. New York: Columbia University Press, 1991.
Adorno, Theodor W. "Goldmann and Adorno: To Describe, Understand and Explain" (1968). Appendix 3 to Lucien Goldmann, *Cultural Creation in Modern Society*, translated by Bart Grahl, 129–45. Oxford: Basil Blackwell, 1976.
Adorno, Theodor W. *Hegel: Three Studies* (1963). Translated by Shierry Weber Nicholsen. Cambridge, MA: MIT Press, 1993.
Adorno, Theodor W. *History and Freedom: Lectures 1964–1965*. Translated by Rodney Livingstone. Cambridge: Polity, 2006.
Adorno, Theodor W. "The Idea of Natural History" (1932). Translated by Robert Hullot-Kentor. *Telos*, no. 60 (Summer 1984): 111–24.

Adorno, Theodor W. *An Introduction to Dialectics (1958)*. Translated by Nicholas Walker. Cambridge: Polity, 2017.

Adorno, Theodor W. *Jargon der Eigentlichkeit: Zur deutschen Ideologie*. In GS 6, 413–526. Frankfurt am Main: Suhrkamp, 1973.

Adorno, Theodor W. *The Jargon of Authenticity* (1964). Translated by Knut Tarnowski and Frederic Will. London: Routledge & Kegan Paul, 1973.

Adorno, Theodor W. *Kant's "Critique of Pure Reason" (1959)*. Translated by Rodney Livingstone. Stanford, CA: Stanford University Press, 2001.

Adorno, Theodor W. *Kants "Kritik der reinen Vernunft" (1959)*. NS IV.4. Edited by Rolf Tiedemann. Frankfurt am Main: Suhrkamp, 1995.

Adorno, Theodor W. *Kierkegaard: Construction of the Aesthetic* (1933). Translated by Robert Hullot-Kentor. Minneapolis: University of Minnesota Press, 1989.

Adorno, Theodor W. *Lectures on Negative Dialectics: Fragments of a Lecture Course 1965/1966*. Translated by Rodney Livingstone. Cambridge: Polity, 2008.

Adorno, Theodor W. *Metaphysics: Concept and Problems* (1965). Edited by Rolf Tiedemann. Translated by Edmund Jephcott. Stanford, CA: Stanford University Press, 2000.

Adorno, Theodor W. *Minima Moralia: Reflections from Damaged Life* (1951). Translated by E. F. N. Jephcott. London: NLB, 1974.

Adorno, Theodor W. *Minima Moralia: Reflexionen aus dem beschädigten Leben*. GS 4. Frankfurt am Main: Suhrkamp, 1996.

Adorno, Theodor W. *Negative Dialectics* (1966, 1967). Translated by E. B. Ashton. New York: Seabury Press, 1973.

Adorno, Theodor W. *Negative Dialektik*. In GS 6, 7–412. Frankfurt am Main: Suhrkamp, 1973.

Adorno, Theodor W. "Notes on Philosophical Thinking" (1965). In *Critical Models: Interventions and Catchwords*, translated by Henry W. Pickford, 127–34. New York: Columbia University Press, 1998.

Adorno, Theodor W. "On the Fetish-Character in Music and the Regression of Listening." In *Essays on Music*, edited by Richard Leppert, 288–317. Berkeley: University of California Press, 2002.

Adorno, Theodor W. *Ontologie und Dialektik (1960/61)*. NS IV.7. Edited by Rolf Tiedemann. Frankfurt am Main: Suhrkamp, 2002.

Adorno, Theodor W. *Ontology and Dialectics 1960/61*. Translated by Nicholas Walker. Cambridge: Polity, 2019.

Adorno, Theodor W. *Philosophische Terminologie I und II* (1962/63). NS IV.9. Edited by Henri Lonitz. Frankfurt am Main: Suhrkamp, 2016.

Adorno, Theodor W. *Philosophy of New Music*. Translated, edited, and with an introduction by Robert Hullot-Kentor. Minneapolis: University of Minnesota Press, 2006.

Adorno, Theodor W. *Schein—Form—Subjekt—Prozesscharackter—Kunstwerk: Textkritische Edition der letzten bekannten Überarbeitung des III. Kapitels der*

"Kapitel-Ästhetik." Edited by Martin Endres, Axel Pichler, and Claus Zittel. 2 vols. Berlin: Walter de Gruyter, 2021.
Adorno, Theodor W. "Theses on the Language of the Philosopher" (1932?). Translated by Samir Gandesha and Michael K. Palamarek. In *Adorno and the Need in Thinking: New Critical Essays*, edited by Donald A. Burke et al., 35–40. Toronto: University of Toronto Press, 2007.
Adorno, Theodor W. *Zur Lehre von der Geschichte und von der Freiheit* (1964/65). NS IV.13. Edited by Rolf Tiedemann. Frankfurt am Main: Suhrkamp, 2001.
Adorno, Theodor W. "Zur Logik der Sozialwissenschaften." GS 8: 547–65.
Adorno, Theodor W. *Zur Metakritik der Erkenntnistheorie: Studien über Husserl und die phänomenologischen Antinomien*. In GS 5, 7–245. Frankfurt am Main: Suhrkamp, 1970.
Adorno, T. W., Else Frenkel-Brunswik, Daniel J. Levinson, and R. Nevitt Stanford, in collaboration with Betty Aron, Maria Hertz Levinson, and William Morrow. *The Authoritarian Personality*. New York: Harper & Brothers, 1950. Chapters 1, 7, and 16–19 appear in Adorno's GS 9.1 (Frankfurt am Main: Suhrkamp, 1975), 143–509, under the title *Studies in the Authoritarian Personality*.
Adorno, Theodor W., Hans Albert, Ralf Dahrendorf, Jürgen Habermas, Harald Pilot, and Karl R. Popper. *The Positivist Dispute in German Sociology* (1969). Translated by Glyn Adey and David Frisby. London: Heinemann, 1976.
Allen, Amy. "Critical Theory and Feminism." In *The Routledge Companion to the Frankfurt School*, edited by Peter Gordon, Espen Hammer, and Axel Honneth, 528–41. New York: Routledge, 2018.
Allen, Amy. *The End of Progress: Decolonizing the Normative Foundations of Critical Theory*. New York: Columbia University Press, 2016.
Allen, Amy. "Feminist Perspectives on Power." *The Stanford Encyclopedia of Philosophy* (Fall 2016 ed.), edited by Edward N. Zalta. <https://plato.stanford.edu/archives/fall2016/entries/feminist-power/>.
Allen, Amy. *The Politics of Our Selves: Power, Autonomy, and Gender in Contemporary Critical Theory*. New York: Columbia University Press, 2008.
Allen, Amy. *The Power of Feminist Theory: Domination, Resistance, Solidarity*. Boulder, CO: Westview Press, 1999.
Allen, Barry. *Truth in Philosophy*. Cambridge, MA: Harvard University Press, 1993.
Anders, Guenther (Stern). "On the Pseudo-Concreteness of Heidegger's Philosophy." *Philosophy and Phenomenological Research* 8, no. 3 (1948): 337–71.
Anderson, Elisabeth. "Feminist Epistemology and Philosophy of Science." In *The Stanford Encyclopedia of Philosophy* (Spring 2020 ed.), ed. Edward N. Zalta. <https://plato.stanford.edu/archives/spr2020/entries/feminism-epistemology/>.
Bauer, Michael. "Adorno and Heidegger on Art in the Modern World." *Philosophy Today* 40, no. 3 (Fall 1996): 357–66.
Beardsley, Monroe C. *Aesthetics: Problems in the Philosophy of Criticism*. New York: Harcourt, Brace & World, 1958.

Beiner, Ronald. *Dangerous Minds: Nietzsche, Heidegger, and the Return of the Far Right*. Philadelphia: University of Pennsylvania Press, 2018.
Benhabib, Seyla. *Situating the Self: Gender, Community and Postmodernism in Contemporary Ethics*. New York: Routledge, 1992.
Benhabib, Seyla, Judith Butler, Drucilla Cornell, and Nancy Fraser. *Feminist Contentions: A Philosophical Exchange*. New York: Routledge, 1995.
Benjamin, Walter. *Origin of the German Trauerspiel* (1928). Translated by Howard Eiland. Cambridge, MA: Harvard University Press, 2019.
Benjamin, Walter. *Ursprung des deutschen Trauerspiels*. Frankfurt am Main: Suhrkamp Taschenbuch, 1978.
Benjamin, Walter. "The Work of Art in the Age of Mechanical Reproduction" (1936). In *Illuminations*, edited by Hannah Arendt, translated by Harry Zohn, 217–51. New York: Schocken Books, 1969.
Berger, Maxi, and Philip Hogh, eds. *Der Vorrang des Objekts: Negative Dialektik heute*. Berlin: J. B. Metzler, 2022.
Bernstein, J. M. *Adorno: Disenchantment and Ethics*. Cambridge: Cambridge University Press, 2001.
Bernstein, J. M. *The Fate of Art: Aesthetic Alienation from Kant to Derrida and Adorno*. University Park: Pennsylvania State University Press, 1992.
Bernstein, J. M. *Recovering Ethical Life: Jürgen Habermas and the Future of Critical Theory*. New York: Routledge, 1995.
Bernstein, J. M. "Why Rescue Semblance? Metaphysical Experience and the Possibility of Ethics." In *The Semblance of Subjectivity: Essays in Adorno's Aesthetic Theory*, edited by Tom Huhn and Lambert Zuidervaart, 177–212. Cambridge, MA: MIT Press, 1997.
Bernstein, Richard J. "Foucault: Critique as a Philosophic *Ēthos*." In *The New Constellation: The Ethical-Political Horizons of Modernity/Postmodernity*, 142–71. Cambridge, MA: MIT Press, 1991.
Bloch, Ernst. *Geist der Utopie* (1918, 1923). Frankfurt am Main: Suhrkamp, 1964.
Bourdieu, Pierre. *The Political Ontology of Martin Heidegger* (1988). Translated by Peter Collier. Stanford, CA: Stanford University Press, 1991.
Bowie, Andrew. *Adorno and the Ends of Philosophy*. Cambridge: Polity, 2013.
Bowie, Andrew. "Adorno, Heidegger, and the Meaning of Music." *Thesis Eleven* 56 (1999): 1–24.
Brunkhorst, Hauke. "Adorno, Heidegger and Postmodernity." *Philosophy and Social Criticism* 14, no. 3–4 (1989): 411–24.
Bubner, Rüdiger. "Concerning the Central Idea of Adorno's Philosophy." In *The Semblance of Subjectivity: Essays in Adorno's Aesthetic Theory*, edited by Tom Huhn and Lambert Zuidervaart, 147–75. Cambridge, MA: MIT Press, 1997.
Buck-Morss, Susan. *The Origin of Negative Dialectics: Theodor W. Adorno, Walter Benjamin, and the Frankfurt Institute*. Hassocks, Sussex, UK: Harvester Press, 1977.
Campbell, Richard. *Truth and Historicity*. Oxford: Clarendon Press, 1992.

Claussen, Detlev. *Theodor W. Adorno: One Last Genius*. Translated by Rodney Livingstone. Cambridge, MA: Belknap Press of Harvard University Press, 2008.
Cook, Deborah. *Adorno, Foucault and the Critique of the West*. London: Verso, 2018.
Cook, Deborah, ed. *Theodor Adorno: Key Concepts*. Stocksfield, UK: Acumen, 2008.
Cook, Deborah. "Through a Glass Darkly: Adorno's Inverse Theology." *Adorno Studies* 1, no. 1 (January 2017): 66–78.
Dallmayr, Fred. *Between Freiburg and Frankfurt: Toward a Critical Ontology*. Amherst: University of Massachusetts Press, 1991.
Dallmayr, Fred. "Phenomenology and Critical Theory: Adorno." *Cultural Hermeneutics* 3 (1976): 367–405.
Dews, Peter. *Logics of Disintegration: Post-Structuralist Thought and the Claims of Critical Theory*. London: Verso, 1987.
Dufrenne, Mikel. *Art et politique*. Paris: Union générale d'éditions, 1974.
Dufrenne, Mikel. *The Phenomenology of Aesthetic Experience*. Translated by Edward S. Casey, Albert A. Anderson, Willis Domingo, and Leon Jacobson. Evanston, IL: Northwestern University Press, 1973.
Düttmann, Alexander Garcia. *The Memory of Thought: An Essay on Heidegger and Adorno* (1991). Translated by Nicholas Walker. London: Continuum, 2002.
Endres, Martin, Axel Pichler, and Claus Zittel, eds. *Eros und Erkenntnis: 50 Jahre "Ästhetische Theorie."* Berlin: Walter DeGruyter, 2019.
Eusterschulte, Anne, and Sebastian Tränkle, eds. *Theodor W. Adorno: Ästhetische Theorie*. Berlin: Walter de Gruyter, 2021.
Farias, Victor. *Heidegger and Nazism* (1987). Edited by Joseph Margolis and Tom Rockmore. Philadelphia: Temple University Press, 1989.
Faye, Emmanuel. *Heidegger: The Introduction of Nazism into Philosophy in Light of the Unpublished Seminars of 1933–1935* (2005). Translated by Michael B. Smith. New Haven, CT: Yale University Press, 2009.
Finlayson, Gordon. "A Critical Notice of *Adorno and Existence*." *International Journal of Philosophical Studies* 25, no. 5 (2017): 723–30.
Florence, Maurice. "Foucault." In *Aesthetics, Method, and Epistemology: Essential Works of Foucault, 1954–1984*, vol. 2, edited by James D. Faubion, translated by Robert Hurley et al., 459–63. New York: The New Press, 1998.
Forum für Philosophie Bad Homburg, ed. *Martin Heidegger: Innen- und Aussenansichten*. Frankfurt am Main: Suhrkamp, 1989.
Foster, Roger S. *Adorno and Philosophical Modernism: The Inside of Things*. Lanham, MD: Lexington Books, 2016.
Foster, Roger S. *Adorno: The Recovery of Experience*. Albany: State University of New York Press, 2007.
Foucault, Michel. *The Archaeology of Knowledge and the Discourse on Language* (1969 and 1971). Translated by A. M. Sheridan Smith. New York: Vintage Books, 1972.

Foucault, Michel. *The Birth of Biopolitics: Lectures at the Collège De France, 1978–79*. Edited by Michel Senellart. Translated by Graham Burchell. New York: Palgrave Macmillan, 2008.

Foucault, Michel. *Discipline and Punish: The Birth of the Prison* (1975). Translated by Alan Sheridan. New York: Pantheon Books, 1977.

Foucault, Michel. *The History of Sexuality*, vol. 1, *An Introduction* (1976). Translated by Robert Hurley. New York: Random House, 1978; Vintage Books, 1990.

Foucault, Michel. "Interview with Michel Foucault" (1980). In *Power: Essential Works of Foucault, 1954–1984*, vol. 3, edited James D. Faubion, translated by Robert Hurley et al., 239–97. New York: The New Press, 2000.

Foucault, Michel. *The Politics of Truth*. Edited by Sylvère Lotringer. Translated by Lysa Hochroth and Catherine Porter. Los Angeles: Semiotext(e), 1997, 2007.

Foucault, Michel. "Powers and Strategies" (1977). In *Power/Knowledge: Selected Interviews and Other Writings 1972–1977*, edited by Colin Gordon, 134–45. New York: Pantheon Books, 1980.

Foucault, Michel. "Questions of Method: An Interview with Michel Foucault" (1980). In *After Philosophy: End or Transformation?*, edited by Kenneth Baynes, James Bohman, and Thomas McCarthy, 100–17. Cambridge, MA: MIT Press, 1987.

Foucault, Michel. *"Society Must Be Defended": Lectures at the Collège de France, 1975–76*. Edited by Mauro Bertani and Alessandro Fontana. Translated by David Macey. New York: Picador, 2003.

Foucault, Michel. "The Subject and Power" (1982). In *Power: Essential Works of Foucault, 1954–1984*, vol. 3, edited by James D. Faubion, translated by Robert Hurley et al., 326–48. New York: The New Press, 2000.

Foucault, Michel. "Truth and Power" (1977). In *Power/Knowledge: Selected Interviews and Other Writings 1972–1977*, edited by Colin Gordon, 109–33. New York: Pantheon Books, 1980.

Foucault, Michel. "Two Lectures" (1976). In *Power/Knowledge: Selected Interviews and Other Writings 1972–1977*, edited by Colin Gordon, 78–108. New York: Pantheon Books, 1980.

Fraser, Nancy. *Justice Interruptus: Critical Reflections on the "Postsocialist Condition."* New York: Routledge, 1997.

Fraser, Nancy. *Unruly Practices: Power, Discourse, and Gender in Contemporary Social Theory*. Minneapolis: University of Minnesota Press, 1989.

Freyenhagen, Fabian. *Adorno's Practical Philosophy: Living Less Wrongly*. Cambridge: Cambridge University Press, 2013.

Fried, Gregory, ed. *Confronting Heidegger: A Critical Dialogue on Politics and Philosophy*. London: Rowman & Littlefield International, 2020.

Gadamer, Hans-Georg. *Truth and Method*. 2nd, rev. ed. Translated and edited by Joel Weinsheimer and Donald G. Marshall. New York: Crossroad, 1989.

Gandesha, Samir. "Leaving Home: On Adorno and Heidegger." In *The Cambridge Companion to Adorno*, edited by Tom Huhn, 101–28. Cambridge: Cambridge University Press, 2004.

Garbrecht, Oliver. *Rationalitätskritik der Moderne: Adorno und Heidegger*. Munich: Herbert Utz, 1999.
Goodman, Nelson. *Languages of Art: An Approach to a Theory of Symbols*. Indianapolis: Bobbs-Merrill, 1968.
Gordon, Peter E. *Adorno and Existence*. Cambridge, MA: Harvard University Press, 2016.
Guyer, Paul. *A History of Modern Aesthetics, Volume 3*: *The Twentieth Century*. Cambridge: Cambridge University Press, 2014.
Guzzoni, Ute. *Identität oder nicht: Zur Kritischen Theorie der Ontologie*. Freiburg/Munich: Verlag Karl Alber, 1981.
Habermas, Jürgen. *The Philosophical Discourse of Modernity: Twelve Lectures* (1985). Translated by Frederick G. Lawrence. Cambridge, MA: MIT Press, 1987.
Habermas, Jürgen. *The Theory of Communicative Action*. Translated by Thomas McCarthy. 2 vols. Boston, MA: Beacon Press, 1984, 1987.
Hammer, Espen. "Adorno's Critique of Heidegger." In *A Companion to Adorno*, edited by Peter E. Gordon, Espen Hammer, and Max Pensky, 473–86. Hoboken, NJ: Wiley Blackwell, 2020.
Hammer, Espen. *Adorno's Modernism: Art, Experience, and Catastrophe*. Cambridge: Cambridge University Press, 2015.
Hammer, Espen. *Philosophy and Temporality from Kant to Critical Theory*. Cambridge: Cambridge University Press, 2011.
Haslanger, Sally. *Resisting Reality: Social Construction and Social Critique*. New York: Oxford University Press, 2012.
Hauser, Arnold. *The Philosophy of Art History*. London: Routledge & Kegan Paul, 1958.
Hauser, Arnold. *The Social History of Art*. 4 vols. Translated by Stanley Goodman. New York: Vintage Books, 1951.
Hauser, Arnold. *The Sociology of Art*. Translated by Kenneth J. Northcott. Chicago, IL: University of Chicago Press, 1982.
Hauser, Arnold. *Sozialgeschichte der Kunst und Literatur*. Munich: C. H. Beck, 1953.
Hegel, G. W. F. *Elements of the Philosophy of Right*. Edited by Allen W. Wood. Translated by H. B. Nisbet. Cambridge: Cambridge University Press, 1991.
Hegel, G. W. F. *Hegel's Logic: Being Part One of the* Encyclopaedia of the Philosophical Sciences (1830). Translated by William Wallace. Oxford: Clarendon Press, 1975.
Hegel, G. W. F. *Phenomenology of Spirit*. Translated by A. V. Miller. Oxford: Oxford University Press, 1977.
Hegel, G. W. F. *The Science of Logic*. Translated and edited by George di Giovanni. Cambridge: Cambridge University Press, 2010.
Heidegger, Martin. *Being and Time*. Translated by Joan Stambaugh. Albany: State University of New York Press, 1996.
Heidegger, Martin. *Contributions to Philosophy (Of the Event)*. Translated by Richard Rojcewicz and Daniela Vallega-Neu. Bloomington: Indiana University Press, 2012.

Heidegger, Martin. *Kant and the Problem of Metaphysics* (1929). Translated by James S. Churchill. Bloomington: Indiana University Press, 1962.
Heidegger, Martin. "Kants These über das Sein." In *Wegmarken*, 3rd ed., 445–80. Frankfurt am Main: Vittorio Klostermann, 1996.
Heidegger, Martin. "Kant's Thesis about Being." In *Pathmarks*, edited by William McNeill, 337–63. Cambridge: Cambridge University Press, 1998.
Heidegger, Martin. "On the Essence of Truth" (1930). Translated by John Sallis. In Martin Heidegger, *Pathmarks*, edited by William McNeill, 136–54. Cambridge: Cambridge University Press, 1998.
Heidegger, Martin. *Pathmarks*. Edited by William McNeill. Cambridge: Cambridge University Press, 1998.
Heidegger, Martin. *Platons Lehre von der Wahrheit: Mit einem Brief über den "Humanismus."* 2nd ed. Bern: A. Francke AG, 1954.
Heidegger, Martin. *Sein und Zeit* (1927). 15th ed. Tübingen: Max Niemeyer, 1979.
Heidegger, Martin. "Vom Wesen der Wahrheit." In Martin Heidegger, *Wegmarken*, 3rd ed., 177–202. Frankfurt am Main: Klostermann, 1996.
Heidegger, Martin. *Wegmarken*. 3rd ed. Frankfurt am Main: Vittorio Klostermann, 1996.
Hogh, Philip. *Communication and Expression: Adorno's Philosophy of Language*. Translated by Antonia Hofstätter. London: Rowman & Littlefield International, 2017.
Honneth, Axel. *The Critique of Power: Reflective Stages in a Critical Social Theory*. Translated by Kenneth Baynes. Cambridge, MA: MIT Press, 1991.
Honneth, Axel. "Performing Justice: Adorno's Introduction to *Negative Dialectics*." In *Pathologies of Reason*, translated by James Ingram et al., 71–87. New York: Columbia University Press, 2009.
Honneth, Axel. *Reification: A New Look at an Old Idea*. Edited by Martin Jay. Oxford: Oxford University Press, 2008.
Horkheimer, Max. *Eclipse of Reason*. New York: Oxford University Press, 1947.
Horkheimer, Max. *Die Sehnsucht nach dem ganz Anderen: Ein Interview mit Kommentar von Helmut Gumnior*. Hamburg: Furche-Verlag, 1970.
Horkheimer, Max, and Theodor W. Adorno. *Dialectic of Enlightenment: Philosophical Fragments* (1947). Translated by Edmund Jephcott. Stanford, CA: Stanford University Press, 2002.
Horkheimer, Max, and Theodor W. Adorno. *Dialektik der Aufklärung: Philosophische Fragmente*. In Max Horkheimer, *Gesammelte Schriften*, vol. 5, *"Dialektik der Aufklärung" und Schriften 1940–1950*, edited by Gunzelin Schmid Noerr, 11–290. Frankfurt am Main: Fischer Taschenbuch, 1987.
Hoy, David Couzens, and Thomas McCarthy. *Critical Theory*. Oxford: Blackwell, 1994.
Huhn, Tom. "The Movement of Mimesis: Heidegger's 'Origin of the Work of Art' in Relation to Adorno and Lyotard." *Philosophy and Social Criticism* 22, no. 4 (July 1996): 45–69.
Huhn, Tom, and Lambert Zuidervaart, eds. *The Semblance of Subjectivity: Essays in Adorno's Aesthetic Theory*. Cambridge, MA: MIT Press, 1997.

Hulatt, Owen. *Adorno's Theory of Philosophical and Aesthetic Truth*. New York: Columbia University Press, 2016.
Husserl, Edmund. *Logical Investigations* (1900/1901). 2 vols. Translated by J. N. Findlay, with a new Preface by Michael Dummett, and edited by Dermot Moran. London: Routledge, 1970, 2001.
Husserl, Edmund. *Logische Untersuchungen*. 2 vols. *Husserliana*, vol. 18 and 19. The Hague: Martinus Nijhoff, 1975, 1984.
Immanen, Mikko. *Toward a Concrete Philosophy: Heidegger and the Emergence of the Frankfurt School*. Ithaca, NY: Cornell University Press and Cornell University Library, 2020.
Ingarden, Roman. *The Cognition of the Literary Work of Art*. Translated by Ruth Ann Crowley and Kenneth R. Olson. Evanston, IL: Northwestern University Press, 1973.
Ingram, David. "Foucault and Habermas." In *The Cambridge Companion to Foucault*, 2nd ed., edited by Gary Gutting, 240–83. Cambridge: Cambridge University Press, 2005.
Jameson, Fredric. *Late Marxism: Adorno, or, the Persistence of the Dialectic*. London: Verso, 1990.
Jarvis, Simon. *Adorno: A Critical Introduction*. New York: Routledge, 1998.
Jay, Martin. *Adorno*. London: Fontana Paperbacks, 1984.
Jay, Martin. *Reason after Its Eclipse: On Late Critical Theory*. Madison: University of Wisconsin Press, 2016.
Kant, Immanuel. *Critique of Practical Reason*. In Immanuel Kant, *Practical Philosophy*, translated and edited by Mary J. Gregor, 133–271. Cambridge: Cambridge University Press, 1996.
Kant, Immanuel. *Critique of Pure Reason*. Translated and edited by Paul Guyer and Allen W. Wood. Cambridge: Cambridge University Press, 1998.
Kant, Immanuel. *Critique of the Power of Judgment*. Edited by Paul Guyer. Translated by Paul Guyer and Eric Matthews. Cambridge: Cambridge University Press, 2000.
Kaufmann, David, "Correlations, Constellations and the Truth: Adorno's Ontology of Redemption." *Philosophy and Social Criticism* 26, no. 5 (2000): 62–80.
Kelly, Michael, ed. *Critique and Power: Recasting the Foucault/Habermas Debate*. Cambridge, MA: MIT Press, 1994.
Kirkham, Richard L. *Theories of Truth: A Critical Introduction*. Cambridge, MA: MIT Press, 1992.
Knowles, Adam. *Heidegger's Fascist Affinities: A Politics of Silence*. Stanford, CA: Stanford University Press, 2019.
Kompridis, Nikolas. *Critique and Disclosure: Critical Theory between Past and Future*. Cambridge, MA: MIT Press, 2007.
Korsch, Karl. *Marxismus und Philosophie* (1923). Edited and introduced by Erich Gerlach. Frankfurt: Europäische Verlagsanstalt, 1966.
Künne, Wolfgang. *Conceptions of Truth*. Oxford: Clarendon Press, 2003.

Langer, Susanne K. *Feeling and Form: A Theory of Art Developed from Philosophy in a New Key*. New York: Charles Scribner's Sons, 1953.
Langer, Susanne K. *Mind: An Essay on Human Feeling*. 3 vols. Baltimore, MD: Johns Hopkins University Press, 1967–82.
Langer, Susanne K. *Philosophy in a New Key: A Study in the Symbolism of Reason, Rite, and Art*. 3rd ed. Cambridge, MA: Harvard University Press, 1957.
Lukács, Georg. *Die Eigenart des Ästhetischen*. 2 vols. Neuwied: Luchterhand, 1963.
Lukács, Georg. *Geschichte und Klassenbewusstsein: Studien über marxistische Dialektik*. Darmstadt/Neuwied: Sammlung Luchterhand, 1968.
Lukács, Georg. *History and Class Consciousness: Studies in Marxist Dialectics* (1923). Translated by Rodney Livingstone. London: Merlin Press, 1971.
Lukács, Georg. *Realism in Our Time: Literature and the Class Struggle*. Translated by Johan and Necke Mander. New York: Harper & Row, 1964.
Lukács, Georg. *Wider den missverstandenen Realismus*. Hamburg: Claassen, 1958.
Lynch, Michael, ed. *The Nature of Truth: Classic and Contemporary Perspectives*. Cambridge, MA: MIT Press, 2001.
Macdonald, Iain. "Adorno's Modal Utopianism: Possibility and Actuality in Adorno and Hegel." *Adorno Studies* 1, no. 1 (January 2017): 1–12.
Macdonald, Iain. " 'What Is, Is More Than It Is': Adorno and Heidegger on the Priority of Possibility." *International Journal of Philosophical Studies* 19, no. 1 (2011): 31–57.
Macdonald, Iain. *What Would Be Different: Figures of Possibility in Adorno*. Stanford, CA: Stanford University Press, 2019.
Macdonald, Iain, and Krzysztof Ziarek, eds. *Adorno and Heidegger: Philosophical Questions*, Stanford, CA: Stanford University Press, 2008.
McCarthy, Thomas. "The Critique of Impure Reason: Foucault and the Frankfurt School." In *Ideals and Illusions: On Reconstruction and Deconstruction in Contemporary Critical Theory*, 43–75. Cambridge, MA: MIT Press, 1991.
McCumber, John. *Time and Philosophy: A History of Continental Thought*. Montreal: McGill-Queen's University Press, 2011.
Medina, José, and David Wood, eds. *Truth: Engagements across Philosophical Traditions*. Malden, MA: Blackwell, 2005.
Mörchen, Herman. *Adorno und Heidegger: Untersuchung einer philosophischen Kommunikationsverweigerung*. Stuttgart: Klett-Cotta, 1981.
Mörchen, Hermann. *Macht und Herrschaft im Denken von Heidegger und Adorno*. Stuttgart: Klett-Cotta, 1980.
Müller-Doohm, Stefan. *Adorno: A Biography*. Translated by Rodney Livingstone. Cambridge: Polity, 2005.
Naeher, Jürgen. "Das ontologische 'Bedürfnis im Denken'; Der Erste Teil der *Negativen Dialektik* (67–136): Zum Verfahren der 'immanenten Kritik.' " In *Die Negative Dialektik Adornos: Einführung—Dialog*, edited by Jürgen Naeher, 204–34. Opladen: Leske Verlag + Budrich, 1984.

Neske, Günther, and Emil Kettering, eds. *Martin Heidegger and National Socialism: Questions and Answers*. New York: Paragon House, 1990.

Nietzsche, Friedrich. *Also Sprach Zarathustra* (1883–1885). In *Nietzsche Werke: Kritische Gesamtausgabe*, part 6, vol. 1. Edited by Giorgio Colli and Mazzino Montinari. Berlin: Walter de Gruyter, 1968.

Nietzsche, Friedrich. *Thus Spoke Zarathustra*. Translated by Walter Kaufmann. New York: Penguin Books, 1966.

O'Connor, Brian. "Adorno, Heidegger and the Critique of Epistemology." *Philosophy and Social Criticism* 24, no. 4 (1998): 43–62.

O'Connor, Brian. *Adorno's Negative Dialectic: Philosophy and the Possibility of Critical Rationality*. Cambridge, MA: MIT Press, 2004.

Petherbridge, Danielle. *The Critical Theory of Axel Honneth*. Lanham, MD: Lexington Books, 2013.

Rockmore, Tom. *On Heidegger's Nazism and Philosophy*. Berkeley: University of California Press, 1992.

Schnädelbach, Herbert. "Dialektik als Vernunftkritik: Zur Konstruktion des Rationalen bei Adorno." In *Adorno-Konferenz 1983*, edited by Ludwig von Friedeburg and Jürgen Habermas, 66–93. Frankfurt am Main: Suhrkamp, 1983.

Scholem, Gershom, and Theodor W. Adorno, eds. *The Correspondence of Walter Benjamin, 1910–1940*. Translated by Manfred R. Jacobson and Evelyn M. Jacobson. Chicago, IL: University of Chicago Press, 1994.

Shuster, Martin. *Autonomy after Auschwitz: Adorno, German Idealism, and Modernity*. Chicago, IL: University of Chicago Press, 2014.

Shuster, Martin. "The Philosophy of History." In *The Routledge Companion to the Frankfurt School*, edited by Peter Gordon, Espen Hammer, and Axel Honneth, 48–64. New York: Routledge, 2018.

Silberbusch, Oshrat C. *Adorno's Philosophy of the Nonidentical: Thinking as Resistance*. Cham, Switzerland: Springer, Palgrave Macmillan, 2018.

Sparshott, Francis E. *The Structure of Aesthetics*. Toronto: University of Toronto Press, 1963.

Stone, Alison. "Adorno and Logic." In *Theodor Adorno: Key Concepts*, edited by Deborah Cook, 47–62. Stocksfield, UK: Acumen, 2008.

Thomä, Dieter. "Verhältnis zur Ontologie: Adornos Denken des Unbegrifflichen." In *Theodor W. Adorno: Negative Dialektik*, edited by Axel Honneth and Christoph Menke, 29–48. Berlin: Akademie, 2006.

Tietz, Udo. *Ontologie und Dialektik: Heidegger und Adorno über das Sein, das Nichtidentische, die Synthesis und die Kopula*. Vienna: Passagen, 2003.

Trawny, Peter. *Heidegger: A Critical Introduction* (2016). Translated by Rodrigo Therezo. Cambridge: Polity, 2019.

Tugendhat, Ernst. "Heidegger's Idea of Truth." In *The Heidegger Controversy: A Critical Reader*, ed. Richard Wolin, 2nd ed., 245–63. Cambridge, MA: MIT Press, 1991.

Weeks, Kathi. *The Problem with Work: Feminism, Marxism, Antiwork Politics, and Postwork Imaginaries*. Durham, NC: Duke University Press, 2011.

Wellmer, Albrecht. "Adorno, Anwalt des Nicht-Identischen: Eine Einführung." In *Zur Dialektik von Moderne und Postmoderne: Vernunftkritik nach Adorno*, 135–66. Frankfurt am Main: Suhrkamp, 1985.

Wellmer, Albrecht. "Metaphysics at the Moment of Its Fall." In *Endgame: The Irreconcilable Nature of Modernity; Essays and Lectures*, translated by David Midgley, 183–201. Cambridge, MA: MIT Press, 1998.

Wellmer, Albrecht. "Truth, Semblance, Reconciliation: Adorno's Aesthetic Redemption of Modernity." In *The Persistence of Modernity: Essays on Aesthetics, Ethics, and Postmodernism*, translated by David Midgley, 1–35. Cambridge, MA: MIT Press, 1991.

Wellmer, Albrecht. "Wahrheit, Schein, Versöhnung: Adornos Ästhetische Rettung der Modernität." In *Zur Dialektik von Moderne und Postmoderne: Vernunftkritik nach Adorno*, 9–47. Frankfurt am Main: Suhrkamp, 1985.

Wilke, Sabine. *Zur Dialektik von Exposition und Darstellung: Ansätze zu einer Kritik der Arbeiten Martin Heideggers, Theodor W. Adornos, und Jacques Derridas*. New York: Peter Lang, 1988.

Wolin, Richard, ed. *The Heidegger Controversy: A Critical Reader*. 2nd ed. Cambridge, MA: MIT Press, 1991.

Wolin, Richard. "On Heidegger's Antisemitism: The Peter Trawny Affair." *Antisemitism Studies* 1, no. 2 (2017): 245–79.

Wolin, Richard. *Walter Benjamin: An Aesthetic of Redemption*. New York: Columbia University Press, 1982.

Wolterstorff, Nicholas. *Art Rethought: The Social Practices of Art*. Oxford: Oxford University Press, 2015.

Zuidervaart, Lambert. *Adorno's Aesthetic Theory: The Redemption of Illusion*. Cambridge, MA: MIT Press, 1991.

Zuidervaart, Lambert. *Art in Public: Politics, Economics, and a Democratic Culture*. Cambridge: Cambridge University Press, 2011.

Zuidervaart, Lambert. *Artistic Truth: Aesthetics, Discourse, and Imaginative Disclosure*. Cambridge: Cambridge University Press, 2004.

Zuidervaart, Lambert. "Methodological Shadowboxing in Marxist Aesthetics: Lukács and Adorno." *Journal of Comparative Literature and Aesthetics* 11 (1988): 85–113.

Zuidervaart, Lambert. *Religion, Truth, and Social Transformation: Essays in Reformational Philosophy*. Montreal: McGill-Queen's University Press, 2016.

Zuidervaart, Lambert. *Shattering Silos: Reimagining Knowledge, Politics, and Social Critique*. Montreal: McGill-Queen's University Press, 2022.

Zuidervaart, Lambert. *Social Domains of Truth: Science, Politics, Art, and Religion*. New York: Routledge, 2023.

Zuidervaart, Lambert. *Social Philosophy after Adorno*. Cambridge: Cambridge University Press, 2007.
Zuidervaart, Lambert. *Truth in Husserl, Heidegger, and the Frankfurt School: Critical Retrieval*. Cambridge, MA: MIT Press, 2017.

Index

the absolute, 8, 26, 60, 92–93, 133, 171n50
accuracy, 35, 54, 132–33, 135
Adorno, Theodor W., ix–xi; as alethic aestheticist, 130–31; as alethic minimalist, 6, 10–12, 14; as alethic negativist, 6, 8–10, 14, 35, 117, 130–31; antisystematic character of, 2, 6–8; as Benjamin-inspired Hegelian, 3, 5, 9, 35, 93, 127; biography of, 55, 141–45, 159n8; contemporary relevance of, 2, 15–17, 21, 77, 80, 99, 105, 122, 124, 130, 140; critical retrieval of, ix, 2–3, 7–13, 16–17, 130–40; dialectical autonomism of, 16, 101, 103–5, 107, 119–20, 125, 127; as ethical minimalist, 11–12; Habermasian critique of, 25, 28, 37, 56, 77–78, 143–44, 154n17; historical metanarrative of, 23–25, 28; modernist aesthetic of, 104–7, 127; negative eschatology of, 28–31; paradoxical modernism of, 104–5, 107, 109–20, 112, 115, 127; pessimism of, 126–27, 176n46; social transformationalist reading of, 14, 22, 28–31, 126; systematic reconstruction of, ix, 7–13, 16–17, 108–20; translation of, 111–12, 117–18, 164n51, 165n60, 175n36, 176n46; truth theory of, 1–6, 16, 31–36, 95, 129–30
aesthetics, 16, 28, 101–9, 112, 114–15, 120–22, 126, 148–49, 176n46; postwar, 102–3
Aesthetic Theory, 1, 3, 16, 19, 101–11, 121, 126–27, 145, 147–49, 173n15; "Coherence and Meaning," 111–14; "Enigmaticalness, Truth Content, Metaphysics," 114–17; main themes of, 101, 104–5, 147–49; "Semblance and Expression," 108–111; untimely timeliness of, 16, 101–5, 121–22, 127
Allen, Amy, 77–81, 83–84, 98, 166n4, 167n9, 168n19, 170n39
Anders, Günther, 66
Anselm, 48–49
antagonism, 85–86, 147–48
Arendt, Hannah, 98
art: dialectical autonomy of, 16, 101, 103–5, 107, 119–20, 125, 127; logicality of, 112; metaphysics of, 114–15, 117, 120; modern, 62, 104–7, 109, 111, 115, 127, 148; and nature, 102–3, 106; politicization of, 122, 124; and politics, 16, 105, 120–27, 140; as promising, 30, 118–20, 124, 127,

art *(continued)*
  140, 176n46; and resistance, 30–31; situated, 104, 173n13; as social antithesis of society, 104–5, 148; social protest, 122–23; and society, 101–2, 104–5, 107; and suffering, 101, 110–11, 120, 124
artistic truth, 1, 16, 95, 101, 105–21, 126, 133, 148, 174n24, 175n38; as cogent imaginative disclosure, 122–23, 125–27; dialectical polarities in, 101, 108–20; and philosophical truth, 115–17, 119; and political truth, 122–25; and politics, 16, 105, 107–8, 120–23, 139–40; and scientific truth, 95; as a social domain, 111, 122–23; transcendence in, 114–19
artworks, 30, 90, 99, 110, 115–16, 118, 122–23; artifactual character of, 109–10, 115, 118; autonomous, 16, 105, 122–23, 125, 140, 148; self-transcendence of, 115–17, 119; as semblance/expression, 108–10, 113–15; and sociohistorical possibility, 118–20
assertions, 14, 25, 36, 38–41, 44, 51–54, 129, 131–33. *See also* propositions
attunement, 112–14
Auschwitz, 22–23
authenticity, 21, 43, 68–69, 144–45
The Authoritarian Personality, 144, 161n16

Beardsley, Monroe, 102
Being *(Sein)*, 14, 155n8, 156n14, 163n42; as *archē*, 63–66; and beings, 43, 48–49, 59, 63–64, 73; as concept, 42–44, 46–49, 65–67; forgetting of, 61, 63; and ideology, 61–62, 64, 70–71; indeterminacy of, 66–67; logical/ontic 44–49, 54, 64–65; meaning of, 45–46, 63–64, 70, 73; predicative, 39, 40, 42–45, 52–54; as third thing, 45–46, 50–51, 65
Benhabib, Seyla, 87–88, 94, 98, 169n37, 170n41
Benjamin, Walter, 3–4, 9, 34–35, 55, 66, 71–72, 93, 103, 142–43, 157n1, 169n35
Bernstein, J. M., 16, 105–7, 111, 114–15, 121, 174n24, 175n37
beyng *(Seyn)*, 15, 73–75
bivalent collectivities, 79–80
Bourdieu, Pierre, 56, 160n15
Bowie, Andrew, 21
Buck-Morss, Susan, xi, 151n7
Butler, Judith, 87–88, 169n37, 171n52

capitalism, 15, 23, 26, 83–84, 86–87, 136–38, 143, 145–46; and art, 104–5, 138, 148; mentioned, 60, 75–76, 97, 136, 163n37
categorial intuition, 14, 37–45, 52, 155n5, 155n8
concepts, 5, 35, 156n16; and art, 111–14, 116; and ideas, 3; and intuitions, 46–47; and the nonconceptual, 4, 9, 15, 29, 39, 44, 66–67, 116; and objects, 4, 25, 46; and things, 5–6, 13–15, 63, 108, 113, 116, 129, 146–47
consciousness: false, 62, 116, 122, 175n42; flashes of, 24–25; liberated, 62; the most advanced, 163n37; philosophy of 37; transformation of, 120–22
constellations, 3–7, 12, 31, 91–95, 129–30, 135, 148, 152n8, 156n11; in art, 108, 116

convergence, 28–31
Cook, Deborah, x–xi, 77–78, 80, 86, 166n5
the copula, 39, 45–50, 53–54, 64, 67, 156n13
Cornell, Drucilla, 88, 169n37, 170n41
correctness, 36, 42, 54, 132
critical retrieval: definition of, 2; of Adorno, ix, 2–3, 7–9, 11–13, 16–17, 21, 130–40; of Kant's transcendental ideas, 12, 22, 26, 28, 31
Critical Theory, xi, 19, 142–43, 160n12. *See also* Frankfurt School
critical theory: and Critical Theory, 167n10, 169n30; feminist, 15–16, 77–80, 83, 92, 99, 167n10
critique, 113; and art, 118–19, 148; of domination, 15, 86–88, 91, 132, 134, 136, 169n35; of falsehood, 9, 11–12; hopeful, 31–36; of ideology, 138; immanent, 37, 58–59, 64–65, 162n28, 164n43; normative, 95–99; of power, 84, 96–97, 99. *See also* metacritique; social critique
Croce, Benedetto, 104

Dallmayr, Fred, 56, 158n4
Dasein, 33, 63, 65–70, 73–74, 165n66
death, 23–24
Derrida, Jacques, 84
determinate/indeterminate, 66–67
determinate negation, 9–10, 21, 134. *See also* self-negation
Dews, Peter, 84
dialectic, 10, 145; of concept/thing, 13–15, 63, 65, 67, 108, 111, 113–14, 116, 119; of domination, 84–85, 92–96, 99, 121; of enlightenment, 23, 22–27, 94; of form/content, 16, 108, 111–15, 148; of Hegel, 92; of history/transcendence, 13–15, 108, 119, 126; negative, 7, 9, 15, 19–21, 33, 36, 38, 58, 61, 64–65, 91–93, 108, 146–47; of semblance/expression, 16, 108–11, 117; of subject/object, 13–14, 21, 37, 63, 65, 69, 108–10, 115, 119
Dialectic of Enlightenment, 15, 84, 87, 143–45
differential transformation, 99
differentiation, 106–7, 111
directional dead ends, 137–39
disclosure, 160n12; and art, 109, 111, 122–23; and fidelity, 132–35; imaginative, 122–25. *See also* self-disclosure; truth, as life-giving disclosure
domination, 8, 27, 91–99, 132, 134, 136, 143–46, 148–49, 169n35; and art, 110–13, 119; blind, 86–87, 92, 134, 143–46; and exchange, 15, 84–86, 139, 146, 148; in Foucault, 80, 82, 86, 168n22, 169n31; masculine, 167n9; of nature, 84–85, 96–97, 110–12, 120; and predicative practices, 130–32; by reason, 169n31; three modes of, 85–86, 92, 94, 96–97, 136, 143–47; mentioned, 12, 34, 71, 98–99
double truth theory, 92, 95–96
Dufrenne, Mikel, 102
dynamic correlation. *See* truth, as dynamic correlation

enlightenment, 23, 26–27, 29, 56, 60, 78, 84, 86–87, 94, 143, 169n31
Eisler, Hanns, 142
exchange, 30–31, 138; principle, 62, 92–93, 146–47; mentioned, 62, 78, 84

existence, 68, 70
experience, 152n20; of art, 119–20, 122; conceptual mediation of, 35; of convergence, 29–31; emphatic, 21; intentional, 38–39; metaphysical, 23–25, 29, 54; philosophical, 25–26; and thought models, 20; of truth, 24–26, 120–22
exploitation, 85–86, 96–97, 136, 143–47
expression (*Ausdruck*), 109–10, 113–14

facts, 38; alternative, 91
Farias, Victor, 56, 160n15
Faye, Emmanuel, 56
feminism, 15–16, 77–78, 169n37; on hope, 87–88, 94, 98; on power, 2, 78–80, 88, 95, 98–99, 167n9; on truth, 16, 78–79, 95, 99, 167n7
fidelity. See truth, as fidelity to societal principles
Finlayson, Gordon, 59
force field (*Kraftfeld*), 5, 12, 37, 93; hermeneutic, 6–13
form and content. See dialectic, of form/content
Foucault, Michel, 77–78, 80–88, 136; differences from Adorno, 3, 13, 84–87, 94, 136; parallels with Adorno, 2, 15, 17, 77–78, 80, 84, 93–97, 98–99; on power, 78, 80–83, 85–86, 88–91, 94–95, 97–99, 168n22, 168n26, 169n28, 169n31, 171n49; on subjection and desubjection, 81, 86–87, 95, 168n19; on truth, 78, 88–91, 93, 95, 170n47; "Truth and Power," 88–91
Frankfurt School, 84, 137, 142, 169n30
Fraser, Nancy, 79–80, 88, 167n12, 169n37, 171n49

freedom, 27, 99, 113, 123, 124–25, 144
Freyenhagen, Fabian, 11, 152n20

Gadamer, Hans-Georg, 102, 104, 173n13
gender, 79–80
God, 26–27, 29–30, 46–48
Goldmann, Lucien, 1
Goodman, Nelson, 102
Gordon, Peter, 36, 59
grammatical subject: and objects, 52–54; and predicates, 45–48, 50, 54
Guyer, Paul, 126, 176n46

Habermas, Jürgen, 28, 37, 56, 77–78, 84, 143, 154n17, 160n12, 166n4, 169n30; mentioned, 106–7
Hammer, Espen, 34–35, 154n17, 164n43
happiness, 24, 29, 31, 119–20, 126–27
Haslanger, Sally, 79
Hauser, Arnold, 103
Hegel, G. W. F., 26, 92, 171n51; Adorno's critique of, 1, 8–10, 15, 22, 29, 58, 65–67, 84–86, 91, 139–40, 145–46, 152n8, 164n45, 164n48; differences from Adorno, 4, 7, 24, 72, 129; influence on Adorno, 3–5, 9–10, 12–13, 20–21, 26, 35, 37, 39, 43, 60, 66, 73, 75, 92–93, 134, 148; and Kant, 48–49, 72–73; *Phenomenology of Spirit*, 1, 5, 142, 177n10; *Science of Logic*, 5, 43, 164n47; mentioned, 2, 14, 103
Hegel: Three Studies, 4–5, 7–9, 11, 20, 58, 133–4
Heidegger, Martin: Adorno's critique of, 2–3, 5, 13–15, 20, 30, 37–39, 42–47, 54, 56–76, 138, 144–45,

157n3, 158n4, 161n16, 163n36, 164n44–5, 164n51, 165n52; Adorno's misreading of, 57, 59, 63–64, 162n23, 162n25, 163n40, 164n43; on Being, 14–15, 37, 39, 43–49, 59–65, 73–74, 155n8, 163n42; *Being and Time*, 37, 53, 57, 60, 63–65, 68, 70, 73–74, 165n53; *Beiträge zur Philosophie*, 73–74; on Dasein, 33, 63, 65–70, 73–74, 165n66; differences from Adorno, 13, 33, 46–49, 59–60, 75, 136; on historicity, 69–72, 165n52; on Kant, 47–49, 156n20; and Nazism, 56–57, 160n14; on other beginning, 15, 62, 73–75, 136; parallels with Adorno, 13, 17, 21, 32, 49–51, 53–56, 59–60, 63, 65, 73–76, 157n2, 162n23; on truth, 59–60, 74–75; mentioned, 160n12, 162n24

historical necessity, 13, 22–26, 28

history, 22, 84–85, 154n17; as continuity/discontinuity, 84–86, 97, 107; and historicity, 15, 69–72; humanly promised other of, 14, 29–30, 75, 94, 115, 117–21, 125, 135–36, 140; and nature, 71–72, 165n60; ontologizing of, 69–72, 165n52; and transcendence, 5–6, 13, 15, 21–25, 29, 31, 69–71, 94, 108, 114–15, 117–19, 126, 129; and truth, 22–25, 31, 75, 134; universal, 84–85, 92, 96

Hogh, Philip, 35

Honneth, Axel, 21, 77–78, 84, 166n4–5

hope, 36, 61, 63, 97–99, 120, 122, 140; and art, 30–31; basis for, 136–37; in feminism, 87–88, 94, 98; future oriented, 63, 134; ill-founded, 98–99, 121–22; in life after death, 23–24; for social transformation, 30–33, 75, 84, 87, 94, 97–99, 120, 126, 132, 134–36; and theology, 29; and truth, 10, 30–33, 75–76, 94, 130; utopian, 10, 87–88, 98–99, 121

Horkheimer, Max, 15, 29, 84, 87, 103, 142–45, 154n17–18

Hulatt, Owen, 8–9, 35

Hullot-Kentor, Robert, 117–18, 172n3, 176n46

Husserl, Edmund: Adorno's critique of, 14, 37–45, 51, 54–55, 155n5, 155n7–8, 171n50; *Logical Investigations*, 37–38; phenomenology of, 38–39; mentioned, 12–13

identity, 24, 53; imposition of, 4, 33–36, 92, 94, 96, 112–13, 130–31, 147; and the nonidentical, 6, 15, 67, 77, 86, 93–94, 131, 133, 146–47; and predicative practices, 34–35, 130–32; principle of, 86–87, 92–93, 96–97; and self-critique, 33–34

ideology, 61–62, 64, 69–70, 115, 138, 163n36, 164n50

illusion (*Schein*), 55, 92, 129, 140; in art, 30, 108–10, 113–15, 117–18; and expression, 108–11; history of Being as, 61–62; necessary, 28, 31, 94; redemption of, 28–30, 109, 114; societally imposed, 25; of transcendence, 28; and truth, 28, 114–120, 140; wrestling free from, 25, 27, 54, 94

import (*Gehalt*): artistic, 111, 113–16, 125; and content (*Inhalt*), 111–14; and semblance, 109, 111

Ingarden, Roman, 102

Institute for Social Research, 142–45

interconnected flourishing, 76, 96, 98–99, 126, 135, 137–39. *See also* truth, as life-giving disclosure
interpretation: and artistic import, 114; of artworks, 115–16
intersubjective recognition, 21
intuition, 38–41, 45; acts of, 38, 40–41; sensible, 46. *See also* categorial intuition

Jameson, Fredric, 103
The Jargon of Authenticity, 20, 57, 144, 164n50
Jaspers, Karl, 68–69
Jay, Martin, xi, 154n17
judgment: analytic/synthetic, 46–47; existential, 45–48, 50–51, 156n12; perceptual, 39; predicative, 35–36, 50–54; process of, 40–42
justice, 26, 70–71, 99, 123–26, 134–35, 137. *See also* societal principles

Kant, Immanuel, 26, 46–49, 72, 156n16; in Adorno, 12–14, 20–21, 26–31, 35, 37, 46, 50, 145–47, 156n17; in Hegel, 72–73; in Heidegger, 47–49; on transcendental amphiboly, 46–49, 156n14; on transcendental apperception, 48–49; mentioned, 2, 102–4, 148
Kant's Critique of Pure Reason, 12
Kaufmann, David, 4, 10–12
Kierkegaard, Søren, 2, 21, 57, 68, 142
knowledge, 39–42, 145–46; absolute, 8, 26, 92–93; artistic, 109–10, 112; conceptual, 110; copy theory of, 39–40; finite/infinite, 26–27; Husserl's theory of, 38–42; in Kant, 145–46; and power, 82; and redemption, 10; scientific conception of, 26–27; and self-negation/critique, 33–34; societal preformation of, 26–27, 35–36
Kompridis, Nikolas, 160n12

Langer, Susanne K., 102, 112, 172n4
liberation, 123–24
life-giving disclosure. *See* truth, as life-giving disclosure
Lukács, Georg, 21, 103, 141, 146, 172n10
Luther, Martin, 23

Macdonald, Iain, 15, 24, 59, 62, 72–74
Mahler, Gustav, 127
Marx, Karl, 22, 145–46, 163n36; mentioned, 2, 20, 22, 72, 83, 103, 145
mass media, 143, 173n13
mediation, 67–68, 94; in art, 108–11, 115–16; and concept of Being, 43, 47, 51, 65, 67; of concept/thing, 60, 65, 67–69, 129; conceptual, 47, 49; of experience, 35; historical, 44; societal, 9, 67–68; of subject/object, 5, 15, 21, 37, 50, 60, 67–69, 108–11, 115, 129; of transcendence, 115–16; and unmediated, 39, 43, 60–61. *See also* dialectic; polarities
metacritique, 20, 52–54
metaphysics, 26, 28–31, 64, 72–74, 76–77, 164n43; of art, 114–15, 117, 120; collapse of, 1, 13, 20–21, 31, 93; end of, 73; experience of, 23–25, 29, 152n20; and history, 72; in Kant, 26–28, 31; as knowledge of the absolute, 92–93, 171n50; materialist, 22; and practical reason, 23–24; and truth, 1, 20–22, 25, 31, 92; mentioned, 62, 76
micrology, 31, 93, 96
mimesis, 33–35, 109–10, 130

Minima Moralia, 1, 10, 32, 141–42, 144
modernity, 84, 91, 107–8, 148
Mörchen, Hermann, 55–56, 75, 157n2, 162n23

nature: and art, 102–3, 106; domination of, 84–85, 96–97, 110–12, 120, 143, 146; and history, 71–72
Negative Dialectics, 1, 3–4, 13–15, 19–29, 31–32, 35, 37–38, 43, 53, 56–59, 64, 67–69, 94, 104, 115, 127, 133, 140, 145–46, 149, 163n36, 164n44; "After Auschwitz," 22; "Being and Existence," 58, 60–61, 63; "On Categorial Intuition," 38, 43–45; "Copula," 38, 43, 45–47, 50–52, 64–65; "Dying Today," 23–24; "Freedom: On the Metacritique of Practical Reason," 20; "Happiness and Waiting in Vain," 24; "Historicity," 69–70; "History and Metaphysics," 71–72; "Meditations on Metaphysics," 13–14, 20–31, 54, 91–92; "Metaphysics and Culture, 22; "Negative Dialectic: Concept and Categories," 20–21; "No Transcendence of Being," 50–51; "The Ontological Need," 60–62; "Ontologizing the Ontic," 66–67; "Protest and Reification" 61–62; "Relation to Ontology," 14–15, 57–59; "Self-Reflection of Dialectics," 91–93; "Semblance of the Other," 28–31; "Weakness and Support," 62; "World Spirit and Natural History," 20, 71–72, 84–85
negativity, 8, 33, 36, 117, 119, 132, 134–35

Nietzsche, Friedrich, 2, 10, 117, 127, 163n36, 171n51
the nonidentical (*das Nichtidentische*), 15, 27–28, 33–35, 58, 66–67, 77, 86, 93, 96, 117, 119, 131, 133–34, 145, 147–48
normative deficiencies, 136–39
normativity, 11, 15–16, 61, 78, 87–88, 91, 95–97, 99, 171n49. See also societal principles; validity

object: and concepts, 4–5, 25, 46; as constellation, 4; epistemic, 33–36; of experience, 49; in Husserl, 40–41; in Kant, 46, 48–49; material, 51–52; and the nonidentical, 33–34; practical, 52–54, 131–32; and predication, 33–36, 42; priority of, 21, 24–25, 27, 36, 42, 104, 121, 130, 145, 147; self-disclosure of, 132–33; societal, 68. See also subject and object
objectivity, 49–53
O'Connor, Brian, 21, 37
the ontological difference, 63, 73. See also Being, and beings
ontological need, 15, 58–63, 163n36
ontological proof, 29–30, 46–48
ontologizing: of history, 70–72, 75; of the ontic, 14–15, 46, 49–50, 63–69, 71, 165n52
ontology, 15, 61, 64; Heideggerian, 15, 30, 33, 37–38, 42–43, 58–68, 74–75
Ontology and Dialectics, 14–15, 46, 57–61, 63–66, 68, 155n8, 156n13

philosophy, 103, 137; and art, 115–17, 119, 148; continental/analytic, ix, 16, 129–30; critical, 20; existential, 20–21, 36, 43, 68, 130;

philosophy *(continued)*
  postmodernist, 87, 169n37, 170n41; poststructuralist, 87–88, 103, 169n30; and resistance, 30–31
polarities, 5–7, 21, 37; in aesthetics, 13, 16, 101, 108–19; conceptual, 13–17; in ontology, 6, 62–63, 65, 68–69, 75–76; in truth, 5–7, 13–17, 21, 37, 93–94, 129
politics, 99, 107–8; and art, 16, 105, 107–8, 120–27, 140; post-truth, 17, 137; as social domain, 99, 122–23; and truth, 77, 89–90, 99, 105, 120–21; utopian, 106
Popper, Karl, 138, 144
possibility, 94; and actuality, 24, 72–4, 118–20; and art, 115, 117–19, 125–26; blocked, 15, 24, 62–63, 72–76, 118–19, 126, 135–36, 139–40; and Dasein, 73, 165n66; formal/real, 72–73; futural, 68, 73–74, 165n66; historical, 16, 24–27, 76, 108, 115, 117–19, 125, 136, 139, 163n37; and historical necessity, 22–26; of life after death, 24; redemptive, 73; temporal direction of, 15, 72–76, 135–36, 139; of transcendence, 22–29, 75, 118–19; and truth, 9–10, 25, 75–76; utopian, 118, 135–36
power, 70, 136, 169n31; and art, 123–25; as collaboration, 98–99, 136–37; disciplinary, 15, 80–83, 85–86, 88–91, 95, 98–99, 168n26; distribution of, 97; in feminism, 15, 79, 87–88; interactional/macrostructural, 15, 78–80, 83, 86, 95, 97–99; juridical/sovereign, 80–82, 90, 168n26; modern, 80–81, 83, 85–86, 89–91, 95; normative critique of, 96–97, 99; political, 99, 123; as relational concept, 78, 90–91; as state biopower, 15, 80–83, 85–86, 169n28; and truth, 15–16, 78, 80, 82, 88–91, 94–96, 99, 136
predication, 14, 39–40, 45–46, 54, 130; logical/ontic, 47–49, 50–52; and the nonidentical, 33–36
predicative availability, 34–36, 42, 52–54, 131
predicative interrelations, 131, 135
predicative practices, 131–32
predicative self-disclosure, 14, 31–36, 54, 131–33
presence, 49
propositional truth, 54, 75–76, 108, 129–30, 166n74; Adorno's account of, 14, 16, 21–22, 31–36, 38–40, 111, 129–32, 135; dynamic correlation in, 132–33; in Husserl, 38–39; importance of, 14, 133
propositions, 14, 32, 54, 112, 129, 132; in Husserl, 38–39; and the use of "is," 64–65, 67. *See also* assertions

race, 79–80
rationality, 143–44, 154n17, 169n31; in art, 112; critique of, 77–78, 84, 112; instrumental, 28; as irrational, 143–44
reconciliation, 61, 94, 147; and art, 106, 111, 113, 149; to death, 24
redemption, 10–12, 114, 120; of illusion/semblance, 28–30, 109, 114; standpoint of, 32
reference, 36, 52–53, 131–32
reflection 49, 107–8; on art, 115–16; critical, 9, 43, 81, 168n19; and judgment, 41–42; in Kant, 46–49, 65–66; philosophical, 115–16; transcendental, 46
reification, 21, 61–62, 68, 146
relativism, 23, 25, 88

repression, 80, 85–86, 96–97, 136, 143–47
resistance, 31, 87, 92, 95, 105, 135, 168n22
resourcefulness, 137–38. *See also* societal principles
Riezler, Kurt, 55, 157n3

Scheler, Max, 71, 164n49
Scholem, Gershom, 20
Schopenhauer, Arthur, 126
scientism, 26, 60
self-critique, 33–34, 92–93, 113, 135
self-disclosure, 54; mimetic, 26, 33–35; of the nonidentical, 27–28; of objects, 132–33. *See also* predicative self-disclosure
self-negation, 26–28, 33–34, 132
semblance (*Schein*). *See* illusion (*Schein*)
sexuality, 80, 83
Shuster, Martin, 26, 169n35
signitive acts, 39–42, 44, 155n7
social critique, 9, 16, 19, 61, 130, 134–40; by Adorno, 1, 8–11, 77–80, 84–88, 92–94, 96–98, 135–36, 144; and aesthetics, 101–5, 107, 125, 139–40, 148; feminist, 87–88, 94–95, 99; by Foucault, 77–78, 80–91, 94, 98, 136; Hegelian, 72; and social hope, 30, 32–33, 125, 132, 134–36, 140
social transformation, 16, 28, 32, 62, 73–75, 86–87, 94, 97–99, 136–37, 139, 142–44, 147–48, 163n37; and art, 30–31, 105, 118, 120, 122, 124, 126–27, 148–49
societal evil, 11, 139
societal principles, 76, 98–99, 125, 132–35, 137–39
society: antagonisms in, 85–86, 147–49; and art, 101–2, 104–5, 107, 148; direction of, 138–39; historically not-impossible, 30, 75, 118, 136; modern, 80–81, 90–91, 95; normalizing, 82; surveillance, 82; as true/untrue, 8–10, 15, 61–62, 73–75, 84, 104, 113, 130, 135, 137, 139–40, 144. *See also* capitalism
sociohistorical evolution, 107
solidarity, 99, 134–35, 137, 167n9. *See also* societal principles
Sparshott, Francis, 102
spirit (*Geist*), 22, 27–28, 30, 84–85, 109, 114
state of affairs (*Sachverhalt*), 38–46, 50–51, 53
Stone, Alison, 4, 152n8
structural distortions, 137–39
subject: hypostatization of, 68; individual, 81; and power, 81, 90; surplus beyond, 14–15, 25, 37, 54, 94, 131. *See also* grammatical subject
subject and object, 14, 25, 27, 37, 48, 70; alienation/reconciliation, 110–11; in art, 108–11; epistemic, 5, 14, 32–36, 54, 65, 91, 93, 132, 134–35; epistemological, 50–51, 54; polarity of, 5–6, 13–14, 68–69, 129; and predication, 48; standpoint beyond, 44–45; in truth theory, 32–34. *See also* mediation, of subject/object
subjectivity, 21, 35, 69, 110, 147, 168n19
subjugation, 85–87, 96, 136, 143–47
sublimation, 97
suffering, 32, 137; and art, 101, 110–11, 120, 124, 127; removal of, 14–15, 29–30, 32, 36, 74–75, 86, 94, 127, 136, 146; and truth, 22–23

synthesis, 45; artistic, 112–13; cognitive, 40–42, 51–54; intrajudgmental, 51–54; of numbers, 43–44; predicative, 50, 53–54
systematic reconstruction, 7–12

temporality. *See* truth, temporality of
theology, 24; and art, 114; and hope, 29; inverse, 20–21; rational, 26
Thomä, Dieter, 59, 163n36
thought, 20, 29; conceptual, 113; exemplary, 44, 156n11; moment of, 39–40, 52; objective mediation of, 68; systematic, 7; utopian potential of, 68–69
Tiedemann, Rolf, 57, 71, 147–48, 165n62
Toward a Metacritique of Epistemology, 20, 38–43, 52
transcendence, 22, 29; and art, 30–31, 115–19, 126; futural, 5; historical/ anthropological, 24–28; and history, 5–6, 13, 15, 21–25, 29, 31, 69–71, 94, 106, 108, 114–15, 117–19, 126, 129; mediated, 115–16; possibility of, 23–5, 29, 118; semblance of, 28; and transience, 22, 55, 70–72
transcendental ideas, 14, 22, 26–28, 30. *See also* Kant, Immanuel
transience, 22, 55, 70–72
truth, ix, 1–2, 16–17, 32; as constellation, 3–7, 12, 69, 77, 91–95, 108, 129–30, 135; as dynamic correlation, 132–35, 137, 139; experience of, 24–26, 28; as fidelity to societal principles, 98–99, 125, 132–35, 137, 139; as historical process, 3, 5, 76, 129, 134; and history, 22–25, 31, 134; holistic conception of, 8–9, 95–96, 129; and hope, 10, 30–33, 75–76, 94, 130; importance of, 17; as life-giving disclosure, 98, 133–35, 137, 139; and metaphysics, 1, 20–22, 25, 31, 92; polarities of, 5–7, 13–17, 21, 37, 93–94, 129; and politics, 89–90, 105, 120–27; and power, 15–16, 78, 80, 82, 88–91, 94–96, 99, 136; public authentication of, 21; redemptive, 10–12; regimes of, 85, 88–91; as relational concept, 90–91, 93, 111; scientific, 26, 89–91, 93, 95, 130, 133, 136, 138, 144; and social critique, 16, 32–33, 87, 130, 132, 134–40; social domains of, 95–96, 99, 111, 122–23, 136–38; as subjectivity, 68–69, 133–34, 164n51; subjunctive conception of, 133–34; temporality of, 3, 15, 22–23, 59–60, 63, 69–72, 75–76; transformative conception of, 6, 13–14, 22, 30–31, 134–40; unfolding of, 74–76, 112–13, 116, 135–37, 139–40; as a whole, 4, 9–12, 14, 16, 19, 31–33, 98–99, 126, 130, 132–35, 138–39, 142, 146. *See also* artistic truth; propositional truth
truth content (*Wahrheitsgehalt*), 1, 105–9, 111, 114–20, 148

universal/particular, 5–6, 34–35, 44–45, 66
the university, 138, 145
utopia, 9–11, 19, 68–69, 84, 98–99, 135–36, 139, 152n20; and art, 106, 114, 117–21, 126; in feminist theory, 87–88, 94, 170n41; and metaphysics, 20; of the whole truth, 9–11, 133

validity: communicative, 106–7, 121; and genesis, 23; logical/inferential, 132–33, 135, 176n5; and power, 88

Wellmer, Albrecht, 16, 105–7, 111, 114, 121, 153n1
Wisser, Richard, 157n2

Zuidervaart, Lambert: *Adorno's Aesthetic Theory*, 151n4, 174n31, 175n44; *Art in Public*, 138, 175n44; *Artistic Truth*, 175n43–44; *Religion, Truth, and Social Transformation*, 166n75, 171n57; *Social Domains of Truth*, 151n3, 166n75, 171n55–56, 177n8; *Social Philosophy after Adorno*, 151n4, 153n1, 176n6; *Truth in Husserl, Heidegger, and the Frankfurt School*, 151n3, 153n10, 155n9, 157n31, 166n72, 176n6